22

D0918732

Campion, Dowland and the
Lutenist Songwriters

016.7824
P644c

Campion, Dowland and the Lutenist Songwriters

Michael Pilkington

ENGLISH SOLO SONG
GUIDES TO THE REPERTOIRE

WITHDRAWN

Indiana University Press

Bloomington and Indianapolis

Copyright © 1989 by Michael Pilkington

All rights reserved.
No part of this book may be reproduced or utilized in any
form or by any means, electronic or mechanical, including
photocopying and recording, or by any information storage
and retrieval system, without permission in writing from
the publisher. The Association of American University
Presses' Resolution on Permissions constitutes the only
exception to this prohibition.

Manufactured in Great Britain

Library of Congress Cataloging-in-Publication Data

Pilkington, Michael.
    Campion, Dowland, and the lutenist songwriters / Michael
Pilkington.
        p.   cm.—(English solo song)
    Bibliography: p.
    Includes indexes.
    ISBN 0-253-34695-9
    1. Songs, English–England–16th century–Bibliography. 2. Songs,
English–England–17th century–Bibliography. 3. Songs with lute–
–Bibliography.   I. Title.   II. Series.
ML128. S3P54   1989
016.78242′0942′09031–dc20   89–11006

Contents

89-6185
ALLEGHENY COLLEGE LIBRARY

ALLEGHENY COLLEGE LIBRARY

Foreword

Even before seeing this book I thought it a marvellous idea, and I was not disappointed. It should prove invaluable to amateurs and professionals alike – to those who may want reassurance and advice as to whether a song is suitable for their vocal range and technical ability, and to those who have a scholarly interest in their repertoire or need help in devising interesting and varied recital programmes.

Milton-under-Wychwood   Catherine Bott

Preface

This book is one of a series, *English Solo Song: a guide to the repertoire*, planned to cover the whole repertoire of English solo song. Songs which cannot be accompanied by piano alone are not included. The series is designed not merely as a practical guide for singers and teachers of singing, but also to be of use to those who wish to study any particular area of English song composition, in relation to the music or the poetry.

A full description of each song is given, as detailed in the Introduction. This may help to answer the question I have often been asked: 'Are there any English songs?' As these guides will show, there is an enormous repertoire available, which is unfortunately only too little known by those who should be most concerned – English singers themselves. It is hoped that the information provided here about variants in the poems, and the sources from which they were taken, will encourage singers to investigate the words as well as the music of the songs they sing. The composers started with the words, after all, and it will be helpful to good performance for the singer to take the same starting-point. Where the words of a song differ from the original poem the singer needs to decide whether this has happened by accident or design. Whether or not the original words are used in performance, it must surely be of value to know what the poet actually wrote. If more than one edition of a song is available any differences are recorded here. The original sources have not been researched, but if published evidence shows an edition to have modified the original this is made clear. So far as possible misprints have been noted, but it is inevitable that some will have been overlooked, and equally inevitable that there will be some errors in this book itself. Any information on this will be gratefully received.

I should like to thank my colleagues in the world of singing teaching for their encouragement. In particular, Jack Coldiron and Bruce Lunkley of Texas, and many members of AOTOS (the Association Of Teachers Of Singing), led me to believe that this series would be of practical use to them in their work. The staff and students at the Guildhall School of Music have made many useful comments, not only in relation to draft versions of these guides, but during the whole course of the twenty-five years I have been teaching the Interpretation of English Song at the School. Finally, I should like to thank my daughter Helen for her assistance with the laborious task of checking the indexes.

Old Coulsdon, 1988   M.P.

Introduction

Though the songs in this volume were designed to be sung with lute they can be performed effectively with a keyboard accompaniment. Lutes are not that plentiful today, nor are lutenists, and if it is reasonable for a pianist to include Bach and Scarlatti in a recital programme it is equally reasonable for a singer to include lute songs. The songs are given in alphabetical order of composer, and then as they appeared in the original collections, each of which is described and its modern edition given with editor and date of publication. Only songs currently in print have been included; when this means that only a selection of songs from a collection is given, the numbering still follows that of the original publication.

Entries are set out as follows:

Title This is the same as the first line in all lute songs.

Poet If known.

Tonality The original key is that given before the vocal ranges, see below. If the original is no longer in print it is given after the title, in roman (ordinary type). Keys other than the original are then listed, after the relevant Coll (Collection) number, in italics. Note that some editions modernise key-signatures and some do not; since the purpose here is to note available transpositions, consistency in this matter may not be found throughout the book, but in any one song the 'key' has been defined on the same basis for all editions.

Collection Volumes in which the song may be found: a key to the numbers used is given on pp. 5-6. The key is original unless otherwise stated.

Range of voice part; optional notes are given in round brackets (); pitches shown in square brackets [] indicate the range of the main body of the song. These are all in relation to the given key, which is original unless given in italics. Key to pitch symbols: C = c below bass clef, c°, c' (middle c), c″, c‴; for example, f′ is the f above middle c.

Meter C is given as 4/4, alla breve as 2/2. However, different editions may vary in this with the same song; the difference between duple and triple rhythms is in any case clear. If more than one time signature is used it implies frequent alternation.

Duration Shown in minutes and seconds. This is clearly a subjective

matter, but the times given will produce satisfactory tempi. They refer
to one stanza only, and figures in square brackets are for performances
omitting repeats.

Difficulty Voice (V) and piano (P) are graded separately as easy (e),
moderately easy (me), moderate (m), moderately difficult (md), and
difficult (d). Again a matter for personal judgment, but a glance at a
few known songs will indicate the standards used. It seems likely that
lutenists would find accompaniments that are difficult on the piano are
also difficult on the lute.

For Most suitable voice or voices; those appropriate to the original key
are in roman type, transposed alternatives are in italics. Square
brackets imply that some such singers might find the text of the song
unsuitable. Voices suited to an original key which is no longer
available appear in round brackets.

Subject A paraphrase of the text, usually suited to programme notes.

Voice Description of vocal line, with reference to shape, size of leaps,
extremes, rhythms, and any special problems. Syllabic word setting is
assumed.

Piano Description of accompaniment, with reference to texture, layout,
harmony, rhythm, and any specific problems. Though given with
pianists in mind, lutenists should find the descriptions informative.

Comment Any further information which might be of value, including
any misprints noticed, and explanations of unusual words. Variant
versions of the words are given in italics; explanations in roman. All
descriptions are based on the complete editions, if available, with notes
on any discrepancies between these and other current versions.
Corrections in square brackets refer to Colls given in square brackets.
Note that all phrasing and dynamic markings in modern editions are
editorial; there were none in the originals.

An example should make the system clear:

(8) Flow not so fast, ye fountains. Colls 6, 17; Coll 18, *D minor*; Coll 20,
   F# minor; Coll 21, *E minor*.

	G minor. g'-g″, [b'-f ″]. 2/2. 1'25″, [1']. 3 St. V/me, P/e.
For:	Sop, Ten; *Mezzo, C-Ten, Bar*.
Subject:	My tears must continue; ordinary sorrows will abate, but true grief remains.
Voice:	Mostly by step; it lies high, and needs long phrasing.
Piano:	Chordal, with melodic bass; simple counterpoint.
Comment:	Repeat optional, and best omitted. A similar song to **46 (15)**: both are beautiful, but not for the same programme. Last word in each stanza: spheres = eyeballs. St. 2, lines 3-4: Neither passage of time (season) nor anything else can appease my sorrow (Doughtie). Colls 6, 17, [18]: bar 14, 1st

half: a° and a', [e° and e'] need flats. Colls 20, 21: accompaniment and introduction to each stanza by Keel.

Explanation

No author of the words known. The song appears in the original key in *English Lute Songs* Book 2 and in Dowland, *50 Songs* Book 2, High key. It appears in D minor in Dowland, *50 Songs* Book 2, Low key; in F# minor in *Elizabethan Love Songs* Book 1, High key, and in E minor in *Elizabethan Love Songs* Book 1, Low key.

The original key is G minor. In this key the lowest note is g', the highest note is g''; there are few notes lower than b' or higher than f''. The song is in duple time. A stanza lasts 1 minute 25 seconds, or 1 minute without repeat. There are three stanzas. The voice part is moderately easy, the piano part is easy.

The original key would suit soprano or tenor, transposed versions would suit mezzo-soprano, counter-tenor or baritone.

In bar 14, first half, the a° and a' need flats added in Colls 6 and 17; in Coll 18 it is the e° and e' that need flats.

Collections and Abbreviations

Collections

Coll 1: *Robert Dowland's 'A musical banquet'*, edited by Peter Stroud, 1986. S & B, *LS* 16.

Coll 2: *Songs from Manuscript Sources* I, edited by David Greer, 1979. S & B, *LS* 17. Tablature included.

Coll 3: *Songs from Manuscript Sources* II, edited by David Greer, 1979. S & B, *LS* 18.

Coll 4: *Twenty Songs from Printed Sources*, edited by David Greer, 1969. S & B, *LS* 19.

Coll 5: *English Lute Songs* I, compiled by Michael Pilkington, 1984. S &B, B 616.

Coll 6: *English Lute Songs* II, compiled by Michael Pilkington, 1984. S & B, B 617.

40 Songs from Elizabethan and Jacobean Songbooks, edited by E.H. Fellowes, 1926; revised by David Scott, 1969. S & B.

Coll 7: Book 1. High key. Out of print.
Coll 8: Book 1. Low key. Out of print.
Coll 9: Book 2. High key. Out of print.
Coll 10: Book 2. Low key. X 2 B.
Coll 11: Book 3. High key. X 3 A.
Coll 12: Book 3. Low key. X 3 B.
Coll 13: Book 4. High key. X 4 A.
Coll 14: Book 4. Low key. X 4 B.

John Dowland; 50 Songs, edited by E.H. Fellowes, 1926; revised by David Scott, 1970. S & B.

Coll 15: Book 1. High key. X 5 A.
Coll 16: Book 1. Low key. X 5 B.
Coll 17: Book 2. High key. X 6 A.
Coll 18: Book 2. Low key. X 6 B.

Coll 19: *An Elizabethan Song Book*, edited by W.H. Auden, C. Kallman, N. Greenberg. 1968. Faber & Faber.

Elizabethan Lovesongs, edited by Frederick Keel. Boosey & Hawkes.
    Coll 20: Book 1. High key. 1909.
    Coll 21: Book 1. Low key.
    Coll 22: Book 2. High key. 1913.
    Coll 23: Book 2. Low key.

Select English Songs and Dialogues of the 16th and 17th Centuries, edited
by Arnold Dolmetsch. Boosey & Hawkes.
    Coll 24: Book 1. 1908.
    Coll 25: Book 2. 1912.

English Ayres, Elizabethan and Jacobean, transcribed and edited by
Peter Warlock and Philip Wilson. Books 1-3: OUP 1927 (originally
published by Enoch in 4 volumes between 1922 and 1925). Books 4-6:
OUP 1931. Though this series is no longer available songs still in print in
other editions have been collated. The 43 songs no longer available
elsewhere have not been included here.
    Coll 26: Book 1.
    Coll 27: Book 2.
    Coll 28: Book 3.
    Coll 29: Book 4.
    Coll 30: Book 5.
    Coll 31: Book 6.

100 Best Short Songs, selected by Elena Gerhardt, Sir George Henschel
and Francis J.Harford. Paterson. 1930.
    Coll 32: Book 2.
    Coll 33: Book 4.

Imperial *New Imperial Edition*, edited by Sydney Northcote. Boosey and
    Hawkes. 1950. A volume for each voice, each containing a lute song.

Davis *The Works of Thomas Campion*.

Abbreviations
For details see Select Bibliography

Arcadia	Sir Philip Sidney, *The Countess of Pembroke's Arcadia*, 1580, 1590, 1598.
Ault	*Elizabethan Lyrics*.
BD	Breton's *Bower of Delights*, 1591.
BL	British Library.
Bullen	*Lyrics from the Song-Books of the Elizabethan Age*.
Campion, On Song	Stephen Ratcliffe, *Campion, On Song*.

Cheerful Ayres	*Cheerful Ayres and Ballads*
Cotgrave	*Wit's Interpreter*, 1655, 1662.
Davis	*The Works of Thomas Campion.*
Davison	*A Poetical Rhapsody*, 1602.
Doughtie	*Lyrics from English Ayres, 1596-1622.*
DP	Diana Poulton, *John Dowland.*
Earle, 1615	Giles Earle, *His Booke*, 1615.
EEL	*Early English Lyrics*, edited by E.K. Chambers and F. Sidgwick
EH	*England's Helicon*, 1600.
EM	*English Madrigalists.*
EMV	*English Madrigal Verse*, edited by E.H. Fellowes.
Filmer, 1629	*French Court Airs.*
Forbes	John Forbes, *Cantus, Songs and Fancies*, 1662, 1666, 1682.
Golden Garland	Richard Johnson's *Golden Garland of Princely Pleasures*, 1620.
LS	*English Lute Songs.*
MB	*Musica Britannica*
New OB	*New Oxford Book of English Verse*, edited by Helen Gardner.
OB	*Oxford Book of English Verse*, edited by Quiller-Couch.
OB 16	*Oxford Book of 16th Century Verse*, edited by E.K. Chambers.
OED	*Oxford English Dictionary.*
Parfitt	Ben Jonson, *The Complete Poems.*
Playford 1652	*Select Musical Ayres and Dialogues.*
1653	*Select Musical Ayres and Dialogues.*
1659	*Select Ayres and Dialogues.*
1660	*A Brief Introduction to the Skills of Musick.*
1667	*The Musical Companion.*
1669	*Select Ayres and Dialogues.*
1672	*An Introduction to the Skills of Musick.*
1673	*The Musical Companion.*
PN	*The Phoenix Nest*, 1593.
Rollins	*see* Select Bibliography: Anthologies.
S & B	Stainer & Bell.
Songs Compleat 3	volume 3, 1719
The Paradyse	*The Paradyse of Daynty Devises*, 1576.
Vivian	*Campion's Works*
Wit and Mirth 1	volume 1, 1699
3	volume 3, 1719
5	volume 5, 1714
6	volume 6, 1720

ANON

1 As at noon Dulcina rested. G major. Colls 3, 5, *Eb major*.
Eb major. e'-g", [g'-f "]. 4/4,6/4. 35". 6 St. V/e, P/e.

For:	*Sop, Ten*; (Cont, C-Ten).
Subject:	Shepherd's wooing described in lively and humorous terms.
Voice:	Steps, some skips; some interesting rhythmic touches.
Piano:	Chordal.
Comment:	Several stanzas could be omitted; the source, Earle, 1615, has fifteen! The song is mentioned in ch.4 of Izaac Walton's *The Compleat Angler*, 1653. Printed in *Wit and Mirth* 5 and 6 with a different tune.

2 Go my flock, go, get you hence (Sir Philip Sidney, *Astrophel and Stella*, 1591, The Ninth Song). Coll 1.
D major. d'-d". 4/4. 25". 10 St. V/e, P/e.

For:	C-Ten, Bar.
Subject:	Go, flock, and leave me to my sorrow; but first let me tell you how fair Stella has refused me.
Voice:	Steps, small skips; short phrases in rather uneven but repeated rhythm; last line legato.
Piano:	Simple chords and a few passing notes.
Comment:	Stanzas 7-9 could be omitted. Poem also printed in *Arcadia*, 1590 and *EH*, 1600.

3 Go now, my soul, to thy desired rest. Coll 3.
D minor. c'-d", [d'-c"]. 4/4. 1'50", [1'05"]. 3 St. V/e, P/e.

For:	C-Ten, Bar.
Subject:	Go, my soul, and tell her how I love her; if she refuses her favours, do not return.
Voice:	Steps, a few skips; varied but simple rhythms; one easy melisma.
Piano:	Chordal, with some decoration.
Comment:	Repeat optional. From Christ Church MS 439.

4 Have I caught my heav'nly jewel? (Sir Philip Sidney, *Astrophel and Stella*, 1591. The Second Song). Coll 2.
Bb major. f'-g", [g'-g"]. 3/4,6/8. 20". 7 St. V/me, P/e.

For:	Ten.

Subject: Shall I take advantage of finding my sweetheart asleep? Only a kiss, but she wakes; and, fool that I am, I flee.
Voice: Steps; a free dance rhythm with some elaborate melismas.
Piano: Chordal.
Comment: Not as easy as it looks, but an effective song. Rhythms need some adjustment: St. 3, bar 6, last beat a crotchet, and bar 8, *tongue* on 5th note; St. 7, bar 1, crotchet and four quavers; St. 2-7, bar 5, 3/4 not 6/8. From BL Add. MS 15117.

5 How now, shepherd, what means that? Coll 3.

G major. e'-e", [f'#-d"]. 4/4. 25". 4 St. V/e, P/e.
For: C-Ten, Bar.
Subject: Two shepherds agree that their unfaithful girls should be left, and others found, rather than waste time weeping over them.
Voice: Steps, small skips; very simple repeated rhythm.
Piano: Chordal.
Comment: Could be performed by two men. St. 3 could be omitted. The poem was printed in *Golden Garland*, 1620, entitled 'The Shepherd's Dialogue of Love between Willy and Cuddy', to be sung to the tune of 'Maying Time'. From BL Add. MS 29481. Song printed in Forbes 1662, 1668, 1682.

6 I prithee leave, love me no more (Michael Drayton, 'To His Coy Love', *Odes, with other Lyric Poesies*, 1619). Coll 3.

C minor. g'-a"b, [g'-g"]. 4/4. 2'10", [1'40"]. V/me, P/e.
For: Ten.
Subject: Tempt me no more with your beauty and kindness, if you will not love me.
Voice: Many skips; 8ve drops and leaps; free rhythm, some melismas.
Piano: Chordal.
Comment: Very much in the new dramatic style of the masque song. Repeat optional. Drayton has another eight-line stanza: 'Clip me no more in those dear arms / Nor thy life's comfort call me; / O these are but too powerful charms / And do but more enthrall me. / But see how patient I am grown / In all this coil about thee, / Come nice thing, let thy heart alone / I cannot live without thee.' The setting has rearranged the order of the 16 lines used: 1-4, 9-12, 5-8, 13-16. From Christ Church MS 87.

7 If floods of tears. Coll 2.

C minor. g'-c", [g'-a'b]. 4/4. 1'05". 4 St. V/e, P/e.
For: C-Ten, Bar.

Subject: I would weep for my sins, but I have no hope; I shall still beg
              for mercy, and if it is granted will sing your praises for ever.
Voice: Steps, broken chords, scales; slow and sustained.
Piano: Chordal, with some decoration.
Comment: First two stanzas printed at the end of the 'Sonnets of Divers
              Noblemen and Gentlemen' in Sidney's *Astrophel and Stella*,
              1591, and set by Dowland, **45 (11)**; first stanza set as a
              madrigal by Bateson, *EM* 22 (12). A good song for a low voice
              in a church setting. Variants in Dowland: bar 4: *Or = And*; bar
              9: *can = will*; bar 11: *But = Than*; bar 19: *fault = faults*. In bar
              10 Bateson has *faults* for *fault*. From Tenbury MS 1019.

8 If I freely may discover (Ben Jonson, *The Poetaster*, 1601. Act II, Scene
   ii). Coll 3.
              F major. c'-c". 4/4. 55". 2 St. V/me, P/e.
For: C-Ten, Bar.
Subject: A description of the ideal mistress; fair, witty, proud, kind.
Voice: Steps, skips, broken chords; rhythmic variety, two bars
              triplets.
Piano: Basically chordal.
Comment: Second stanza supplied from the play source. Also set by
              Henry Lawes. From Earle, 1615. Line 8: *her* (Earle) = *the*, in
              play; line 10: *But all* (Earle) = *All*, in play.

9 If I seek to enjoy the fruits. Coll 3.
              G minor. d'-d". 6/8. 35". 2 St. V/me, P/e.
For: C-Ten, Bar.
Subject: I love her who rejects me, a situation only the planets can
              alter.
Voice: Steps, scales, many paired semiquavers; almost a patter-
              song.
Piano: Chordal.
Comment: Set by Bateson as a madrigal, *EM* 22 (4). The editor points
              out three missing syllables in stanza 1; he gives Bateson's
              version, but says it does not fit the music. It would seem to
              fit quite well, with the same underlay as the equivalent
              syllables in St. 2. Other variants in Bateson: St. 1, bar 11:
              frail = air; St. 2, bars 2-3: *You powers and you planets
              which*; bar 5: *your = you*; last three lines of poem omitted.
              From Christ Church MS 439.

10 If the deep sighs (Michael Drayton, based on parts of the Ninth
   Eclogue in *The Shepherds' Garland*, 1593). Coll 2.
              A minor. f°#-g', [g°-f']. 4/4,3/4,4/4. 1'15". 2 St. V/me, P/e.
For: [Sop], Ten.

Subject: All Nature shares my grief.
Voice: Steps, skips; small melisma; irregular long-lined phrasing;
                some rhythmic variety.
Piano: Chordal, some decoration.
Comment: Crotchet = crotchet throughout. This adaptation of an
                eclogue by Drayton was set as a madrigal by Ward, *EM* 19
                (23-24). Controlled singing needed. Original written in tenor
                range, but could be sung an 8ve higher by soprano. Variants
                in Ward: St. 1, bar 23: *whence* = *whom*; bar 26: *Who* = *Now*.
                St. 2, bar 3: *wond'dreth* = *wonders*; bar 12: *echo* = *echoes*.
                From Tenbury MS 1019.

11 Most men do love the Spanish wine. Coll 2.
                G major. G-d', [G-g°]. 4/4. 1'15". V/me, P/me.
For: Bass.
Subject: In praise of ale as distinct from wine.
Voice: Steps, skips, broken chords; many quaver runs, both scales
                and Handelian figures; one sustained d' approached and left
                by running steps, otherwise g° is the highest note.
Piano: Basically chordal, but many imitative quaver runs.
Comment: A real drinking song, many nonsense syllables; a good
                bravura piece. From Cambridge, Rowe MS 2.

12 Music, thou soul of heav'n (Robert Herrick, *Hesperides*, 1648). Coll 3.
                G minor. d'-e"b, [f'-d"]. 4/4. 1'25". V/e, P/e.
For: Mezzo, C-Ten, Bar.
Subject: Music, come from heaven and charm our souls.
Voice: Steps, a few skips; sequences; varied rhythms and
                phrase-lengths.
Piano: Mainly chordal.
Comment: Has two more lines (bars 6-11) than the poem as printed in
                Hesperides, where the first line runs: 'Music, thou Queen of
                Heaven', with several other variants. From Christ Church
                MS 87.

13 My lytell pretty one. Coll 29; Coll 24, *Bb major*, Coll 33, *F major*.
                C major. g'-a", [g'-g"]. 3/4. 30". V/e, P/e.
For: Ten; *C-Ten, Bar*.
Subject: My pretty one is very special.
Voice: Steps, small skips, broken chord; small melisma; simple
                rhythm.
Piano: Chordal.
Comment: Dolmetsch has a four-bar introduction not given by Warlock,
                and has added a third part to the accompaniment
                throughout, while Warlock is mostly in two parts. Other

differences, numbering bars from the start of the voice: bar 9: 2/4 bar [W], 3/4 bar [D]; bar 15, bass: c° d° c° [W], f° g° f° [D]; bar 18, beat 2, RH: g' [W], a' [D]; bar 16, beat 2, voice: d″ [W], b′*b* [D]; beat 3, RH quavers: b′*b* a' [W], a' a' [D]. Coll 33 has a four-bar introduction and a freely composed accompaniment, the melody follows Dolmetsch but omits both bars rest for the voice. An attractive little song. Line 3: When beckoned she comes at once. Line 4: alone = unique. From BL Add. MS 4900.

14 O dear life, when shall it be? (Sir Philip Sidney, *Astrophel and Stella*, 1591. The Tenth Song). Coll 1.

G minor. d'-d″. 4/4. 45″, [35″]. 8 St. V/e, P/e.

For: C-Ten, Bar.

Subject: In his love's absence he sends his thoughts to her, that he may remember their previous happiness together.

Voice: Steps, small skips, broken chords; four-square rhythms and regular phrases.

Piano: Chordal, with a fair amount of decoration.

Comment: Repeat best omitted. Stanzas 1-4 and 8 of this song were printed by Robert Dowland, and appear in *Astrophel and Stella*, the other three have been added by the editor from *Arcadia*, 1598. Some stanzas could well be omitted. St. 1-3 were set by Byrd, *EM* 15 (33), and St. 8 by Ward, *EM* 19 (8). St. 2, line 6: aims at = guesses at. St. 3, line 1: thee, refers to thought.

15 O death, rock me asleep. A minor. Coll 25, *G minor.*

G minor. f'-d″, [g'-d″]. 3/2. 2'15″. 3 St. V/e, P/e.

For: (Sop, Ten); *Mezzo, C-Ten, Bar.*

Subject: Though innocent I am about to die; let the passing bell tell of my death.

Voice: Steps, small skips; much repetition of phrases; simple rhythm.

Piano: Chordal.

Comment: Has been attributed to Anne Boleyn, and more commonly to her brother George, Viscount Rochford, but only by conjecture (*OB 16*). There are a number of MS sources of the poem, giving some useful variants: Page 1, bars 21-22: *woeful* = *careful*, with the same meaning. Page 2, bar 2: *the* = *thou*; bar 5: *the* = *my*; bars 8/12: *the* = *thy*. St. 2, line 2: *wayle* = *wait*; refrain as St. 1. St 3, line 5; *the* = *thou*; line 7: *For thou my death dost tell*. Sources: Ault, *OB 16, EEL*. Coll 25 omits St. 2, which runs: 'My pains who can express? / Alas they are so strong; / My dolour will not suffer strength /

my life for to prolong. / *Refrain*.' The last line of each stanza should only occur in the last stanza; to allow this it is possible to take a repeat from page 2, bar 20, back to page 1, bar 5. An alternative would be simply to repeat page 1 from bar 5 until the last stanza. Much of the song is based on a one-bar ground, and can easily become monotonous, but in the right hands it could be very moving. From BL Add. MS 15117. Another setting, as a consort song with viols, is given in *MB* XXII.

16 O Lord, whose grace (Mary Herbert, Countess of Pembroke). Coll 2.
G major. c'-e″, [e'-e″]. 4/4. 1′20″. 3 St. V/me, P/e.

For:	Mezzo, C-Ten, Bar.
Subject:	A prayer for mercy, with a confession of sin.
Voice:	Steps and skips; rhythms mostly simple, some ties; fairly long phrasing required.
Piano:	Basically chordal, but strong contrapuntal suggestions.
Comment:	Needs a real controlled line. Possibly by Antony Holborne, it is in the old viol-song style. The original poem, a paraphrase of Psalm 51 by Sir Philip Sidney's sister, has 8 stanzas; only 1, 2, and 8 are given here. From BL Add. MS 15117.

17 Phyllis was a fair maid. Coll 20; Coll 21, E major.
G major. f'#-g″, [g'-e″]. 4/4. 30″. 3 St. V/e, P/e.

For:	Sop; Mezzo.
Subject:	Phyllis had her Corydon, but I have no one, and keep my sheep alone.
Voice:	Steps, repeated notes, scales, sequences; rhythm easy.
Piano:	Chordal, with bouncy bass.
Comment:	Accompaniment and introduction to each stanza by Keel. The melody and first stanza come from Earle, 1615; the remaining stanzas have by added by Percy Pinkerton. A cheerful little number. Bar 12: *A = I* in Earle, 1615. A version edited by Warlock is given in *Four English Songs of the Early Seventeenth Century*, OUP 1925. Pages 91, 92 and 93, bars 3-4: all fs [ds] should be naturals.

18 Shall I weep or shall I sing? Coll 3.
G minor. d'-d″, [f'-d″]. 4/4. 40″. 4 St. V/e, P/e.

For:	Mezzo.
Subject:	A girl bemoans her betrayal by a faithless lover.
Voice:	Steps, some skips; some rhythmic freedom, but mostly simple.
Piano:	Basically chordal.
Comment:	Some might prefer to omit the fourth stanza! From BL Add. MS 29481. Words in Cotgrave, 1655.

19 Sleepe, sleepe. Coll 21; Coll 20, *A major.*

        F major. d'-d", [f'-c"]. 2/2. 1'45". V/me, P/e.

For:	*Sop, Ten*; Mezzo, C-Ten, Bar.
Subject:	Sleep will release you from your grief.
Voice:	Steps, small skips, free rhythms, long sustained e" at end.
Piano:	Chordal, with decoration.
Comment:	Accompaniment and introduction by Keel. Melody from Earle, 1615. Line 5: true affects do cumber = destroy true feelings; line 7: *and* = *sad* in Earle, 1615. Bar 11, beats 2-3, voice: rhythm, dotted crotchet quaver; bars 12 and 14: no rests; bar 27: should be 3/2 not 4/2, omit second minim beat.

20 Sweet muses, nurses of delights. Coll 3.

        C major. c'-c". 4/4. 30". 3 St. V/e, P/e.

For:	Mezzo, C-Ten, Bar.
Subject:	Celebration of Apollo.
Voice:	Steps, skips; simple but lively rhythms.
Piano:	Slightly contrapuntal.
Comment:	Probably a masque song; from Earle, 1615. Warlock comments, 'Something seems to be missing between the second and third stanzas'.

21 Sweet, stay awhile. Colls 3, 5.

        G minor. f'#-g", [g'-e"b]. 4/4. 1'30". V/me, P/e.

For:	Sop, Ten.
Subject:	Do not leave me, it is not yet dawn.
Voice:	Steps, some skips; many short climbing phrases; some chromatics.
Piano:	Simple two-part counterpoint has been added to the original unfigured bass by David Greer.
Comment:	An intense and emotional setting of a famous poem. Care must be taken to maintain continuity of thought despite the many rests. Also set by Dowland, **47 (2)**; Henry Lawes (S & B, B 325); and as a madrigal by Gibbons, *EM* 20 (15). For notes on the poem see **47 (2)**. From BL Add. MS 29481.

22 The poor soul sat sighing. Colls 9, 26; Coll 10, D minor.

        G minor. g'-g". 3/4. 1'. 8 St. V/e, P/e.

For:	Sop, Ten; *Mezzo, C-Ten, Bar.*
Subject:	A man is seen mourning his lost love.
Voice:	Steps and skips; slightly chromatic; simple rhythms.
Piano:	Chordal, with some simple counterpoint.
Comment:	The Willow Song. Shakespeare used stanzas 1 and 3 in *Othello*, with some alterations. Colls 9 and 10 omit stanzas 4-7, which are in Coll 26 and *OB 16*. From BL Add. MS 15117.

ALLEGHENY COLLEGE LIBRARY

23 Why dost thou turn away? Coll 21; Coll 20, A major.
F major. c'-d", [f'-c"]. 4/4. 45". 2 St. V/e, P/e.

For: *Sop, Ten*; Mezzo, C-Ten, Bar; Cont, Bass.

Subject: A dialogue: Why do you refuse me? – Because I do not trust you.

Voice: Steps, small skips, scale; 8ve drop; simple rhythms.

Piano: Chordal, melodic bass.

Comment: Accompaniment and introduction to each stanza by Keel. From Earle, 1615. St. 2, line 3: *jealous = yellow* in Earle. Bars 9 and 30, beats 3-4, bars 20 and 41, beats 1-2 and 3-4, voice: rhythm, dotted crotchet quaver.

RICHARD ALISON
fl. 1592 – 1606

24 THE PSALMES OF DAVID IN METER. Coll 4. 1599. In the two songs given below only the first stanzas are given by Alison; the remainder have been added by the editor from *The Whole Book of Psalms collected into English Metre by Thomas Sternhold, John Hopkins and others*, 1586. They are both set for four voices, or for solo voice with instrumental accompaniment.

Voice: Mostly by step, with simple but varied rhythms.

Piano: Chordal.

Comment: The singer should take due note of the direction of stems, and the pianist should play the lute part.

(1) O Lord, turn not away thy face (John Markant). Coll 4.
G minor. f'-f ", [g'-e"b]. 4/4. 55". 2 St. V/e, P/e.

For: Sop, Ten; Mezzo, Bar.

Comment: Called 'The Lamentation', this is a prayer for mercy on a sinner.

(2) When as we sat in Babylon (William Whittingham). Coll 4.
Bb major, f'-g", [f'-e"b]. 4/4. 1'. 5 St. V/e, P/e.

For: Sop, Ten.

Comment: A setting of Psalm 137, By the Waters of Babylon.

JOHN ATTEY
fl. 1622; d. 1640

25 THE FIRST BOOKE OF AYRES of Foure Parts, With Tableture for the Lute: So made, that all the parts may be plaide together with the Lute, or one voice with the Lute and Base-Vyoll. 1622. S & B edition by E.H. Fellowes, 1926. Out of print.

(1) **On a time the amorous Silvy.** Colls 5, 13, 20; Coll 14, *D major*; Coll 21,
     E major.

	G major. d'-g'', [g'-e'']. 2/2,3/4. 1', [45'']. 3 St. V/me, P/e.
For:	Sop, Ten; *Mezzo, C-Ten, Bar*; *Cont, Bass.*
Subject:	Describes lovers parting happily at morning.
Voice:	Steps, many simple leaps, one 3-bar melisma; change of metre.
Piano:	Chordal.
Comment:	Repeat optional. Underlay needs re-arranging in stanzas 2 and 3: first two notes to *With, that* on the semibreve, and make the minim in bar 4 two crotchets. Coll 5 gives minim = dotted crotchet, Colls 13 and 14 give semibreve = dotted crotchet; crotchet = crotchet also works well. The poem is a translation from the French of Pierre Guedron, 'Un jour l'amoureuse Silvie', 1613. The French words are given in full in Doughtie, with the translation by Filmer, 1629. Colls 20, 21: accompaniment by Keel. Bar 10, all stanzas, voice: rhythm should be – dotted crotchet quaver dotted crotchet two semiquavers. St. 2, bar 2: *faire = fairest*, two crotchets, all other editions. St. 3, bar 2, *he waked from = the shepherd waked from*, all other editions, minim and four crotchets.

(14) **Sweet was the song.** Colls 19, 22; Coll 23, *F minor.*

	A minor. e'-a'', [g'#-g'']. 2/2. 1'45''. V/m, P/me.
For:	Sop, Ten; *Mezzo, Bar.*
Subject:	Mary's lullaby for the infant Jesus.
Voice:	Steps and repeated notes; several highlying phrases; many melismas.
Piano:	Contrapuntal, often very thin.
Comment:	Charming tune to good words, but a disappointing accompaniment. BL Add. MS 17786-91 has an anonymous setting of this poem for voice and a quartet of viols, published in *MB* XXII. Line 7: eke = also; line 8: vouchsafed = granted. Coll 19: page 3, bar 3, beats 3 and 4: add e'd'e'f', dotted quaver semiquaver two quavers, according to Fellowes; bars 3-6: Fellowes omits second and third *lulla's* in both phrases. Colls 22, 23: introduction and accompaniment by Keel, and it must be admitted that it is more effective than Attey's original! Line 1: *sang = sung*, all other editions; last line: *gently = sweetly*, all other editions.

WILLIAM BARLEY
d. 1614

26 SONGS TO THE BANDORA. Coll 4.
Printed in an instruction book called *A New Booke of Tabliture*, 1596.
The music is in fact anonymous. The accompaniment for all these
songs was written to sound an 8ve lower. David Greer advises
ignoring these 8ve lower signs when using a piano, as the result will
be 'turgid'. This is good advice when sung by women, but when sung
an 8ve lower by men an incorrect bass line results. The solution might
be to play the bass line in the lower 8ve, leaving the rest of the
accompaniment in the higher one.

(1) Those eyes that set my fancy on a fire. Coll 4.

	D minor. a°-b′*b*, [c′-a″]. 4/4. 1′15″, [1′]. 3 St. V/e, P/e.
For:	C-Ten, Bar, Bass.
Subject:	Description of beloved, who is such as no heart could withstand.
Voice:	Steps, simple skips; repeated notes; very simple rhythms.
Piano:	Chordal.
Comment:	See notes in Coll 4. Since this is a sonnet it might be better to leave the last seven bars until all three stanzas have been sung, and then sing them with repeat. Otherwise repeat optional. The words are a fairly close translation of Desportes' sonnet from *Diane*, 1, 11: 'Du bel oeil de Diane est ma flamme empruntée.' Printed in *PN*, 1593. A somewhat pessimistic alternative poem from *PN*, 1593, is also given in Coll 4. Line 13: *there withstand = therewith stand*, in source. Doughtie suggests *thee withstand*; Collier suggests *these withstand*.

(2) How can the tree but waste (Thomas, Lord Vaux). Coll 4.

	C minor. b°-b′*b*, [c′-a′*b*]. 4/4. 1′10″, [50″]. 3 St. V/e, P/e.
For:	Mezzo, C-Ten, Bar; Cont, Bass.
Subject:	Life is a misery if there is no response to one's words and deeds.
Voice:	Steps, simple skips, repeated notes; simple rhythm and phrasing.
Piano:	Chordal.
Comment:	Repeat optional. Poem printed in *The Paradise*, 1576, with the following variants: St. 1, line 3: *the = that*. St. 2, line 3: *sight = light*. All stanzas, line 5: *I = you*, also in Earle, 1615. Bar 12, beat 2: e′*b* not d′ in piano. St. 1, lines 1 and 3: but = do anything except. St. 2, line 1: plight = condition. St. 3,

lines 2-4: What use is a head (with its senses), which has no inclination (device) save to complain, since sorrow is the basis of the heart's misery. St. 2, line 4: *that*, missing in sources (Doughtie).

(3) **Sweet are the thoughts that savour of content** (Robert Greene, *Greene's Farewell to Folly*, 1591). Coll 4.

> D minor. d'-f ". 3/2,6/4. 1'30", [45"]. 2 St. V/e, P/e.

For:	Mezzo, Bar.
Subject:	The poor are often happier than princes; a contented mind is in itself a crown and a kingdom.
Voice:	Steps, simple skips, broken chords; simple rhythms.
Piano:	Chordal, some decoration.
Comment:	Not the original words, which cannot be traced; David Greer has found a pleasant poem to fit. The first poem in Barley's book also fits quite well, and can be found in *EMV* p. 349. Repeat both halves or neither.

(4) **But this, and then no more** (Sir Arthur Gorges). Coll 4.

> C major. c'-c", [c'-a']. 4/4. 35". 7 St. V/e, P/e.

For:	[Mezzo], C-Ten, Bar; [Cont], Bass.
Subject:	These are my last words; I do not hope they will make you kinder, my wounds are too deep for cure, but they will show how ingratitude can kill.
Voice:	Almost entirely by step; rhythms obscured by barlines – there are several 3/4 phrases, otherwise simple.
Piano:	Chordal, rhythms as for voice.
Comment:	Some stanzas could be omitted. Women might wish to omit or modify the last stanza. For this last stanza the music must be repeated from bar 9, last beat. The poem is not printed in Barley but has been found by David Greer among the *Poems* of Sir Arthur Gorges.

JOHN BARTLET
fl. 1606 – 1610

27 **A BOOKE OF AYRES** the First Part is for the Lute or Orpharion and the Viol de Gambo and 4 Partes to sing. 1606. S & B edition by E.H. Fellowes, 1925. Out of print. The four-part versions of all Bartlet's songs are given in *MB* LIII.

(1) **O Lord, thy faithfulness.** Coll 5.

> D minor. g'-g", [b'*b*-f "]. 4/4. 1'15". V/me, P/e.

For:	Sop, Ten.

Subject: The praise of God. Psalm 71:22-3.
Voice: Mostly by step; some chromatics; longish phrases.
Piano: Simple counterpoint, mostly in three parts.
Comment: Lies on the high side. A dignified song, useful for church. Line 7: eke = also.

(2) If ever hapless woman. Coll 19.

A minor. f'-f ", [g'-e"]. 2/2. 2', [1'30"]. 4 St. V/me, P/me.
For: Sop; Mezzo.
Subject: A lament on the death of a brother in battle.
Voice: Mostly by step; longish phrases with some rhythmic variety.
Piano: Three-part counterpoint throughout.
Comment: Repeat optional. A moving song; the poem is thought by some to have been written by Mary Herbert in memory of her brother, Sir Philip Sidney, who died in battle in the Netherlands in 1586. There are a few problems of underlay: St. 2, line 2: repeat *pleasing motions* and treat *motions* as three syllables the second time. Similarly *inundations* in line 4 has five syllables. St. 3, line 2: repeat *his mortall life*; line 3, *woe* takes two notes. St. 4, line 2: repeat *mourning* and *sorrowes. EMV* and Fellowes have a comma after *mourning*, not after *dayly* as in Coll 19. St. 3, line 2: lewdly = wickedly. St. 4, line 2: portes = doors, portals.

(3) When from my love. Colls 5, 22; Coll 23, *A major.*

C major. e'-g", [g'-f "]. 4/4. 35", [25"]. 2 St. V/e, P/me.
For: Ten; *C-Ten, Bar.*
Subject: Complaining cheerfully of women's fickleness.
Voice: Mostly by step, simple rhythms.
Piano: Chordal; some counterpoint; one awkward phrase.
Comment: Repeat optional. Given in Earle, 1615. Colls 22, 23: accompaniment and introduction to each stanza by Keel. Bar 7, first half of each stanza, voice: dotted crotchet quaver, not two crotchets. Printed in Forbes, 1662, 1666, 1682.

(4) Who doth behold my mistress' face. G major. Coll 22, *A major*; Coll 23, *F major.*

A *major.* a'-f "#. 4/4. 30". 4 St. V/e, P/e.
For: Ten; *C-Ten, Bar.*
Subject: Praise of a mistress.
Voice: Steps, small skips, sequence; simple rhythm.
Piano: Chordal.
Comment: St. 1, line 2: hap = luck (since she will enslave all others). A lively little song. Colls 22, 23: accompaniment and introductions to each stanza by Keel. St. 4, line 1: *is mixt =*

mixed is, all other editions. Printed in Forbes, 1662, 1666, 1682.

(5) If there be anyone. Coll 23; Coll 22, *Bb major*.

         G major. d'-d", [f' #-d"]. 4/4. 45". 3 St. V/me, P/e.

For:	*[Sop], Ten*; [Mezzo], C-Ten, Bar.
Subject:	If anyone is suffering the pangs of love, let him join me.
Voice:	Repeated d"s; steps and 3rds; rhythms simple.
Piano:	Chordal, with melodic bass.
Comment:	Colls 22, 23: accompaniment by Keel, with four bars introduction to each stanza to Bartlet's one. Bartlet has a fourth stanza: 'If there be any one that fraud hath perplexed, / Or burst his heart at love's command; / If there be any one whom all griefs have vexed, / Or in hell's pains do daily stand, / Such is my case. Let him come sit with me and mourn, / That feels hell's pain and lover's grief with love's great scorn.' St. 1, line 6: gripe = grip. St. 2, line 5: *come let him sit* = thus in source, but almost certainly an error for *let him come sit*, as in other stanzas. St. 3, line 2: to be drowned under the stress of misfortune (*too* = *to*). Colls 22, [23]: bar 15, note 2: b'*b* not c", [g' not a'], all stanzas.

(6) I heard of late. Coll 22; Coll 23, *Eb major*.

         G major. d'-g", [g'-e"]. 4/4. 45". 3 St. V/me, P/e.

For:	Sop, Ten; *Mezzo, C-Ten, Bar.*
Subject:	Love is a dangerous fellow, full of tricks.
Voice:	Steps, small skips; 8ve leaps, sequences; rhythm simple but varied.
Piano:	Chordal, with melodic bass.
Comment:	Colls 22, 23: accompaniment by Keel. St. 1, line 1: *had* = *was*, all other editions; line 6: *awake* (Coll 22) = *awaked*, all other editions. St. 2, line 3: tickle = difficult; line 4: it is = there is; line 5: in his fetters fall = in the trap of his fetters. St. 3, line 2: worm – here meaning a harmless creature; line 3: coy conceit = disdainful idea; line 6: parlous = perilous.

(9) A pretty duck there was. Coll 5; Coll 22, *F major*; Coll 23, *D major*.

         G major. g'-a". [b'-g"]. 2/2. 45". [35"]. 3 St. V/m, P/e.

For:	Sop, Ten; *Mezzo, C-Ten, Bar.*
Subject:	Describes a young girl looking to find a lover.
Voice:	Steps, simple skips, repeated notes; bouncy rhythms, semi-patter; high-lying.
Piano:	Mostly chordal.
Comment:	Repeat optional. Needs clear diction, difficult with the high tessitura; but great fun for a high light soprano with a sense of humour. Colls 22, 23: accompaniment by Keel. Bar 15:

slur notes 2-3, not 1-2. St. 2, line 2: *lonely* = *lovely*, all other
editions, however, this seems quite a reasonable emendation. St. 3: invented by Keel to replace the original, which
runs: 'A tickling part that maidens love, / But I can never
get; / Yet long have sought, and still do crave, / At rest my
heart to set.'

(10) Of all the birds (George Gascoigne, *Poesies*, 1575). Colls 7, 19; Coll
8, *D major.*

G major. g'-g", [a'-e"]. 3/4. 45", [35"]. 5 St. V/e, P/e.

For:	Sop, Ten; *Mezzo, C-Ten, Bar.*
Subject:	My sparrow behaves delightfully, and has no equal.
Voice:	3rds, steps, many repeated notes, rhythms simple.
Piano:	Chordal.
Comment:	Repeat optional. A cheerful little number. Stanzas can be omitted – the original poem has nine, of six lines each, Bartlet's refrain being the final couplet of stanza 7. Only stanzas 1-4 and 8 are given in the song; stanza 9 would make things clearer: 'Wherefore I sing and ever shall / To praise as I have ever proved / There is no bird amongst them all / So worthy for to be beloved. / Let others praise what bird they will / Sweet Philip shall be my bird still.'

Published in *A Hundred Sundrie Flowres*, 1573, headed:
'He wrote (at his friends request) in prayse of a
Gentlewoman, whose name was Philip, as followith'
(Doughtie). Both John Skelton (see Vaughan Williams, *Five
Tudor Portraits*), and Philip Sidney wrote poems on 'Philip
Sparrow'. Fellowes states that this is 'a skit on Philip
Sparrow, the poet'. St. 1, line 3: *or sit* = *or lie* in poem
(Doughtie). St. 3, line 3: lays on load = does something with
vehemence and energy, *EMV*, 'lays it on', Coll 19. St. 4, line
4: pricke and praunce = ride gaily, *OED*; line 5: fend cut =
maintain modest conduct, *EMV*, parry a thrust, Coll 19; line
6: peate = pet, Coll 19. St. 5, line 3: make ... game = make
fun of; line 4: suspect = suspicion.

(14) What thing is love? (George Peele, *The Hunting of Cupid*, 1591).
Coll 5; Coll 22, *A major;* Coll 23, *F major.*

G major. d'-e", [g'-d"]. 2/2. 35". V/e, P/e.

For:	*Sop, Ten*; Mezzo, C-Ten, Bar; *Cont, Bass.*
Subject:	Humorous description of love.
Voice:	Steps, broken chords, sequences, repeated notes; simple varied rhythms.
Piano:	Simple counterpoint.
Comment:	Useful encore. Line 6: devise = guess. Ault, *New OB* and *OB*

16 have the following variants: lines 1-2: *What thing is love? for sure (for, well I wot*, Ault) *love is a thing. It is a prick, it is a sting*; line 6: *wits = wit*; line 7: *dwelling is = darling lies*; and provide eight more lines: 'From whence do come love's piercing darts / That make such holes into our hearts / And all the world herein accord (agree) / Love is a great and mighty Lord. / And when he list (wishes) to mount so high / With Venus he in heaven doth lie / And evermore hath been a God / Since Mars and she played even and odd.' With some adjustments the whole poem could be sung to Bartlet's music. Though Venus was married to Vulcan she was caught having an affair with Mars. Colls 22, 23: accompaniment and introduction by Keel. Line 1: repeat *what thing is love*, not *I pray thee tell*.

DANIEL BATCHELOR
c. 1574 – after 1610

28 To plead my faith (Robert Devereux, Earl of Essex). Colls 1, 31.
C minor. f'-f ", [g'-f "]. 3/2,6/4. 2'20". V/e, P/me.

For:	Ten.
Subject:	I loved too high, my hopes are buried; forget me since you have scorned me; I do not repent, though I despair.
Voice:	Steps, repeated notes, broken chords; galliard-type rhythms.
Piano:	Basically chordal, but with fully written out 'divisions'.
Comment:	The accompaniment indicates Batchelor's calibre as a lutenist. He seems to have been Sir Philip Sidney's page. The poem (which appears in Earle, 1615, with some variants) is clearly addressed to Queen Elizabeth. See DP, pp. 226-8. Line 11: do all mischief prove = experience all misfortune. Use the second line of words for each repeat, and the third section must be repeated for balance. Coll 31 gives lute part only, Coll 1 gives viol part also. Coll 1, bar 11, beats 3-4: no naturals to a's in Coll 31 (bars 20-21); bar 14, beat 3: no natural to a° in Coll 31 (bar 26).

THOMAS CAMPION
1567 – 1620
The words of all Campion's songs are by Campion himself.

29 A BOOKE OF AYRES [Philip Rosseter], Set foorth to be sung to the Lute, Orpherian, and Base Viol. 1601. S & B edition by E.H. Fellowes,

1922; revised by Thurston Dart, 1960; revised by David Scott, 1969. Tablature provided (*LS* 8).

(1) My sweetest Lesbia. Davis; Colls 5, 8, *F major*; Coll 7, *Bb major*.
         G major. d'-e", [f' #-d"]. 3/2. 1'10", [50"]. 3 St. V/me, P/e.
For: *Sop, Ten*; C-Ten, Bar.
Subject: Let us be happy in our love, whatever others may think.
Voice: Steps, small skips; fluid rhythm; long phrasing desirable.
Piano: Chordal; a few contrapuntal bars.
Comment: Repeat optional. A charming tune, though not quite as simple as appears at first sight. Translated from Catullus' *Vivamus, mea Lesbia, atque amemus*. Another translation, possibly also by Campion, was set by Corkine, 41 (11). St. 1, line 3: weigh = value; line 6: ever-during = everlasting. Ben Jonson also made a translation of the same poem, see **49 (6)**.

(2) Though you are young. Davis.
         D minor. d'-f ", [f'-f "]. 3/2. 50", [35"]. 3 St. V/e, P/e.
For: Mezzo, Bar.
Subject: Age speaks to youth, claiming the value of experience.
Voice: Steps, small skips; all four phrases in the same simple rhythm.
Piano: Simple three-part counterpoint.
Comment: Repeat optional. St. 2, line 4: stubs = tree stumps. Copies in Earle, 1615, and Christ Church MS 439. Printed by Playford, 1669 and 1672, in a setting by Henry Playford. Bar 4, beat 2: Davis has no flat to b°.

(3) I care not for these ladies. Colls 19, 28, Davis.
         G major. d'-e", [e'-d"]. 3/2. 50", [35"]. 3 St. V/e, P/e.
For: C-Ten, Bar.
Subject: Court ladies are artificial and require expensive presents; I prefer the natural country girl who wants only love.
Voice: Steps, small skips; dance rhythms, mostly simple.
Piano: Chordal, with slight decoration.
Comment: Second repeat optional. Note: Amaryllis was a name used for a shepherdess by Theocritus, Virgil and Ovid. Variants in Earle, 1615: St. 1, line 1: *these* = *those*. St. 2, lines 2, 3: *We* = *I*. The tune is a jig, suitable for a song dealing with what Hamlet called 'country matters', as in the sexual pun in line 2, backed up by line 5 of the first stanza.

(4) Follow thy fair sun. Colls 19, 30, Davis; Coll 13, *B minor*; Colls 5, 14, *F# minor*.
         G minor. d'-d", [f'-d"]. 2/2. 50", [30"]. 5 St. V/me, P/e.

For: *Sop, Ten*; Mezzo, C-Ten, Bar; *Cont, Bass*.
Subject: Serious advice to the unhappy lover to keep faith in spite of rejection.
Voice: Steps, 3rds; one chromatic phrase; rhythms simple; long phrasing desirable but not essential.
Piano: Chordal, with decorations.
Comment: Repeat optional, better omitted. Some stanzas may be cut, Colls 11 and 12 only give 1, 4 and 5. Campion used the same music for 'Seek the Lord', 30 (8). A simple but beautiful song. St. 2-5, line 2: first two syllables to be repeated. St. 4, line 4: divineth = realises. St. 5, lines 2-3: the sun creates the shadow; line 4: proved = approved – but Vivian gives *proud*, without comment, and *EMV*, though giving *proved* in the text, following Bullen, notes that the original reads *prou'd* – which would seem to allow Vivian's more convincing reading. Ault and Coll 30 follow Vivian. Davis gives *prov'd* with a note that it means *approved*, but since he has 'regularised *u* and *v*' this may not refute *EMV*.

(5) **My love hath vowed**.
            G minor. d'-d'', [f'-d'']. 2/2. 55'', [40'']. 4 St. V/e, P/e.
For: Mezzo.
Subject: My lover will leave me, having had his desire. If I had known I would not have believed his promises; men are not to be trusted, and 'I will go no more a-maying'.
Voice: Steps; some rhythmic variety.
Piano: Three-part counterpoint, then chordal.
Comment: Repeat optional; some stanzas may be omitted. St. 1, line 2: sped = undone. St. 2, line 2: prove = experience; line 4: event = unhappy result. St. 4, line 3: importune = beset with requests. BL Add. MS 34608.

(6) **When to her lute Corinna sings**. Coll 31, Davis; Coll 9, *A minor*; Colls 5, 10, *E minor*.
            G minor. d'-f'', [d'-d'']. 2/2. 50'', [35'']. 2 St. V/me. P/e.
For: *Sop, Ten*; Mezzo, Bar; *Cont, C-Ten, Bass*.
Subject: Describes the effect of well-played music on the listener.
Voice: Steps, broken chords, sequence; 8ve leap; very varied rhythms; short melismas.
Piano: Chordal, with some decoration.
Comment: A marvellous matching of words and music; Campion's art at its best. Repeat optional. Words printed in Davison, 1602, and set by Jones as a madrigal, *EM* 35a (16-17). St. 1, line 2: leaden = heavy; line 4: challeng'd echo – a call must be made for an echo to respond. Coll 31: many bass notes an 8ve

lower, following the viol part; bar 12, beat 4, LH: quaver rest quaver, for crotchet of *LS* 8.

(7) Turn back you wanton flyer. Colls 19, 30.

G minor. f'#-f ″, [g'-f ″]. 2/2. 50″, [40″]. 2 St. V/e, P/e.

For:	Sop, Ten.
Subject:	Come back to me, for 'hearts with hearts delighted should strive to be united'; let us exchange our kisses.
Voice:	Steps, small skips; simple bouncy rhythms, with unusual final phrase.
Piano:	Chordal; some decoration.
Comment:	Second repeat optional, but better included. See **31 (10)** for a closely related song. St. 1, line 1: wanton = frisky; line 5: *shines still, LS* 8 = *still shines*, all other editions; still = always; line 11: entertaining = holding mutually together. St. 2, line 8: *swerving = changing*, in source, Davis, and Fellowes' original edition; altered by both Bullen and Vivian to maintain the rhyme; lines 10 and 11: commas after sow and reap, as given in *EMV*, Vivian and Fellowes, make the sense clearer and match the first stanza. Coll 30: bar 5, beat 3, voice: sharp given to c″ in brackets, not in other editions.

(8) It fell on a summer's day. Coll 5.

G major. f'#-e″, [g'-d″]. 2/2. 30″, [20″]. 4 St. V/me, P/me.

For:	Sop, Ten; Mezzo, C-Ten, Bar.
Subject:	Delightful tale of seduction welcomed by the seduced.
Voice:	Steps, small skips, short melisma; rhythmically full of subtle variations which need careful study.
Piano:	Chordal, some decoration; rhythmic traps, and an awkward cadence.
Comment:	Repeat optional. Coll 5 has revised barring. Perhaps the most enchanting of all Campion's songs, this needs a light touch by a singer with a sense of humour. St. 1, line 3: bow'r = bedroom. St. 2, line 6: dump = reverie. St. 4, line 3: sleight = trickery; line 4: her pretence allows him to act as though she were really asleep; line 5: trance = dazed state or ecstasy. Campion wrote two Latin versions of the poem.

(9) The cypress curtain of the night. Colls 5, 11; Coll 12, *D minor*.

G minor. g'-f ″. 3/2. 1'25″, [1']. 3 St. V/me, P/me.

For:	Sop, Ten; *Mezzo, Bar*; *Cont, C-Ten, Bass*.
Subject:	My sorrow is too great to be eased by sleep.
Voice:	Steps; simple rhythm; long sustained phrases.
Piano:	Three-part counterpoint.
Comment:	Repeat optional. A serious and deeply felt song. St. 1, line 1:

cypress – thin crape-like material, originally from Cyprus, died black and used for mourning; line 5: Morpheus – the Greek God of Dreams. St. 2, line 4: bands = fetters; line 5: reft = bereft, robbed. St. 3, line 2: crazed = broken; line 4: tire upon = feed greedily upon – a term used in hawking.

(10) Follow your saint. Colls 9, 19; Colls 5, 10, *E minor.*
G minor. f'-f ", [a'-d"]. 3/2. 45". 2 St. V/e, P/e.
For: Sop, Ten; Mezzo, Bar; *Cont, C-Ten, Bass.*
Subject: The pleasure and pain of worshipping the beloved, or possibly St Cecilia, patron saint of music.
Voice: Steps, 6th leaps; simple rhythms.
Piano: Chordal; occasional decoration.
Comment: Almost the same tune as **33 (10)**. St. 1, line 3: pity move = cause (her) to feel pity. St. 2, line 4: sympathy = harmony, concord; agreement in quality, likeness.

(11) Fair, if you expect admiring. Colls 19, 28.
G major. d'-e", [g'-d"]. 2/2. 45", [35"]. 2 St. V/e, P/e.
For: Mezzo, C-Ten, Bar.
Subject: If you wish to be loved you should respond, otherwise leave me alone; but even if grief is my lot I will try again.
Voice: Steps, small skips; lively and fairly varied rhythm.
Piano: Chordal, some decoration.
Comment: Second repeat optional. *Her* three lines from the end could be changed to *him*. St. 1, line 3: grace love by returning it in kind (Davis); line 4: fond = infatuated; but if = unless; line 6: false if you show your 'love' of unkindness by fleeing from love and delight (Davis). St. 3, line 2: importune = beset with requests.

(12) Thou art not fair. Davis.
C minor. g'-f ". 3/2. 1'10", [50"]. 2 St. V/e, P/e.
For: Ten.
Subject: 'Beauty is no beauty without love'; do not kiss me if you do not love me.
Voice: Steps, small skips; occasional short melismas; varied rhythm.
Piano: Chordal with decoration.
Comment: Repeat optional. Barlines are misleading. Set as a madrigal by Vautor, *EM* 34 (13-14). Reprinted in Playford, 1652, 1653, 1659, reset by Nicholas Lanier; and appears in several MSS, including a version in sonnet form, probably an early version by Campion (Davis). Campion wrote a Latin version which makes the point of the second stanza clear – the

man's rejection of the woman in the first four lines should make the woman, if truly a woman, embrace him just because he no longer wants her! St. 1, line 3: mere = pure, perfect; line 5: prove = find. St. 2, line 1: *seek not*, *LS* 8, = *seek thou*, *EMV* and Davis; line 6: in despite = in spite of all I have just said!

(13) See where she flies.

G major. e'-e″, [f' #-d″]. 2/2,3/2. 55″. 2 St. V/me, P/me.

For: C-Ten, Bar.
Subject: Terrifying when she is angry, when pleased a pure delight; my happiness depends on her mood.
Voice: Steps and repeated notes; varied rhythms.
Piano: Chordal; some decoration.
Comment: Choice of tempo rather difficult; perhaps the middle section should be dotted semibreve = semibreve, in spite of the hemiola. St. 2, line 3: blowne = full-blown like flowers; line 8: froward = unreasonable.

(14) Blame not my cheeks. Davis.

D minor. d'-d″. 3/2. 1′05″, [50″]. 2 St. V/e, P/e.

For: Mezzo, C-Ten, Bar.
Subject: Pale cheeks show a warm heart, and vice versa.
Voice: Steps, small skips, 8ve drop; simple rhythms.
Piano: Simple three-part counterpoint.
Comment: Repeat optional. Barlines misleading. Set by Jones, **59 (9)**. Printed in Davison, 1602. St. 1, line 4: *are* = *art*, Vivian, Davis and Fellowes.

(15) When the god of merry love.

G minor. f'-d″, [g'-d″]. 2/2. 35″, [25″]. 2 St. V/e, P/e.

For: Mezzo, C-Ten, Bar.
Subject: When Cupid was a babe his old nurse kissed him; inflamed with love she cried until she died.
Voice: Steps, small skips; very simple rhythm.
Piano: Chordal with decoration.
Comment: Repeat optional. The last two lines of each verse are a rare example of awkward word-setting by Campion. St. 1, line 4: wanton = mischievous.

(16) Mistress since you so much desire.

G major. d'-d″. 2/2. 1′10″, [45″]. 2 St. V/e, P/e.

For: C-Ten, Bar.
Subject: Love lies not in your heart or your lips, but in your eyes.
Voice: Steps, skips; four-fold sequence; rhythmic variety.
Piano: Chordal, and contrapuntal.

Comment: Repeat optional. See **33 (22)** for a rather more bawdy
               version.

(17) Your fair looks. Coll 31.

               G minor. d'-d''. 2/2. 55'', [35'']. 3 St. V/me, P/e.
For: Mezzo, C-Ten, Bar.
Subject: You arouse my desires; come to the quiet grove and embrace
               me; if you must now leave, come again when it is safe.
Voice: Steps and skips; simple rhythms except for a tricky last line.
Piano: Simple three-part counterpoint.
Comment: Repeat optional. An effective song if the last line can be
               handled convincingly. See **33 (23)** for another working of this
               subject. St. 2, line 8: die = reach consummation. Coll 31: line
               7, the f' on the first syllable of *grovy* is given a sharp.

(18) The man of life upright.

               G minor. g'-d''. 2/2. 40'', [25'']. 6 St. V/me, P/e.
For: Sop, Ten; Mezzo, C-Ten, Bar.
Subject: Only the virtuous man can defy fate.
Voice: Steps; rhythms of second part difficult to make convincing.
Piano: Simple counterpoint.
Comment: Repeat optional; some stanzas could be omitted. The first
               four stanzas are based on Horace *Odes* 1.22, *Integer vitae
               scelerisque purus*. See **30 (2)** for another setting by Campion;
               also set as a madrigal by Alison, 1606, *EM* 33 (1-2). The
               poem appears in several MSS, sometimes attributed to
               Francis Bacon.

(19) Hark all you ladies. Coll 19, Davis.

               G major. g'-g'', [g'-e'']. 2/2. 40'', [25'']. 5 St. V/e, P/e.
For: Sop, Ten.
Subject: Ladies, Proserpina bids you wake and have pity on your
               lovers, or her fairies will punish you. If you obey she will
               make you more beautiful, but those who do not love shall
               lead apes in hell.
Voice: Steps, small skips, repeated notes; simple but lively rhythm.
Piano: Chordal with decoration.
Comment: Repeat optional; some stanzas could be omitted. A cheerful
               and entertaining song. St. 1, line 2: Proserpina – wife of
               Pluto and Queen of the Underworld. St. 2, line 6: rue =
               regret and pity; line 7: paramours = lovers. St. 4, line 3:
               Dione – a consort of Zeus, worshipped at Dodona, where the
               oracle spoke through doves, and the priestesses were called
               'pigeons'; line 5: damask hue – damask roses are pink. St. 5,
               line 7: Avernus – the entrance to Hades, the underworld.

Bar 1, beat 4: c′ in *LS* 8 is misprint for d′, see tablature. The idea that old maids were condemned to go with apes in hell after death was common at this time. The poem was first printed in the appendix to the 1591 edition of Sidney's *Astrophel and Stella*. It also appears in two MS versions.

(20) When thou must home. Coll 19, Davis.

G minor. d′-e″*b*, [e′-d″]. 3/2. 1′10″, [50″]. 2 St. V/e, P/e.

For: C-Ten, Bar.

Subject: When you die and meet Helen and the other spirits in Elysium tell them how much honour was done to your beauty, and then how you murdered me.

Voice: Steps, small skips; simple smooth rhythms.

Piano: Simple three-part counterpoint.

Comment: Repeat optional. One of Campion's most beautiful poems, based on Propertius 2.28, *Sunt apud infernos tot milia formosarum*. St. 1, line 3: ingirt = encircle; line 4: Iope – ?Io, loved by Zeus; Helen – Helen of Troy; line 5: finished = perfect, completed. St. 2, line 1: tourneys = tournaments. Bar 14, bass, beat 2: the c° in *LS* 8 is an editorial addition, see tablature; Davis and Coll 19 have semibreve B*b*.

(21) Come let us sound with melody. Davis.

G minor. f′#-d″, [g′-d″]. 2/2. 35″. 6 St. V/me, P/me.

For: Mezzo, C-Ten, Bar.

Subject: Let us praise God and his Holy Spirit. Guide my soul and have mercy on my sins, and I will give thee honour in heaven.

Voice: Steps, small skips; rhythm controlled entirely by words.

Piano: Chordal.

Comment: An experiment in classical metre (Sapphic), in the manner of the French 'vers mesurés'. It is a very free paraphrase of Psalm 19: The heavens declare the glory of God. Barlines misleading. A very unusual song, more effective than is sometimes suggested. Some stanzas could be omitted. St. 4, line 1: thy bespotted image – man, made in the image of God, but bespotted by sin.

30 THE FIRST BOOKE OF AYRES Containing Divine and Morall Songs. To be sung to the Lute and Viols, in two, three, and foure Parts; or by one Voyce to an Instrument. c. 1613. S & B edition by E.H. Fellowes, 1925. Revised by David Scott, 1979 (*LS* 5).

V/e, P/e, for almost all the songs, which have simple hymn-like melodies with chordal accompaniments; exceptions are noted in the Comments below.

(1) **Author of light.** Coll 5.

G minor. d′-e″b, [d′-d″]. 4/2. 1′10″. 2 St.

For: Mezzo, C-Ten, Bar.

Subject: A prayer for mercy, in the belief that God will grant it.

Comment: Melodically fairly elaborate, with some chromatics; free and varied rhythm not always related to word accent, so care is needed. Campion's most ambitious religious song. St. 1, line 1: sprite = spirit; line 2: confounding = destroying; line 5: underlights = lights from below, such as volcanoes? St. 2, line 1: recure = restore to health; line 4: place the heart in joy's bosom; line 6: assuage = relieve. See Wilfrid Mellers 'Words and Music in Elizabethan England', *The Age of Shakespeare*, ed. Boris Ford, Pelican Guides to English Literature 2, London 1955.

(2) **The man of life upright.**

C major. e′-e″. 4/2. 20″. 6 St.

For: Mezzo, C-Ten, Bar.

Subject: Only the virtuous man can defy fate.

Comment: Some stanzas could be omitted. See also **29 (18)**.

(3) **Where are all thy beauties now.**

G minor. g′-g″, [g′-f″]. 2/2. 40″, [30″]. 4 St.

For: Sop, Ten.

Subject: An eulogy for a dead ruler; with all his faults he was better than his detractors.

Comment: Repeat optional. St. 2, line 1; state = throne with canopy; bays = baize, a coarse cloth, according to Davis; Scott suggests the alternative of a wreath of bay-leaves as also possible.

(4) **Out of my soul's depth.**

G minor. f′#-f″, [g′-e″]. 4/2. 35″. 4 St.

For: Sop, Ten.

Subject: A cry for mercy, and a trust in God.

Comment: Paraphrase of Psalm 130: Out of the deep have I cried unto Thee (*De profundis*). St. 3, line 3: the night watch stands down at dawn. St. 4, line 4: recure = cure.

(5) **View me, Lord, a work of thine.**

G minor. d′-d″, [d′-c″]. 4/2. 25″. 5 St.

For: Mezzo, C-Ten, Bar.

Subject: I am a sinner; cleanse me, O Lord.

Comment: One or two stanzas could be omitted. St. 2, line 1: surfeits = overfeeds; line 4: is = *in* in source; Vivian's emendation followed by all other editors.

(6) Bravely deck'd, come forth bright day.
C major. c'-e", [d'-e"]. 4/2. 40". 4 St.

For: Mezzo, C-Ten, Bar.

Subject: A celebration of King James's escape from the Gunpowder Plot of November 5th, 1605.

Comment: One or two stanzas could be omitted. The final stanza refers to the death of Prince Henry in 1612, which caused Charles to become heir to the throne. St. 1, line 8: ember – ember days are fast-days in the church. Davis gives ember as 'period or revolution of time', but *OED* only gives this in relation to a possible Old English source *ymbryne*. St. 2, line 8: oblations = offerings of thanksgiving. St. 3, line 9: No one could have imagined such wickedness; *treason of* = *treason or*, *EMV* and Davis. St. 4, line 2: disclose = uncover, reveal; Davis gives *disperse*, but this meaning is not given in *OED*.

(7) To music bent is my retired mind.
C minor. f'-c", [g'-c"]. 4/2. 25". 3 St.

For: Mezzo, C-Ten, Bar.

Subject: I would turn to music, but to sing of heaven, not earth.

Comment: Repeat optional. St. 1, line 2: fain = gladly; lines 5-6: to record God's power and mercies will sweeten the song (Davis).

(8) Tune thy music to thy heart. Davis.
C minor. g'-e"b, [g'-c"]. 4/2. 25". 3 St.

For: Sop, Ten; Mezzo, C-Ten, Bar.

Subject: Sing with devotion; to love is the highest art.

Comment: St. 1, line 2: so = in the same way. Line 4: *sometime* = *sometimes* in Vivian. St. 2, line 1: curious = elaborate; line 3: affects = desires. St. 3, line 1: *effect* (do) = *affect* (aim at) in Vivian.

(9) Most sweet and pleasing are thy ways.
G minor. f'-d", [g'-d"]. 4/2. 1'05", [45"]. 2 St.

For: Mezzo, C-Ten, Bar.

Subject: God's paths are only for the good; there is no evil in paradise.

Comment: Repeat optional.

(10) Wise men patience never want.
C major. d'-e", [d'-d"]. 4/2. 40", [30"]. 4 St.

For: Mezzo, C-Ten, Bar.

Subject: Forgiveness is a great virtue, which once came naturally to men.

Comment: Repeat optional. St. 1, line 1: want = lack; line 3: vaunt = boast; line 5: only he that can forgive. St. 4, line 1: Deeds and words that flow from love (Davis); line 6: *whereon = where on* in Vivian and Davis, who gives – His gentle rays make thrive all things over which the water of human love has spread itself.

(11) Never weatherbeaten sail. Coll 19, Davis.

                G major. d'-e", [e'-d"]. 2/2. 50". 2 St.

For: Mezzo, C-Ten, Bar.

Subject: Lord, come quickly, and carry my tired soul to heaven.

Comment: Many paired quavers in this lovely tune; one of the most beautiful hymns ever written. There is an MS copy of the poem, clearly written out from memory, dated November 1707, which testifies to its enduring popularity. St. 1, line 2: affected = aspired to, was drawn to; line 3: sprite = spirit.

(12) Lift up to heaven.

                G minor. g'-e'b. 4/2. 1'20", [55"]. 2 St.

For: Sop, Ten; Mezzo, C-Ten, Bar.

Subject: Do not fear to repent, for God is merciful.

Comment: Repeat optional. St. 1, line 4: ruth = pity.

(13) Lo, when back mine eye.

                F major. e'-e", [f'-d"]. 4/2. 20". 6 St.

For: Mezzo, C-Ten, Bar.

Subject: When I look back I see the hell I have escaped, and praise God for his mercy.

Comment: Some stanzas could be omitted. St. 5, line 4: ever-during = everlasting. St. 6, line 3: *humbly = humble* in source, amended by Vivian and all subsequent editors.

(14) As by the streams of Babylon.

                G minor. g'-f ", [g'-d"]. 4/2. 45", [30"]. 6 St.

For: Sop, Ten; Mezzo, Bar.

Subject: Paraphrase of Psalm 137: By the waters of Babylon we sat down and wept (*Super flumina*); how shall we sing the Lord's song in a strange land?

Comment: Repeat optional. St. 5/6 could well be omitted. St. 1, line 4: begat = created. St. 2, line 1: aloft = on top of. St. 3, line 3: Salem = Jerusalem. St. 4, line 4: ground = both the earth, and the ground bass of a melody. St. 5, lines 3-4: these two lines should be in quotes, being the words cried by the Children of Edom, long-time enemies of Israel; line 4: *stone by stone = stone and by stone* in source, amended by Vivian and all subsequent editors. St. 6, line 1: Babel's seed – the daughters of Babylon.

(15) Sing a song of joy.
G major. g′-e″. 4/2. 15″. 7 St.

For: Sop, Ten; Mezzo, C-Ten, Bar.
Subject: A hymn of praise. A free paraphrase of verses 1-5 of Psalm 104: Bless the Lord, O my soul (*Benedic, anima mea*).
Comment: Some stanzas could be omitted. St. 2, line 4: renown = celebrate. St. 6, line 2: hests = behests, commands.

(16) Awake, awake, thou heavy sprite.
G major. d′-e″, [d′-d″]. 2/2. 1′, [45″]. 2 St.

For: Mezzo, C-Ten, Bar.
Subject: Rise and seek heaven, before it is too late.
Comment: Repeat optional. A rather more elaborate melody, with several paired quavers, 6th and 8ve leaps, and a melisma. St. 1, line 6: still = always. St. 2: You think life long, but your fate may be decided at any moment. Davis gives the following interpretation of the first three lines: Your daily steps are leading you towards eternal reward or punishment, *but* they are minute (a span, the measure of a hand) compared to the extent of time they foreshadow.

(17) Come cheerful day. Davis.
G major/minor. d′-f ″, [d′-e″]. 4/2. 1′30″, [1′05″]. 2 St.

For: Mezzo, Bar.
Subject: Every day and every night brings us nearer death.
Comment: A very unusual song, in that the (optionally) repeated section has a new key signature. Davis, bar 9: sharp to f° missing. *LS* 5, bar 11, bass, last crotchet should be f°.

(18) Seek the Lord.
G minor. d′-d″, [f′-d″]. 4/2. 45″, [30″]. 4 St.

For: Mezzo, C-Ten, Bar.
Subject: Seek the Lord and you will triumph; leave the world and you will be saved.
Comment: Repeat optional. Stanza 3 could be omitted. Almost the same music as **29** (4). St. 3, line 3: foils = adornments. St. 4, line 3: sovereign = powerful, and superlative as medicine.

(19) Lighten, heavy heart, thy sprite.
G major. d′-e″, [d′-e″]. 2/2. 45″. 2 St.

For: Mezzo, C-Ten, Bar.
Subject: Lift up your spirit and act; sloth is a great sin.

Comment: St. 1, line 4: temper = temperament, mental or musical. St. 2, line 1: distastes = unpleasantness; line 6: moorish = sluggish, used of water found in boggy soil.

(20) **Jack and Joan**. Colls 19, 28; Coll 11, A major; Coll 12, F major.
        G major. f'#-e", [g'-d"]. 2/2. 35". 4 St.

For: *Sop, Ten*; Mezzo, C-Ten, Bar.

Subject: Country folk lead a better and happier life than courtiers.

Comment: A dance tune rather than a hymn, with many paired quavers in lilting rhythm. Stanzas 2/3 may be omitted. St. 1, line 7: lash out = squander money (*OED* gives this meaning as obsolete!). St. 2, line 1: nappy = strong and foaming; line 4: crabs = crab-apples. St. 3, line 3: tutties = bouquets, nosegays – Dorset dialect, according to Vivian; line 7: which others break – Davis points out that it is the nobility who break the hedges while hunting. St. 4, line 4: silly = simple. Coll 28 has a number of passing notes in RH: bar 1: beat 2: a°g° quavers; bar 6: beat 4: a°b° quavers; bar 7, beats 1-2: c'd'e'd' quavers.

(21) **All looks be pale**. Coll 19.
        G minor. d'-f ", [f'-f "]. 2/2. 55". 4 St.

For: Mezzo, Bar.

Subject: An elegy on the death of Prince Henry, much loved eldest son of James I, who died in 1612.

Comment: Like the first song in this *Booke* in its free and varied rhythms; melismas, 6th leap. A stanza could be omitted. St. 2, line 5: want = lack. St. 4, line 1: wished sight = desired appearance. For the death of Prince Henry see **38**.

31 **THE SECOND BOOKE OF AYRES** Containing Light Conceits of Lovers. To be sung to the Lute and Viols, in two, and three Parts: or by one Voyce to an Instrument. c. 1613. S & B edition by E.H. Fellowes, 1925. Revised by David Scott, 1979 (*LS* 6). Tablature provided.

(1) **Vain men whose follies**. Coll 5.
        F major. f'-f ". 4/2. 45", [35"]. 3 St. V/me, P/me.

For: Ten; Bar.

Subject: Advice to men not to put women on pedestals, but to accept them as they are.

Voice: Steps and some 3rds; fairly long smooth line in first section, then two short rhythmic phrases.

Piano: Chordal, some decoration; rhythms need care.

Comment: Repeat needed for balance. Misleading barring revised in
             Coll 5. Tempo must be carefully judged to allow a constant
             crotchet for both sections. St. 1, line 3: prove = put to the
             test. St. 2, line 5: brake = broke. St. 3, line 3: consent = agree
             together. Copies appear in several MSS.

(2) How eas'ly wert thou chained. Davis.
             C minor. g'-f ". 2/2. 1'. 3 St. V/e, P/e.
For: Ten.
Subject: It is no woman but a goddess who has left me, no wonder I
             now grieve.
Voice: Steps, small skips; lies high; some rhythmic variety.
Piano: Chordal.
Comment: A remarkable match of harmony and words. St. 2, line 7: he
             – the god of Love. Davis, bar 9, voice: 7th crotchet should be
             c' not b°.

(3) Harden now thy tired heart.
             G minor. g'-f ", [g'-e"b]. 2/2. 1'20", [1']. 2 St. V/e, P/e.
For: Ten; Bar.
Subject: Once you and I were truly happy; now you have betrayed me
             where will you find a man to love and admire you as I did?
Voice: Steps and skips; 6th leap; simple rhythms.
Piano: Chordal, with some decoration.
Comment: Repeat optional. St. 1, line 2: assuage = soothe, relieve. St. 2,
             line 1: trai'tress – the original spelling *Tray-tresse* points the
             pun; line 5: wot = knows.

(4) O what unhoped for sweet supply. Coll 5.
             F minor. f'-f ", [f'-e"b]. 2/2. 45", [30"]. 2 St. V/e, p/e.
For: [Sop], Ten; [Mezzo], Bar.
Subject: Joy at finding love unexpectedly returned.
Voice: Steps; 6th drop; simple rhythms.
Piano: Chordal.
Comment: Repeat optional. Words from masculine viewpoint, but could
             be easily reversed.

(5) Where she her sacred bow'r adorns. Coll 21; Coll 20, *Bb major*.
             G major. d'-d", [e'-c"]. 2/2. 40". 5 St. V/e, P/e.
For: *Ten*; C-Ten, Bar.
Subject: She is so lovely I must adore her, whether she responds or
             no.
Voice: Steps, a few skips, 6th drop; simple rhythms, many paired
             quavers.
Piano: Chordal.

Comment: Some stanzas could be omitted. St. 2, lines 2, 4: love =
             affection, grace = material favours; line 8: let me die, or, let
             me be damned (Davis). St. 4, line 5: *womb* = *worth*, *EMV* and
             Davis. Colls 20, 21: accompaniment and introduction to each
             stanza by Keel. The first word should be *Where*, not *Here*. The
             repeats in the tune have been wrongly organised, the phrases
             should run AABB not ABAB. Stanzas three and four omitted.

(6) Fain would I my love disclose.
             G major. f'#-d", [g'-d"]. 2/2. 40". 4 St. V/e, P/e.
For: C-Ten, Bar.
Subject: If I tell her of my desires I might lose her; but they are so
             strong I must do so, and she is wise enough to know the
             effect she has on men.
Voice: Steps, small skips; simple rhythms with many paired
             quavers.
Piano: Chordal.
Comment: Fourth stanza rather complex, and could be omitted. St. 1,
             line 1: fain = gladly. St. 2, line 2: school'd = disciplined
             (Davis), accustomed (Scott); line 8: recure = curing; *past* =
             most, in source; this sensible seeming emendation men-
             tioned by Scott, first made by Bullen, and followed by all
             other editors. St. 3, line 8: deserts = merits. St. 4, line 1:
             have the hand = have the ability; line 2: distaste = dislike;
             line 4: want = lack; their wills embraced = they desired; line
             8: they are deliberately trying to be caught (Davis).

(7) Give beauty all her right.
             F major. c'-d", [f'-c"]. 2/2. 55", [35"]. V/me, P/e.
For: C-Ten, Bar.
Subject: Beauty takes many forms, and my love is as fair as any.
Voice: Steps, small skips; scale, broken chords, sequences; varied
             rhythms, paired quavers.
Piano: Chordal, with some decoration.
Comment: Repeat optional. Barlines misleading – the rhythm is very
             free in this fairly elaborate melody. An interesting song. St.
             1, line 6: Ros'mund – Rosamond Clifford, mistress of Henry
             II, a favourite romantic heroine with the Elizabethans. St. 2,
             line 2: *swelling* = *smelling*, in source; emendation by Bullen
             followed by Vivian and *EMV*; Davis gives *smelling* with
             note: sweetly smelling – the unfavourable connotation is
             modern; Scott also gives *smelling* with note: *?swelling,
             ?smiling.*

(8) O dear that I with thee might live. Coll 23; Coll 22, *B minor*.

> G minor. d'-d". 2/2. 1', [40"]. 3 St. V/e, P/e.

For: *Sop, Ten*; Mezzo, C-Ten, Bar.

Subject: If we could live alone we could avoid jealousy, but in any case our love is strong enough to survive it.

Voice: Steps, sequences; paired quavers in simple rhythms.

Piano: Chordal, occasional decoration.

Comment: Repeat optional. St. 1, line 5: may colour find = may find supporting evidence; line 6: diseased = uncomfortable. St. 2, line 3: *other* = *others* in Davis, *other's* in *EMV*; line 5: suspect = suspicion; line 6: of force = of necessity. St. 3, lines 3-4: when a lover relents from his jealous hate it melts away as quickly as snow in the sun; line 5: kindness = love. Colls 22, 23: accompaniment and introduction to each stanza by Keel. St. 2, line 4: *all* = *thee*, all other editions.

(9) Good men, show if you can tell.

> C minor. c'-e"b, [c'-d"]. 2/2. 25". 5 St. V/e, P/e.

For: Mezzo.

Subject: Where is pity? I am young, but have learnt that men cannot be trusted, and my friends do but laugh.

Voice: Steps and skips; 8ve drop; short simple tune.

Piano: Chordal.

Comment: Some stanzas could be omitted, though all are worth singing. St. 1, line 3: *would I* = *I would* in Vivian; line 6: only = especially. St. 5, line 3: rue = pity.

(10) What harvest half so sweet is? Coll 19, Davis.

> G minor. f'-f', [g'-e"]. 2/2. 50", [35"]. 2 St. V/e, P/e.

For: Ten; Bar.

Subject: Kisses given and returned are harmless, though they may be disapproved of by others.

Voice: Steps, small skips; simple rhythms, many paired quavers, an extended cadence.

Piano: Chordal.

Comment: Second repeat optional; in any case there seems to be some uncertainty as to whether it includes the last four lines of the stanza or only the last two. St. 2, line 8: envie = regard with disapproval; pronounced to rhyme with deny. See **29 (7)**, where lines 1-6 of stanza 2 are the same as lines 1-6 of this song, with similar music.

(11) Sweet, exclude me not.

> G minor. d'-f ", [d'-e"b]. 2/2. 1'10", [45"]. 3 St. V/e, P/e.

For: Bar.

Subject: Since we are now engaged you should open your door; after all, rents are paid in advance!

Voice: Steps, small skips; sequences; varied rhythms and phrase-
           lengths.
Piano: Chordal, with some imitation of voice.
Comment: Repeat optional. Barring misleading – the first phrase is
           grouped 3/4,2/4,3/4,2/2, in all stanzas. A persuasive little
           song, suggesting more than it actually states. St. 1, line 4:
           sure = engaged. St. 2, line 2: quarter = quarter-day, when
           rents are paid.

(12) **The peaceful western wind.** Coll 5, Davis; Coll 23, *F major*; Coll 22,
      Bb major.
           G major. d'-e", [g'-d]. 2/2. 1', [40"]. 4 St. V/e, P/e.
For: *[Sop], Ten*; [Mezzo], C-Ten, Bar.
Subject: A celebration of spring for three stanzas; the fourth is a
           lover's complaint, which women could omit.
Voice: Steps, skips; simple rhythm with many paired quavers.
Piano: Chordal.
Comment: A charming folksong-like melody (the first phrase being
           based on 'The Westerne Winde' used by Taverner and others
           in Mass settings) which Campion also used for **34 (2)**. St. 1,
           line 1: wind – should be rhymed with kind; line 3: kind =
           sort; line 4: kind = loving; line 5: forward = early; line 6:
           earthly, in text = *earthy*, in music; line 8: fain = gladly. St. 2,
           line 8: overflown = flooded. St. 3, line 1: Saturn – equated by
           the Romans with the Greek god Chronos, who swallowed his
           children, thus destroying life, but was later forced by Zeus to
           bring them up again, illustrating the rebirth of the seasons.
           The original Roman Saturn was a god of agriculture, which
           may be more relevent in this context; line 2: love's queen –
           Venus; line 3: naked boy – Cupid. Another version of this
           poem, in BL Add. MS 15117, has a slightly different metrical
           scheme and a different tune; it omits St. 4, making it
           suitable for women, and substitutes *Nature* for *Saturn* in St.
           3. This poem is given in both Vivian and Davis. Colls 22, 23:
           accompaniment and introduction to each stanza by Keel. St.
           3 omitted.

(13) **There is none, O none but you.**
           F major. f'-d". 2/2. 30". 5 St. V/e, P/e.
For: C-Ten, Bar.
Subject: You are my only joy; if you are kind I will write such a book
           that all will wonder at your beauty and my faith.
Voice: Steps, two small skips; simple rhythm with many paired
           quavers.
Piano: Chordal.

Comment: Stanzas 2/3 could be omitted. St. 1, line 3: affect = aspire to.

(14) Pin'd I am, and like to die.
                 C major. c'-c". 2/2. 40", [25"]. 3 St. V/e, P/e.
For: Mezzo, Cont.
Subject: I lack what I refuse, and fly what I desire; but I shall try it
                 before long.
Voice: Steps, skips; 8ve leap, scale; simple rhythms, some paired
                 quavers.
Piano: Chordal, but some melodic movement in bass.
Comment: Repeat optional. The audience, and the singer, must be
                 carefully chosen; this song is full of double meanings,
                 depending on what 'it' may be! St. 3: see *Romeo and Juliet*,
                 Act II, Scene i, 23-26.

(15) So many loves have I neglected.
                 G major. d'-d". 2/2. 45". 4 St. V/e, P/e.
For: Mezzo.
Subject: Having rejected so many lovers I am now alone and would
                 repent; but men can speak their passions and women may
                 not.
Voice: Steps; 8ve drop and leap; simple rhythms with many paired
                 quavers.
Piano: Chordal.
Comment: Fourth stanza a little obscure, and could be omitted. Also set
                 by John Wilson, in *Cheerful Ayres*, 1660. St. 3, line 8: *roving
                 = moving*, in source, emended by Vivian, and followed by all
                 other editors. St. 4, line 1: strangeness = reserve; line 8:
                 strange = reserved.

(16) Though your strangeness frets my heart. Coll 19, Davis.
                 G minor. d'-d". 2/2. 50", [30"]. 4 St. V/e, P/e.
For: Mezzo, C-Ten, Bar.
Subject: Because our love must be kept secret you stay away, and
                 pretend to favour another; this is not fair to me.
Voice: Steps and many small skips; mostly crotchets, but a slightly
                 irregular final phrase.
Piano: Chordal.
Comment: Repeat optional. Also set, with several variants, by Jones, **60**
                 (1), John Wilson, *Cheerful Ayres*, 1660, and in Forbes 1662,
                 1666, 1682, perhaps by Thomas Davidson. Several MS
                 versions include BL Egerton MS 2230. St. 1, line 1:
                 strangeness = reserve; line 5: affect = aim at; line 6: suspect
                 = suspicion. St. 2, line 4: attend = wait. St. 4, line 6: alone =
                 merely. St. 4, line 2: *Some else your = Or else your*, in Coll 17,

Vivian, and Scott's note; an old MS copy has *Or else some your*; Vivian thinks perhaps it should read *Or else some*. As Davis points out, this reverses Campion's meaning. The two lines are complaining that the singer's rivals are getting all the benefits and the 'secret friend' nothing, so he would rather change places and become a 'rival' and let someone else be a 'secret friend'.

(17) Come away, come away.

G major. e'-e", [g'-d"]. 2/2. 55", [35"]. 2 St. V/me, P/e.

For: [Mezzo], C-Ten, Bar.

Subject: Come quickly; you are late and I want to embrace you while we have time.

Voice: Steps, skips; 6th leap and drop; considerable rhythmic variety, many paired quavers.

Piano: Chordal.

Comment: Repeat optional. Barring misleading in second half. *He* could replace *she* in the second stanza. St. 1, line 3: *love and longing* in music = *loves longing* in text; lines 3-4: meaning doubtful, perhaps: your graces must be the umpires to separate the combatants in the war of love's longing – that is – desire; or, they must be the seconds to the duellists in the lists of love. *Sticklers* can mean arbiters or supporters, umpires or seconds. Somewhat strangely Davis, having chosen *loves longing* as his main reading, explains the passage thus: 'Her graces must umpire the erotic battle between her (armed with love's delights) and him (armed with love's longing).' St. 2, line 6: the starry flower – the heliotrope 'which always inclineth to that place where the sun shineth, and being deprived of the sun dieth', Lyly, *Euphues and His England*, 1580. Davis suggests that the first song in *The Lords Maske* (see **35**) may well have used this setting.

(18) Come you pretty false-eyed wanton. Coll 5; Coll 22, *A minor*; Coll 23, *F minor*.

G minor. f'#-e", [g'-d"]. 2/2. 30" 3 St. V/e, P/e.

For: *Tenor*; C-Ten, Bar.

Subject: Cheerful flirtation; now I have caught you I will kiss you.

Voice: Some skips, many repeated notes; regular rhythms.

Piano: Chordal.

Comment: St. 2, line 3: tell the osiers = count the willows; line 4: Goodwin's sands – a submerged sandbank in the straits of Dover; line 10: *trustless* = *fruitless*, in Earle, 1615, which has ten other variants; Vivian tentatively suggests the emendation *thriftless*. Davis keeps *trustless*, giving the meaning as undependable or treacherous. Colls 22, 23: accompaniment and introduction to each stanza by Keel. St. 3, line 5: *desire = desires*, all other editions. Bullen relegated the third stanza to his notes – 'Occasionally Campion does not know when to stop. The poem reads better without it'.

(19) A secret love or two. Coll 5.
G minor. d'-e″*b*, [e'-d″]. 3/4. 45″, [35″]. 3 St. V/me, P/e.

For:	Mezzo.
Subject:	Lively defence of extra-marital affairs, by a wife!
Voice:	Steps, small skips; paired quavers; some unexpected phrases.
Piano:	Chordal.
Comment:	Repeat optional; last 8 bars, not marked as a repeat in Coll 5. St. 1, line 2: close playing = love-making; line 5: redress = satisfaction; line 6: wants = lacks; line 7: keep not touch = fail to keep marriage vows *and* fail to make love. St. 2, line 1: spring is drawn = water is taken from a spring; line 4: waste treasure smothers = hides his wealth like a miser; line 5: scent = smell *and* impregnate with perfume. St. 3, line 2: venturer = merchant engaged in foreign trade; line 4: slipping = taking a cutting from a plant. An unusual subject, but an entertaining song for a singer with the self-confidence to bring it off. Compare Chaucer's 'Wife of Bath'.

(20) Her rosy cheeks. Coll 28; Coll 22, *A major*; Coll 23, *F major*. G major.
d'-e″, [e'-e″]. 3/4. 1'10″, [50″]. 2 St. V/me, P/e.

For:	*Ten*; C-Ten, Bar; *Bass*.
Subject:	She is too lovely to describe, and though she is cold, I must praise her.
Voice:	Steps, some small skips; rhythms apparently very simple, but very varied in accentuation; many paired quavers and dotted crotchets.
Piano:	Chordal.
Comment:	Barring misleading throughout. Repeat optional. St. 1, line 3: rubine = ruby-coloured. St. 2, line 2: pretend = signify (Davis has 'claim as reward'); line 5: i.e. a virgin (Davis). Colls 22, 23: accompaniment and introduction to each stanza by Keel.

(21) Where shall I refuge seek?
G minor. d'-e″*b*, [f'-d″]. 4/2. 1'30″, [1']. 2 St. V/me, P/e.

For:	Mezzo, C-Ten, Bar.
Subject:	Once you loved me, and now without reason reject me.

Voice: Steps, skips; 6th drop; slightly chromatic; rhythms mostly simple, but some fairly long phrases.
Piano: Chordal, somewhat chromatic.
Comment: Repeat optional. Musically more ambitious than most of Campion's songs. St. 2, line 3: without my deserving it you now look on my vows and love with disfavour.

32 **THE THIRD BOOKE OF AYRES** Composed So as they may be expressed by one Voyce, with a Violl, Lute, or Orpharion. 1618. S & B edition by E.H. Fellowes, 1926; Revised by Thurston Dart, 1969 (*LS* 7).

(1) **Oft have I sighed**. Colls 5, 23, 31, New Imperial (Contralto); Coll 22, *F minor*.
             D minor. d'-d", [d'-c"]. 4/4. 1'. 2 St. V/me, P/e.
For: *Sop*; Mezzo, Cont.
Subject: Sadness at absence of beloved.
Voice: Steps and small skips; some chromatics; short melismas.
Piano: Chordal, with some contrapuntal decoration.
Comment: A beautiful and original song, rewarding to a singer of sensitivity. St. 1, line 4: when wished...day – when longed for friends fail to keep appointments. St. 2, line 1: common = ordinary; use = do; line 2: stay = absence. *LS* 7 and Coll 5: bar 10, voice: rest should be quaver, not crotchet. Colls 22, 23: accompaniment by Keel. Imperial has a slightly rearranged layout of the accompaniment; under the second *languish* e°b should be e° natural; St. 2, last two lines: *constant I mourn For him that vows can break* = *still constant mourn For him that can break vows*, all other editions.

(2) **Now let her change**. Davis.
             G minor. d'-d". 2/2. 35", [25"]. 3 St. V/e, P/e.
For: C-Ten, Bar.
Subject: Let her go. I was faithful, she is false; let her now betray others.
Voice: Steps, a few small skips; fairly regular bouncy rhythm.
Piano: Chordal, some decoration.
Comment: Repeat optional. Editor's 'moderate speed' must surely apply to minims, not crotchets. Set by Pilkington, **70** (8) (copy in BL Add. MS 29291), and Jones, **59** (17). See **70** (8) for variants. There is a parody of the first stanza in Thomas Heywood's 'The Rape of Lucrece', 1608, second song, given in *EMV* and Doughtie.

(3) **Were my heart as some men's are**.
             C minor. g'-f ", [g'-e"b]. 2/2. 25". 3 St. V/e, P/e.

For:　　　　　Ten; Bar.
Subject:　　　Some would ignore your faults, but not I, because I love you;
　　　　　　　true friends speak out, and do not flatter.
Voice:　　　　Steps, skips; 6th leap; simple square rhythm.
Piano:　　　　Chordal.
Comment:　　Simple but effective. St. 1, line 1: errors = transgressions
　　　　　　　(Davis); line 2: curious = strange. St. 3, line 2: observer =
　　　　　　　follower, not spy (Davis), but *OED* gives both 'an obsequious
　　　　　　　follower' and 'one who watches, marks or takes notice', as
　　　　　　　meanings in use at this time.

(4) Maids are simple. Coll 30.

　　　　　　　G minor. d'-d", [e'-d"]. 2/2. 20". 4 St. V/me, P/e.
For:　　　　　Mezzo.
Subject:　　　We girls would be foolish to trust men, especially young ones.
Voice:　　　　Steps, small skips; 6th drop; quick melisma.
Piano:　　　　Chordal.
Comment:　　Editor's 'rather fast' may cause trouble with the melisma; a
　　　　　　　steady crotchet beat is preferable, and gives scope to the
　　　　　　　words. St. 1, line 3: wills = desires. St. 2, line 4: deserts =
　　　　　　　merits.

(5) So tired are all my thoughts.

　　　　　　　D minor. d'-c". 2/2. 30". 4 St. V/me, P/e.
For:　　　　　Mezzo, C-Ten, Bar; Cont, Bass.
Subject:　　　The grief that comes from having nothing to do. The pains of
　　　　　　　lovers and soldiers have some value, mine have none.
Voice:　　　　Steps, skips; very variable rhythm, almost recit.
Piano:　　　　Chordal.
Comment:　　All four stanzas are necessary to sustain the argument. St. 2,
　　　　　　　line 1: forespoke = foretold; Davis gives 'bewitched', but this
　　　　　　　meaning does not appear in *OED*; distaste = discomfort and
　　　　　　　disliking. St. 3, line 1: mover – the woman the singer loves.

(6) Why presumes thy pride?

　　　　　　　G minor. f'#-f ", [g'-d"]. 4/4. 25". 5 St. V/e, P/e.
For:　　　　　Sop, Ten; Mezzo, Bar.
Subject:　　　A philosophic discourse on the dangers of beauty.
Voice:　　　　Steps; 6th drop; simple repeated rhythm.
Piano:　　　　Chordal, some decoration.
Comment:　　St. 3/4 could be omitted. Reprinted in Playford, 1660. St. 3,
　　　　　　　line 2: poor effect = little gain. A play on the various meanings
　　　　　　　of *good* and *goods*.

(7) Kind are her answers. Coll 19, Davis.

	F major. e'-e"b, [e'-c"]. 4/4. 50". 2 St. V/me, P/e.
For:	C-Ten, Bar.
Subject:	She speaks kindly to me, but will not accept my love; O why do we submit to women, who at best cause us sorrow?
Voice:	Steps, small skips; 6th leap; some unexpected moments in rhythm and melody.
Piano:	Chordal.
Comment:	One of Campion's most original songs, and very successful. The tempo suggestions in Coll 19 seem rather fussy. St. 2, line 6: prefixed = predetermined.

(8) O grief, O spite.

	G minor. d'-e"b. 4/4. 1'05". 2 St. V/me, P/me.
For:	Mezzo, C-Ten, Bar.
Subject:	There are no virtues today; only old stories contain true goodness.
Voice:	Steps, small skips; 6th drop; considerable rhythmic variety.
Piano:	Chordal, some decoration, one definitely tricky bar.
Comment:	Curious, and interesting. St. 1, line 4: cast = overthrown; line 6: ? possessions can only be retained by bribery. St. 2, line 2: desert = merit; line 3: styles = titles; one of the frequent allusions to the buying of knighthoods under James I (Davis).

(9) O never to be moved. Davis, Coll 30.

	G minor. d'-f ", [d'-e"b]. 2/2. 1'15". 2 St. V/e, P/e.
For:	Mezzo, Bar.
Subject:	You are hard-hearted, but hear my prayer; pity me before I die.
Voice:	Steps, small skips; melisma; some rhythmic variety,
Piano:	Chordal.
Comment:	Viol and lute cannot play together; the harmony of the last phrase is quite different for the two instruments. St. 2, line 2: distaste = offence, your scorn causes offence; line 4: mean = moderation. Coll 30: the first chord of the third phrase has no sharp to the f' in LH.

(10) Break now, my heart. Colls 19, 23, Davis; Coll 22, *B minor.*

	G minor. c'-e"b, [d'-d"]. 2/2,3/4. 55". 2 St. V/e, P/e.
For:	*Ten*; C-Ten, Bar.
Subject:	I would die; but no, she might relent.
Voice:	Steps, small skips, broken chords; varied rhythms.
Piano:	Chordal.
Comment:	Crotchet = crotchet might well be better than minim =

dotted crotchet. An interesting song, which almost has the effect of a miniature recit. and aria. The classical reference in the last two lines is to Achilles: his mother Thetis sought to give him invulnerability by dipping him in the Styx, the river of Hades, when a baby; she had to hold him by the heel, and he was killed when Paris' arrow pierced that heel. Colls 22, [23]: bars 24, 27 of each stanza: dotted crotchet c″, [a′], quaver minim b′s, [g″#s]. Accompaniment and introduction to each stanza by Keel.

(11) If Love loves truth. Coll 5.

	G major. d′-d″, [g′-d″]. 4/4. 1′. 2 St. V/me, P/e.
For:	C-Ten, Bar.
Subject:	Cheerful philosophy: women's unfaithfulness is only natural.
Voice:	Steps and skips; 6th leap; simple rhythms, some paired quavers.
Piano:	Chordal, melodic bass line.
Comment:	St. 1, line 2: dissembled = pretended; lines 3 and 4: if they appear to be kind this kindness is immediately upset by a storm of emotion. St. 2, line 6: use = habit or training. Reprinted in Playford, 1660 and 1673. Several MS versions, including BL Add. MS 29386.

(12) Now winter nights enlarge. Coll 19.

	G major. g′-g″. 4/4. 1′. 2 St. V/me, P/e.
For:	Sop, Ten.
Subject:	'Tis winter, but much pleasure may still be had, in speech, music, dancing, and love-making.
Voice:	Steps, small skips; 8ve drop; simple rhythms with many paired quavers; lies high.
Piano:	Chordal.
Comment:	Subject of a extremely detailed analysis in *Campion, On Song*. St. 2, line 1: dispense with = allow, excuse.

(13) Awake thou spring.

	C minor. c′-e″b, [c′-d″]. 2/2. 40″. 3 St. V/e, P/e.
For:	Mezzo, C-Ten, Bar.
Subject:	Wake and speak, for your voice is music, and speech is the best of graces.
Voice:	Steps, small skips; simple rhythms.
Piano:	Chordal.
Comment:	Not very interesting. St. 3, line 1: brutish lives = animals.

(14) What is it all?

	G major. d′-d″, [f′#-d″]. 4/4. 30″. 4 St. V/e, P/e.

For: C-Ten, Bar.
Subject: In praise of good wives.
Voice: Steps, small skips; simple rhythms.
Piano: Chordal, some decoration.
Comment: An unusual and worthwhile subject; even if based on an assumption of male superiority, it expresses genuine gratitude. St. 1, line 1: possess = have knowledge of; conversing – living together in society, according to Davis, but the normal meaning of making conversation seems to fit better. St. 3, line 3: governing the performance of their household tasks according to whether they seem to please us or not (Davis).

(15) Fire that must flame.

F major. d'-d", [e'-c"]. 2/2. 30". 4 St. V/e, P/e.

For: C-Ten, Bar.
Subject: Love needs hope to live, so respond to my pleas.
Voice: Steps, skips; 8ve leap; simple but varied rhythms.
Piano: Chordal.
Comment: More clearly modal than most of Campion's songs. St. 2, line 4: churl = miser.

(16) If thou long'st so much to learn. Colls 5, 19.

C minor. c'-e"*b*, [e'*b*-c"]. 2/2. 30". 4 St. V/me, P/e.

For: Mezzo.
Subject: Experienced young woman mocks a young man and warns him of the dangers of love.
Voice: Steps, small skips; 6th leap; simple rhythms, but many paired quavers and even semiquavers.
Piano: Chordal.
Comment: Good song for an actress. St. 1, line 2: prove = find out by experience; line 6: salamander – a lizard-like creature supposed to be able to live in fire. St. 2, line 3: *otherwhiles* (*other whiles*, in Vivian, Davis and Coll 19) = at other times. St. 3, line 6: forward = generous. Coll 19 marks the last four bars to be repeated; optional.

(17) Shall I come, sweet love, to thee? Coll 28.

F minor. f'-f ". 4/4. 45", [30"]. 3 St. V/e, P/e.

For: Ten.
Subject: If I come will you let me in, or make me suffer cold and danger outside while you mock me from your bed?
Voice: Steps, skips; simple rhythms.
Piano: Chordal with decoration.
Comment: Repeat optional. An attractive little song. St. 1, line 4: let =

hindrance; line 6: tell = count. St. 2, lines 3-4: will work my woe either for booty (if a thief) or to satisfy his spite (if a foe) (Davis). Earle, 1615, has four stanzas, and slightly lengthens line 5 in each, see Vivian and Davis; BL Add. MS 29481 gives the first strophe, with lengthened lines and much vocal decoration, given in Davis.

(18) Thrice toss these oaken ashes. Colls 19, 29; Coll 22, *A minor*; Coll 23, *F minor*.

G minor. d'-f ", [f' #-d"]. 4/4. 45", [30"]. 3 St. V/e, P/e.

For:	*Ten*; Bar.
Subject:	The first two stanzas are a spell for ending the fears and cares of love; the third admits her eyes can break any such charm.
Voice:	Steps, descending scale; 8ve leap; simple rhythms, many paired quavers.
Piano:	Chordal
Comment:	A wide-ranging melody, but rhythmically rather monotonous. Vivian and Davis give another version of the poem in sonnet form from BL Harl. MS 6910. Colls 22, 23: accompaniment and introduction to each stanza by Keel. St. 1, line 3: *then*, in music = *and*, in text and all other editions. Coll 22: St. 3, line 1: *around* = *a round*, in all other editions.

(19) Be thou then my beauty named.

G minor. f'-g", [g'-g"]. 4/4. 35", [25"]. 3 St. V/e, P/e.

For:	Ten.
Subject:	Be my beauty, my Queen, or my Goddess: I will love, serve, and adore.
Voice:	Steps and skips; rhythm almost entirely in crotchets.
Piano:	Chordal.
Comment:	Somewhat four-square, but a neatly turned piece of flattery. Repeat optional.

(20) Fire, fire. Colls 19, 31, Davis.

G major. e'-e", [g'-e"]. 4/4,3/4,4/4. 55", [45"]. 2 St. V/me, P/e.

For:	Mezzo, C-Ten, Bar.
Subject:	I burn with desire; the rivers and oceans must quench the flames, or drown me in my love.
Voice:	Steps, small skips; 6th drop, 8ve leap; very varied rhythms: broken phrases, dance rhythms, suspensions, melismas.
Piano:	Chordal, with some decoration.
Comment:	One of Campion's few attempts at an extended and varied musical setting. Repeat optional, but advisable, at least for the last stanza. Also set by Lanier in Playford, 1669. Vivian

notes, in error, that there is a setting by Morley; the title is the same, but not the poem, though it may have given Campion the idea for this one. There are several MS versions of this poem, with many minor variants, some with the music by Nicholas Lanier. St. 2, line 2: *hell to* – two of the MS have convincing alternatives: *help to*, or *help for*. Coll 31: bar 20 (*all*), voice: bracketed sharp to g'; bar 26 (*me*), voice: crotchet crotchet rest, not minim.

(21) Oh sweet delight.

	C minor. d'-e″b, [e'b-d″]. 4/4. 55″. 2 St. V/e, P/e.
For:	C-Ten, Bar.
Subject:	To live thus loved is bliss.
Voice:	Steps, small skips; 6th leap; rhythms simple but varied.
Piano:	Chordal.
Comment:	A romantic evocation of happy love. St. 2, line 4: distaste = unpleasantness; line 5: So = thus; line 6: let men of this present age of iron (as distinct from the golden age) envy. In BL Egerton MS 2013 the last line reads: 'Which till eyes ache, let you fond men envy.'

(22) Thus I resolve.

	G minor. d'-f ″, [d'-d″]. 2/2. 1'. 2 St. V/e, P/e.
For:	Bar.
Subject:	Since she is fair and kind I will not try to restrain her, for that is the way to lose her.
Voice:	Steps, skips; 6th leap; rhythms simple, though those of prose rather than verse.
Piano:	Chordal, but many contrapuntal suggestions.
Comment:	Some harmonic surprises at times. St. 2, line 1: 'It is proper for the palm-tree to mount; the heavier you load it the higher it sprouteth' (Lyly, *Euphues: The Anatomy of Wit*, 1578).

(23) Come, O come, my life's delight.

	G minor. f'-f ″, [g'-e″]. 3/4,2/2. 55″, [40″]. 2 St. V/e, P/e.
For:	Sop, Ten; Mezzo, Bar.
Subject:	Come to me quickly, for I love you.
Voice:	Steps, small skips; melisma; not much rhythmic variety, though phrase lengths vary.
Piano:	Chordal, some decoration.
Comment:	Repeat optional. A rather strange setting of these well-known words, surprisingly lacking in energy. No tempo relationship is suggested by the editor, and indeed, could be dotted minim = minim or semibreve, though crotchet = crotchet would perhaps be more convincing.

(24) Could my heart more tongues employ.
              F major. c′-d″, [f′-c″]. 2/2. 45″, [35″]. 3 St. V/e, P/e.
For: Mezzo, C-Ten, Bar.
Subject: True hearts despair when treated unkindly; it would be
              wiser not to hope; it is better never to be blessed than to lose
              all later.
Voice: Steps and 5th drop; very simple rhythm.
Piano: Chordal, with a little decoration.
Comment: Repeat optional. St. 2, line 1: happy minds = happy are the
              minds; redeem their engagements = escape from emotional
              ties. BL Add. MS 10309 has two versions of this poem; one,
              in a different metre, may well be a first draft; the other is as
              here with a few variants; see Vivian and Davis.

(25) Sleep, angry beauty.
              F major. f′-f″, [f′-e″b]. 4/4. 55″. 2 St. V/e, P/e.
For: Bar.
Subject: Sleep in peace, and maybe when you wake you will pity me.
Voice: Steps, small skips; melisma; simple but varied rhythms.
Piano: Chordal, a little decoration.
Comment: A pleasant little song. St. 2, line 1: secure – free from anxiety
              (as if she were actually sinless) (Davis).

(26) Silly boy, 'tis full moon yet. Coll 19.
              G major. d′-e″, [d′-d″]. 4/4. 35″. 4 St. V/e, P/e.
For: Mezzo, C-Ten, Bar.
Subject: First love is innocent, and will soon learn better; but it is
              worth a try, since true love for life is the greatest of all
              blessings.
Voice: Steps, small skips, broken chord; simple rhythms, some
              variety.
Piano: Chordal, a little decoration.
Comment: A good poem, though St. 2 could be omitted. St. 1, line 2: wit
              = intelligence; line 3: bereaved = taken from you. St. 2, line
              4: want = lack. St. 3, line 2: cheer = countenance; read =
              indicate (grief, by looking at the ground). Earle, 1615, has
              slight variants, see Davis.

(27) Never love unless you can. Coll 5.
              Bb major. f′-f″, [f′-d″]. 2/2. 20″. 3 St. V/e, P/e.
For: Mezzo, Bar.
Subject: Light-hearted advice to girls about men.
Voice: Steps, skips; 6th leaps; simple rhythm.
Piano: Chordal; some melodic bass phrases.
Comment: Enjoyable. St. 1, line 6: straight = immediately; line 4: ever

= always. St. 2, lines 3-6: quoting the man's excuses. St. 3, line 2: *awhile* = *a while*, in Vivian and Davis.

(28) So quick, so hot, so mad. Coll 19.

G major. g'-g". 3/4. 45", [35"]. 3 St. V/me, P/e.

For: Sop.

Subject: A firm rejection of an importunate lover.

Voice: Steps and 3rds; many small melismas require a flexible voice.

Piano: Chordal.

Comment: Repeat optional. An entertaining verse for an actress who can handle the vocal decoration. St. 1, line 1: quick = lively; line 3: fain = gladly; line 5: I care not = I don't mind. St. 2, line 1: roofs – signifying indoors as distinct from outdoors; line 2: unused pace = unaccustomed step; line 3: charged = loaded. St. 3, line 6: in bed (as lovers), in the grave (as husband and wife at the end of a long happy marriage) (Davis); may also imply his hot love would cause them both to 'die'.

(29) Shall I then hope?

G major. d'-e", [g'-d"]. 4/4. 45". 3 St. V/e, P/e.

For: C-Ten, Bar.

Subject: Since she has betrayed me love is dead; she is faithless, so I am free.

Voice: Steps, small skips; 8ve drop; simple rather repetitive rhythm.

Piano: Chordal, with hints of counterpoint.

Comment: A good song for a divorced man! Based on 'Faith, Hope and Charity (Love)'. St. 2, line 1: events = experiences; line 6: 'loosing' is Campion's usual spelling of 'losing', but here 'loosing' or letting go may also apply (Davis). St. 3, line 4: as = so long as.

33 THE FOURTH BOOKE OF AYRES Composed So as they may be expressed by One Voyce, with a Violl, Lute, or Orpharion. 1618. S & B edition by E.H. Fellowes, 1926. Out of print.

(4) Veil, love, my eyes. Coll 5.

G minor. f'#-e"b, [g'-d"]. 4/4. 50". 2 St. V/e, P/e.

For: C-Ten, Bar.

Subject: Let me not know of her unfaithfulness, for she is kind to me.

Voice: Steps, some skips; simple rhythms with paired quavers.

Piano: Chordal, with occasional counterpoint.

Comment: Repeat optional. A good poem. St. 1, line 2: curious =

inquisitive; line 3: private = true to one only (Davis). St. 2, line 1: recure = cure; line 6: still = always.

(5) Every dame affects good fame. Coll 22; Coll 23, *D major*.
                       F major. e′-g″, [g′-f″]. 4/4. 40″. 3 St. V/e, P/e.
For: Sop, Ten; *Mezzo, C-Ten, Bar*.
Subject: Description of a good wife.
Voice: Steps, small skips; 6th leap; simple rhythm, some paired quavers.
Piano: Chordal.
Comment: St. 1, line 1: affects = aims at; line 2: bays = rewards; line 4: becomes = is becoming to; line 5 and last line: toys = trifles. St. 2, line 3: lawne = fine linen; The Fawne – 'A corridor in the Royal Exchange which served as a bazaar, where at this time fashionable Ladies made their purchases', *EMV*. St. 3, line 1: Astrea – daughter of Zeus and Themis, and goddess of justice, lived among men during the Golden Age, but then withdrew to the stars, under the name of Virgo; line 2: their – the Good-men, whose tide of fortune is on the ebb thanks to their wives' expensive flowing dresses. Colls 22, 23: accompaniment and introduction to each stanza by Keel. Allotted to Campion Book 3 in error.

(6) So sweet is thy discourse. Coll 31, New Imperial (Soprano).
                       G minor. f′#-g″, [g′-g″]. 4/4. 1′, [40″]. 2 St. V/m, P/e.
For: Sop, Ten.
Subject: My love for you has overshadowed all memories of past joys.
Voice: Octave leap, 6th leap and fall, somewhat chromatic; many paired quavers, high lying.
Piano: Chordal.
Comment: Rather modified rapture in face of this new love! Slight modification of accompaniment in Imperial; bar 2, voice: last note has no natural in Fellowes; bar 11, beat 3, piano: crotchet, not quaver rest and quaver, in Fellowes; bars 12-13, voice: underlay in Fellowes gives *That* to last quaver of 12 and *her graced* to the first two crotchets of 13.

(7) There is a garden in her face. Colls 5, 29, Davis. Coll 7, *A major*; Coll 33, *Ab major*; Coll 8, *F major*.
                       G major. d′-e″, [g′-d″]. 4/4. 40″. 3 St. V/me, P/e.
For: *Sop, Ten*; Mezzo, C-Ten, Bar; *Cont, Bass*.
Subject: Description of pretty girl in terms of a garden.
Voice: Steps, many skips; 8ve drop; melisma; varied rhythms.
Piano: Chordal, with a fair amount of counterpoint.
Comment: Also set by Jones, **59 (10)**, and as a madrigal by Alison, *EM*

33 (19-21). Compare Herrick's well known poem 'Cherry Ripe'. St. 1, line 6: cherry-ripe = a street cry. St. 2, lines 1-2: cherries are lips, and pearls, teeth. Coll 33: accompaniment composed by Michael Diack. Coll 29: bar 15, beats 3-4: rhythm – quaver quaver crotchet instead of crotchet quaver quaver in accompaniment, which must be an error.

(8) To his sweet lute. Coll 19.

G major. g'-g'', [a'-e'']. 2/2. 35''. 3 St. V/me, P/e.

For:	Sop, Ten.
Subject:	Apollo's revenge on king Midas for preferring the music of Pan.
Voice:	Steps, simple skips; simple rhythms with many paired quavers.
Piano:	Chordal.
Comment:	Apollo – the Sun-God, also God of Art and Music. Pan – God of the pastures. He loved the nymph Syrinx, who fled from him, and was changed into reeds, from which came pan-pipes. Midas was king of Phrygia; asked to judge the performances of Apollo and Pan he choose Pan, and was given a pair of ass's ears by Apollo as a reward for his stupidity. It was this same Midas of whom it was said everything he touched turned to gold.

(10) Love me or not. Colls 5, 26.

G minor. g'-f'', [a'-d'']. 3/4. 40'', [30'']. 3 St. V/e, P/e.

For:	Ten, Bar.
Subject:	A gentle love-song.
Voice:	Steps; simple rhythms with some paired quavers.
Piano:	Chordal.
Comment:	Repeat optional. Nearly the same tune as **29 (10)**, but the second part is shorter, with more rhythmic variation. St. 1, line 2: needs must I = I am compelled to.

(14) Beauty is but a painted hell. G major. Coll 22, *A major*; Coll 23, *F major*.

A major. g'-f''#, [f'#-e'']. 4/4. 30''. 3 St. V/e, P/me.

For:	*Ten*; (C-Ten, Bar); *Cont, Bass*.
Subject:	Admiring a ruthless beauty only leads to madness.
Voice:	Repeated e''s, steps; 6th drop; simple rhythms; should be slightly chromatic, see Comment.
Piano:	Chordal.
Comment:	Colls 22, 23: accompaniment and introduction to each stanza by Keel. Allotted to Campion Book 3 in error. Bars 9 and 11 of each stanza, second half, voice: dotted crotchet

quaver, not two crotchets; bar 12 note 1 and bar 13 note 4 in voice: should be flattened in all stanzas, this means modifying Keel's accompaniment.

(17) I must complain. Coll 5, Davis.
> G minor. g'-f ", [a'-f "]. 2/2. 50", [35"]. 2 St. V/e, P/e.

For: Ten, Bar.
Subject: Resigned acceptance that a beautiful mistress will not also be a faithful one.
Voice: Steps, skips; 6th leap; simple rhythms.
Piano: Chordal, some slight decoration.
Comment: Repeat optional, but recommended. Also set by Dowland, **46** (17), where the few variants are given. St. 1, line 1: love = beloved. St. 2, lines 3 and 4: Many new lovers come to her, which daily relights the fires of forgetful love (in me); line 5: resolve = accept. BL Add. MS 15117 has some variants: St. 1, line 2: *lovely parts = beauty's parts*; line 3: *Thence = Hence*; line 5: *form = frame*. St. 2, line 1: *Should I aggrieved then wish = Should I have grieved and wished*; line 4: *That = This*. This MS has a third stanza: 'Thus my complaints from her untruth arise, / Accusing her and nature both in one. / For beauty stained is but a false disguise / A Common wonder which is quickly gone. / A false fair face cannot with all her feature / Without a true heart make a true fair creature.' Christ Church MS 439 has two versions, one with stanzas 1 and 3 (above), the other with stanzas 1, 3, and: 'What need'st thou plaine, if thou be still rejected / The fairest creature sometime may prove strange / Continual plaints will make thee still rejected / If that her wanton mind be given to range; / And nothing better fits a man's true parts / Than with disdain t'encounter their false hearts.'

(18) Think'st thou to seduce me then. Coll 19.
> G minor. g'-g", [a'-f "]. 2/2. 35". 4 St. V/me, P/e.

For: Sop.
Subject: Your attempts to seduce me are much too obvious; flattering speeches need practice!
Voice: Steps, simple skips; variable rhythms, with many paired quavers.
Piano: Chordal.
Comment: Good song for an actress. St. 1, line 2: prate = talk too much (followed by comma in *EMV* and Fellowes). St. 2, line 2: *faineth* (*feigneth*, *EMV* and Fellowes) = pretends; line 3: glances at the notes of his speech. St. 3, line 3: Gudgeons, a

genus of small fish easily caught; hence, slang for gullible persons (cf. the modern term 'sucker', also the name of a fish) (Davis). St. 4, line 1: ruth = pity. Coll 19, bar 8, RH, notes 3-4: dotted crotchet quaver in Fellowes. Also set by Corkine, **41** (11), the first two verses with only slight variants, a different third verse, and no fourth verse. Corkine's third verse runs as follows: 'If with wit we be deceived, our falls may be excused. / Seeming good with flattery graced is but of few refused. / But of all accursed are they that are by fools abused.'

(22) Beauty since you so much desire. Coll 5, Davis.

G major. d'-e'', [e'-d'']. 2/2. 35''. 2 St. V/me, P/e.

For: C-Ten, Bar.

Subject: Slightly bawdy indication of what some men look for in a woman!

Voice: Steps, skips; 6th leap; very varied rhythms with many paired quavers and a sequence.

Piano: Chordal, but much melodic imitation in the bass line.

Comment: The singer must be confident of making the right suggestions without being suggestive. See **29** (16) for original version here parodied.

(23) Your fair looks. Coll 5.

G minor. d'-d'', [f' #-d'']. 4/4. 50'', [35'']. 3 St. V/me, P/e.

For: C-Ten, Bar.

Subject: Come into this grove and embrace me, and I shall remember the place for ever.

Voice: Steps, some skips; slightly chromatic; simple rhythms; start of second half needs care to make it convincing.

Piano: Chordal, some decoration.

Comment: A revision of an earlier poem **29** (17), with new music; an improvement all round. Repeat optional. St. 1, line 1: urge = incite.

34 THE DESCRIPTION OF A MASKE Presented before the Kinges Majestie at White-hall, on Twelfth Night last, in honour of the Lord Hayes, and his Bride, Daughter and Heire to the Honourable the Lord Dennye, their Marriage having the same Day at Court solemnized. 1607. Coll 4.

'James Hayes or Hay, the son of Sir James Hay of Kingask, was a Scotch gentleman who came to Court on James's accession and was a great favourite with the King. He was knighted, created Lord Hay of the Scotch peerage in 1606, Baron Hay of Sawley in 1615, Viscount Doncaster in 1618, and Earl of Carlisle in 1622. He married, first, on the occasion of this masque, Honora, daughter of Lord Denny, and secondly, in 1617, Lucy Percy. He was employed on several important missions, to France in 1616, and to Germany in 1619 to support the Elector Palatine' (Vivian).

(1) **Now hath Flora robb'd her bowers.** Coll 4.

	G major. d'-e". 4/4. 1'15", [1']. 2 St. V/e, P/e.
For:	Mezzo, C-Ten, Bar.
Subject:	There are flowers everywhere; roses are best, but the red and white must be mixed.
Voice:	Steps, small skips; simple rhythms, varied phrase-lengths.
Piano:	Chordal, some decoration.
Comment:	Repeat optional. 'As soon as they came to the descent towards the dancing place, the consort of ten ceased, and the four Sylvans played the same ayre, to which Zephyrus and the two other Sylvans did sing these words in a bass, tenor and treble voice and going up and down as they sung, they strowed flowers all about the place' (Campion's note). It can be sung as solo, duet or trio.

(2) **Move now with measured sound.** Coll 4.

	G major. d'-e", [e'-d"]. 4/4. 55". 2 St. V/e, P/e.
For:	Mezzo, C-Ten, Bar.
Subject:	Apollo (God of Art) made the trees move, but it is Hymen (God of Marriage) should lead you.
Voice:	Steps, few skips; simple rhythm.
Piano:	Chordal.
Comment:	'This spoken, the four Sylvans played on their instruments the first strain of the song following, and at the repetition thereof the voices fell in with the instruments which were thus divided: a treble and a bass were placed near his Majesty, and another treble and bass near the grove, that the words of the song might be heard of all, because the trees of gold instantly at the first sound of their voices began to move and dance according to the measure of the time which the musicians kept in singing, and the nature of the words which they delivered' (Campion's note). The same music is used for 31 (12). St. 2, line 4: hayes = dances (cf. 'Shepherd's Hay'), besides being a compliment to Lord Hayes.

(3) **Shows and nightly revels.** See 63.

(4) **Triumph now with joy and mirth.** See 51.

(5) **Time, that leads the fatal round.** See 63.

35 THE DESCRIPTION, SPEECHES, AND SONGS, OF THE LORDS MASKE presented in the Banquetting-house on the marriage night of the high and mightie Count Palatine and the royally descended the Ladie Elizabeth. 1613. The Count Palatine married Princess Elizabeth, daughter of James I, who became the 'Winter Queen'.

(5) **Woo her and win her**. Coll 4.

	G minor. d'-e", [f'-d"]. 6/4,3/2. 35". 2 St. V/e, P/e.
For:	Mezzo, C-Ten, Bar.
Subject:	Women have two loves: you need both words and music for courtship.
Voice:	Steps, skips, broken chords; 8ve drop; only two phrases, each repeated, in the same slightly irregular rhythm.
Piano:	Chordal.
Comment:	The rhythm holds the attention in this otherwise simple song. St. 1, line 2: in the masque four women are wooed by eight men; lines 7-8: if fair women were rarer they would be even more the subject of men's aspirations. St. 2, line 8: venter = venture.

MICHAEL CAVENDISH
c. 1565 – 1628

36 14 AYRES IN TABLETORIE TO THE LUTE expressed with two voyces and the base Violl or the voice & Lute only. 6 more to 4 voyces and in Tabletorie. 1598. S & B edition by E.H. Fellowes, 1926. Out of print. Nos 15-20 given in *MB* LIII.

(1) **Stay, Glycia, stay**. Coll 5.

	G major. g'-e", [g'-d"]. 2/2,3/4. 45". V/e, P/e.
For:	Ten, C-Ten, Bar.
Subject:	Lively pursuit of a girl.
Voice:	Steps, small skips; rhythm simple apart from change of metre.
Piano:	Simple counterpoint in three parts.
Comment:	Repeat essential. The final triple time section is based on a version of the popular dance, Lavolta; minim = dotted minim.

(5) **Finetta, fair and feat**. Coll 14; Coll 13, *B minor*.

	G minor. d'-d". 3/4. 50". V/me, P/me.
For:	*Ten*; C-Ten, Bar.
Subject:	Finetta's charms make me love and grieve.
Voice:	Steps, skips, broken chords; lively and at times unexpected rhythms.

Piano: Contrapuntal.
Comment: Light and tuneful, with some nonsense syllables. St. 1, line 1:
                feat = neat.

(6) Love is not blind. Colls 5, 26.
                G major. f'#-e", [g'-d"]. 3/4,3/2. 40", [30"]. 5 St. V/e, P/me.
For: Mezzo, C-Ten, Bar.
Subject: A lively denunciation of the power of love.
Voice: Steps, small skips, broken chords; rhythm quite simple.
Piano: Contrapuntal, a little awkward at the fast tempo
                appropriate.
Comment: Repeat optional. Some stanzas could be omitted. St. 2, line 1:
                fancy = fancies, EMV; line 4: *fence = sense*, Coll 26, though no
                other editor; St. 3, line 1: *yet = it, EMV* as emendation, not
                used by any other editor; mine only = only my. St. 4, lines 3-4:
                love has no power to enslave the free, unless given him by us;
                nor can his power last if we do not wish it. St. 5, line 1: *poet's =
                poet*, Coll 26; line 2: *ignorant's = ignorant*, Coll 26; line 4: Love
                has strange manners, so visits strange places, as described in
                the first two lines of this stanza. Based on a sonnet from
                Gaspar Gil Polo's *Diana Enamorada*, 1564, 'No es ciego
                Amor'. Coll 26: bar 9, beats 2-3, RH: quaver rest crotchet
                quaver for dotted crotchet quaver.

(8) The heart to rue. Colls 5, 26.
                G minor. d'-e"b, [f'#-d"]. 4/4. 1'15". 2 St. V/e, P/me.
For: Mezzo, C-Ten, Bar.
Subject: My heart is wounded by the beauty my eye sees, so have pity.
Voice: Steps, skips, simple but varied rhythms.
Piano: Contrapuntal, mostly in three parts.
Comment: An interesting though somewhat complex song. St. 1, line 5:
                desert = good deed. St. 2, lines 1-2: The eye sees much beauty,
                grace and honour, for such beauty grace and honour require
                as much; or, The eye sees as much as beauty, grace and
                honour require, but (line 3) the heart finds more. St. 1, line 3:
                own = owe, in *EMV*, Coll 26 and Doughtie: if *own*, lines 3-4
                might mean: what can the one that owns them both (heart
                and eye) say but that both do him harm; if *owe*, line 3 might
                mean: what can he say that for this reason (lines 1-2) owes
                them both (to the beloved). Doughtie, curiously, gives the first
                interpretation, though not amending *owe* to *own*.

(12) Wandering in this place. Coll 19.
                G minor. f'#-f", [g'-e"b]. 2/2,3/2. 2'20". V/me, P/me.
For: Mezzo, Bar.

Subject: I have no comfort here.
Voice: Steps, skips, slightly chromatic; simple rhythms.
Piano: Contrapuntal.
Comment: Longer than most lute-songs, serious and moving. Fellowes gives the sections written in 3/2 in Coll 19 in crotchets not minims, with no change of time-signature, that is, the minim of the 3/2 = the previous crotchet; this seems a convincing solution. Coll 19, page 66, line 3, bar 1, beat 1: no flat to a° in Fellowes. Page 68, line 3, bar 3, voice: Fellowes sensibly advises adding a natural to the first b'. The final Latin phrase translates: O Lord, Lord, there is no sorrow like unto my sorrow. See Lamentations 1:12, Vulgate. Also arranged as a five-part madrigal, No 28 in Cavendish's original volume, *EM* 36.

(13) Everie bush new springing. Coll 19.
                  C major. b°-c″, [d′-c″]. 2/2. 1′. V/me, P/me.
For: Mezzo, C-Ten, Bar.
Subject: Love in springtime.
Voice: Mostly by step; varied rhythms.
Piano: Contrapuntal, in varying numbers of parts.
Comment: Lively and enjoyable. Madrigal version: *EM* 36 (27)

(14) Down in a valley. Colls 19, 29.
                  F major. e′-f″, [g′-e″]. 3/4. 1′10″. V/me, P/me.
For: Mezzo.
Subject: We met the shepherd lads in the valley.
Voice: Steps, many skips; slightly modal; simple rhythms.
Piano: Chordal, with occasional decoration.
Comment: A lively dance number. Poem printed as one long verse in *EMV*. Line 2: ports = havens. Line 3: meet resorts = proper meeting-places. Line 4: hap = luck; swain = young man. Line 6: Flora – Goddess of flowers and spring. Line 8: his = the swain's; dyde in grain = brightly coloured as in their natural state. Line 9: dyde = colourful. Coll 29: bar 8 and similar, beat 3, LH: adds f° from viol part.

(15) Wanton, come hither. Coll 5.
                  G minor. c′-f″, [f′#-d″]. 3/4,3/2. 1′35″, [1′15″]. V/me, P/me.
For: Bar.
Subject: Boy chases girl; boy gives up chase; girl accepts boy.
Voice: Steps, occasional skips, scales; much variety of rhythm and tempo.
Piano: Alternately contrapuntal and chordal; some neat fingering needed.

Comment: Repeat optional but recommended. An effective little drama.
              Line 8: prove = test. Line 9: stayed = stopped.

JOHN COPRARIO
c. 1570/80 – 1626

37 **FUNERAL TEARES** For the death of the Right Honourable the
   Earle of Devonshire. Figured in seaven songes, whereof six are so set
   forth that the wordes may be exprest by a treble voice alone to the
   Lute and Base Viole, or else that the meane part may be added, if any
   shall affect more fulnesse of parts. The Seaventh Is made in forme of a
   Dialogue, and cannot be sung without two voyces. 1606. S & B edition
   by Gerald Hendrie and Thurston Dart, 1959. Tablature included (*LS*
   9).

   Charles Blount, Earl of Devonshire and eighth Lord Mountjoy, was
   born in 1563. In 1601 he succeeded Essex as commander in Ireland,
   and within a year defeated the Earl of Tyrone. In 1605 he married
   Penelope Devereux Rich, after her divorce from Lord Rich. He died in
   1606.

(1) Oft thou hast.
              C major. g'-g". 4/4. 1'10", [55"]. 2 St. V/me, P/e.
For: Sop, [Ten].
Subject: You often shared my happy songs; now in death hear those
              of sorrow; music helps mourning.
Voice: Steps, skips; 8ve leap; simple rhythms, but some long
              phrases.
Piano: Chordal, with some decoration; melodic bass.
Comment: Repeat optional. Each phrase tends to cover a wide range.
              Bar 6: the last bass note is surely an error – make previous
              G minim, as in tablature.

(2) O sweet flower. Coll 29, (under the English name of Cooper).
              C major. e'-g", [g'-g"]. 4/4. 1'15", [1']. 2 St. V/e, P/e.
For: Sop, [Ten].
Subject: We only saw half your life; how wondrous would the rest
              have been had you not died too young (aged 43).
Voice: Steps, skips, sequence; simple rhythms with varying
              phrase-lengths.
Piano: Chordal with decoration, melodic bass.
Comment: Repeat optional. Simpler than 37 (1).

(3) O th'unsure hopes.
              C major. g'-g". 4/4. 1'20", [1']. 2 St. V/me, P/e.

For: Sop, [Ten].
Subject: The hopes of men and women are unsure, and may be destroyed before fulfilment.
Voice: Steps, skips; 8ve leap, 6th leap, melisma; variable rhythms and some long phrases.
Piano: Chordal, some decoration; melodic bass.
Comment: Repeat optional. A passionate song, opening with the 8ve leap. The bass prelude quotes the opening phrase of the tune to Ophelia's song in *Hamlet*, 'He is dead and gone, lady' (Doughtie).

(4) In darkness let me dwell.

A minor. e'-g", [e'-f"]. 4/4. 2'35", [1'55"]. 2 St. V/me, P/me.

For: Sop, [Ten].
Subject: Let me now embrace the dark, so that I may quickly join you in death.
Voice: Steps, skips, broken chords; slightly chromatic; some sequences; irregular rhythms and phrase-lengths.
Piano: Chordal, much decoration; some chromatics; melodic bass.
Comment: Repeat optional. An interesting comparison with Dowland's more famous setting of the first stanza, **48 (3)**. St. 1, line 5: *in* = *to* in Dowland; line 6: *dying live* = *living die* in Dowland; *doth* = *do* in Dowland.

(5) My joy is dead.

G minor. d'-e"b, [d'-d"]. 4/4. 1'20", [1']. 2 St. V/me, P/e.

For: Mezzo, [C-Ten, Bar].
Subject: Let no tender hearts hear my sad songs; they are meant to move the hard-hearted.
Voice: Steps, skips; slightly sequential; one melisma; simple rhythms and fairly regular phrases.
Piano: Chordal with some decoration; melodic bass.
Comment: Repeat optional. The simplest in this set.

(6) Deceitful fancy.

G minor. d'-e"b, [d'-d"]. 4/4. 1'20", [1']. 2 St. V/me, P/e.

For: Mezzo, [C-Ten, Bar].
Subject: I seem to see your shade; either you should be real, or I too should be a ghost.
Voice: Steps, skips, broken chords; 6th leap; starts with irregular rhythm in sequence, becoming smoother, melodically and rhythmically.
Comment: Repeat optional. Interesting in that it begins almost in recit. style, and ends as a normal lute song.

(7) **Foe of mankind**. A duet, outside the scope of this volume.

38 SONGS OF MOURNING Bewailing the untimely death of Prince
 Henry. Worded by Tho. Campion. And set forth to bee sung with one
 voyce to the Lute, or Violl. 1613. S & B edition by Gerald Hendrie and
 Thurston Dart, 1959. Tablature included (*LS* 9).

 Henry, Prince of Wales, was the eldest son of James I. He died in
 1612, aged only 18, just before the marriage of his sister Princess
 Elizabeth to the Elector Palatine. He was a patron of the arts,
 particularly of music. John Coprario taught music to the children of
 James I.

(1) **O grief**.

	G minor. d'-f ", [d'-e"*b*]. 4/4. 1'25", [1'05"]. 2 St. V/me, P/e.
For:	Mezzo, Bar.
Subject:	Our joys are uncertain; fate takes happiness even from kings.
Voice:	Steps, skips, repeated notes; 6th drop, 8ve leap; rhythm very free in recit. style; phrase-lengths fairly regular.
Piano:	Chordal, with some decoration.
Comment:	Headed 'To the most sacred King James'. Repeat optional. St. 1, line 7: surety = certainty. St. 2, line 3: raze = obliterate.

(2) **'Tis now dead night**.

	G minor. d'-g", [f'-e"*b*]. 4/4. 2'10", [1'40"]. 2 St. V/me, P/e.
For:	Sop, Ten.
Subject:	Let a mother now mourn her peerless son; never was there more reason for a queen to weep.
Voice:	Steps, many skips, broken chords; some chromatics; dim. 4th drop; very angular line; the only g" starts a phrase; recit. style with varying phrase-lengths.
Piano:	Chordal, with some decoration, some melodic bass; contrapuntal ending; chromatic.
Comment:	Headed 'To the most sacred Queen Anne'. Repeat optional. St. 1, line 6: note that the music fills the space in the middle of this line, as line 7 states; line 10: sire of Troy = King Priam.

(3) **Fortune and glory**.

C minor. e'*b*-g", [g'-g"]. 4/4. 1'50", [1'25"]. 2 St. V/me, P/e.

For:	Sop, Ten.
Subject:	What is the gain of a crown compared with the loss of a brother? You must now take his place, and receive the honours we offered him.
Voice:	Steps, many skips, broken chords; 8ve and 6th leaps; recit. style rhythms and irregular phrase-lengths.
Piano:	Chordal, with some decoration and melodic bass.
Comment:	Headed 'To the most high and mighty Prince Charles'. Repeat

optional. St. 2, line 4: prevented = preceded. Bar 12: 4th note in voice should have a flat.

(4) So parted you. Coll 30 (under the English name of Cooper).

	G major. d'-e", [e'-e"]. 4/4. 1'25", [1'05"]. 2 St. V/me, P/e.
For:	Mezzo, C-Ten, Bar.
Subject:	Your tears would move stones; alas that such a love should be ended.
Voice:	Steps, skips, broken chords, repeated notes; 6th drops, 6th and 8ve leaps; more continuous than the first three songs, but still fairly free rhythms.
Piano:	Chordal, with some decoration.
Comment:	Headed 'To the most princely and virtuous the Lady Elizabeth'. Repeat optional. A very romantic song, the most touching of the set. St. 1, line 3: ruth = pity; line 6: *fate = love* in original, amended in BL copy in a contemporary hand to *fate*, which is followed by Bullen and Vivian, Davis takes *love* as being the god of Love, and retains it. Bar 10: the repeat marks refer to the second section, not the first, and are the wrong side of the double bar-line. Coll 26: bar 12, last note, voice: c" not d" as in *LS 9*.

(5) How like a golden dream.

	G major. d'-e", [e'-e"]. 4/4. 1'40", [1'15"]. 2 St. V/me, P/e.
For:	Mezzo, C-Ten, Bar.
Subject:	Though you did not know each other long you must weep for him; though in days to come your sadness will turn to joy.
Voice:	Steps, skips; 6th drops, 6th and 8ve leaps; free rhythms, but fairly regular phrasing.
Piano:	Chordal, with decoration and bass melodic line.
Comment:	Headed 'To the most illustrious and mighty Frederick the fift, Count Palatine of the Rhine'. Repeat optional. The Count landed in England on 16th October, 1612, and Prince Henry died the following November 6th. The Count married Princess Elizabeth a few weeks later. St. 1, line 2: straight = immediately.

(6) When pale famine.

	G minor. d'-f ", [e'-d"]. 4/4. 1'20", [1']. 2 St. V/me, P/e.
For:	Mezzo, Bar.
Subject:	When famine and war ravaged the land affliction was not as great as now, when lords and commons mourn what might have been.
Voice:	Steps, skips, broken chords; some chromatics; irregular rhythms, but fairly regular phrase-lengths.
Piano:	Chordal, with hints of counterpoint; a melodic bass.

Comment: Headed 'To the most disconsolate Great Britain'. Repeat
            optional. St. 1, line 2: *unsatiate*, in text = *insatiate*, in music
            = insatiable; line 4: contemning = holding in contempt; line
            8: *Then now for ones fate*, in music = *Thou now for ones fall*,
            in text. St. 2, line 1: States = rulers.

(7) O poor distracted world.

            C major. e'-g", [g'-e"]. 4/4. 1'30", [1'10"]. 2 St. V/e, P/e.
For: Sop, Ten.
Subject: Poor world, troubled by religious controversy, how happy
            you would have been had this Prince lived; he would have
            defended truth.
Voice: Steps, skips, broken chords, repeated notes; 6th leap;
            rhythm fairly continuous quavers in verbally controlled
            rhythm.
Piano: Chordal, with some elaboration at cadences.
Comment: Headed 'To the World'. Repeat optional. The 30 Years War
            in Germany, involving Frederick, Count Palatine, was
            shortly to begin. St. 1, line 6: King James had published, in
            1609, 'Premonitions to all most mighty Monarchs, Kings,
            Free Princes and States of Christendom'. St. 2, line 2:
            Thrace – part of the Mohammedan empire; line 8: In your
            (remaining younger) brothers we expect (await) the
            fulfilment of the hopes you were ready to realise.

39 SONGS FROM THE MASKE OF SQUIRES Presented in the
Banqueting roome at Whitehall, on St Stephens night last, At the
Mariage of the Right Honourable the Earle of Somerset: and the right
noble the Lady Frances Howard. Written by Thomas Campion. 1614.
The first song Made and expressed by Nicholas Lanier. The three
songs following were composed by Mr Coprario, and sung by Mr John
Allen and Mr Lanier. S & B edition by Gerald Hendrie and Thurston
Dart, 1959. Tablature included (*LS* 9).

(1) Bring away this sacred tree. See 62.

(2) Go happy man. Davis.

            G minor. g'-g". 4/4. 45", [30"]. 2 St. V/me, P/e.
For: Sop, Ten.
Subject: Go, happy bridegroom, none can now prevent you.
Voice: Steps, skips, melismas; subtle variations of dance rhythms.
Piano: Chordal; the rhythms are easier than in the voice.
Comment: Repeat optional. The rhythmic subtleties are tricky but very
            effective. 'The three destinies set the Tree of Golde before
            the Queene. – The Queene puld a branch from the Tree and

gave it to a Nobleman, who delivered it to one of the Squires. A Song while the Squires descend with the bough toward the Scene' (Campion's stage directions).

(3) While dancing rests. Davis.

       G minor. d'-g", [g'-f "]. 3/8,3/4,4/4. 40", [30"]. 3 St. V/me, P/e.

For: Sop, Ten.

Subject: Rest from dancing and listen to music, it weaves spells to bring good fortune; love is best at spring-time, so praise Hymen, God of Marriage.

Voice: Steps, small skips; melismas; normal 3/8,3/4 time, with written out rallentando at end.

Piano: Chordal, some melodic bass.

Comment: Repeat optional. 'The third Song of three partes, with a Chorus of five partes, sung after the first Daunce' (Campion's note). However, it can clearly be sung as a solo. The tempo relationship suggested is satisfactory, but a possible alternative would be to take ending as quaver = quaver, and then repeat, taking dotted crotchet = crotchet this second time. St. 2, line 3: persever = endure. Campion's own *Description of a Maske* has an extra word at the end of line 3 of each stanza: 1, chanting; 2, ever; 3, closing; although omitted in the setting printed at the end of the Maske, it is a pity to lose the subtle echo effect with its changing meaning, and there seems no reason why the last two notes of the cadence should not be repeated.

(4) Come ashore. Davis.

       F major. f'-f ". 2/4. 1', [40"]. 2 St. V/e, P/e.

For: Mezzo, Bar.

Subject: The celebrations are now over; some will sleep, Venus will call others. Hymen prefers long nights, so goodnight to all.

Voice: Steps, a few skips; 6th and 8ve drops; regular dance rhythm rather like a hornpipe.

Piano: Chordal.

Comment: Repeat optional. 'Stright in the Thames appeared foure Barges with skippers in them, and withall this song was sung' (Campion's stage direction before the first stanza). 'The Squires speeches being ended, the Song is Sung while the Boates passe way' (Campion's direction before the second stanza). St. 1, line 2: pates = heads, brains; line 5: the sea-born goddess = Venus. St. 2, line 3: affect = desire.

40 Send home my long-strayed eyes (John Donne, *Songs and Sonnets*, 1633). *LS* 9.

G minor. d'-f ", [f'-e"]. 4/4. 55". V/me, P/e.

For:	Mezzo, Bar.
Subject:	Return my eyes to me; but if you have taught them ill by your bad behaviour, keep them to yourself.
Voice:	Steps, small skips; arpeggios, melismas; free recit. style; arioso.
Piano:	Chordal.
Comment:	An MS source which has been freely corrected by the editors. An interesting setting of the first stanza of this fine poem. The other two stanzas run: 'Send home my harmless heart again, / Which no unworthy thought could stain, / Which if it be taught by thine / To make jestings / Of protestings, / And break both / Word and oath, / Keep it, for then 'tis none of mine. // Yet send me back my heart and eyes, / That I may know, and see thy lies, / And may laugh and joy, when thou / Art in anguish / And dost languish / For some one / That will none, / Or prove as false as thou art now.'

WILLIAM CORKINE
fl. 1610 – 1612

41 AYRES To Sing and Play to the Lute and Basse Violl. 1610. S & B edition by E.H. Fellowes, 1926. Out of print.

(5) Sweet, let me go. Colls 5, 28.

C major. c'-a", [g'-g"]. 2/2. 1'05". V/m, P/me.

For:	Sop. [Cont, C-Ten; see below].
Subject:	Fast and funny version of 'Stop it, I like it!'.
Voice:	Steps; many offbeat rhythms; words vital though often placed high at crucial moments.
Piano:	Fairly simple chords, some running bass, all fast.
Comment:	For a singer with clear diction in the upper register and a sense of humour this is a winner. The original was printed an 8ve lower in the alto clef; if bars 8½- 10½ were raised an 8ve, and the whole then sung in the lower 8ve by a contralto, or even counter-tenor, it might well be even more effective. Bars 25-28, voice: quavers phrased 1 and 3 in Coll 5 and Fellowes, 2 and 2 in Coll 28. Bar 31, beats 1-2, LH: minim G, Coll 5 and Fellowes, G F crotchets, Coll 28.

(6) He that hath no mistress. Coll 5.

F major. c'-e"*b*, [e'-c"]. 3/2. 50". V/me, P/e.

For:	C-Ten, Bar.
Subject:	Angry complaint at desertion by his lady.

Voice: Steps, small skips; 8ve leap; scales; variable rhythms.
Piano: Chordal.
Comment: Line 1: favour = gift to a lover; line 4: Joan – generic name for
      female rustic; line 6: carted: harlots were carried through the
      streets in a cart to expose and punish them; line 5: *are* = *am* in
      source, according to Doughtie.

(7) Sweet Cupid. Coll 5. Coll 20, *B major*; Coll 21, *G major*.
      B*b* major. f'-f ". 2/2. 40". 3 St. V/e, P/e.
For: Ten; *Bar*.
Subject: Let us make love now, before we are too old.
Voice: Steps, small skips; simple rhythms.
Piano: Chordal, some decoration.
Comment: Some inoffensively bawdy double meanings in this attractive
      little song. St. 2, line 1: lay = overthrow. St. 3, line 2: shale =
      to drop out, of seed or grain; here meaning to spill, or to be
      wasted. Colls 20, 21: accompaniment and introduction to
      each stanza by Keel. Bar 6 of each stanza, notes 3-5, voice:
      should be quaver quaver crotchet.

42 THE SECOND BOOKE OF AYRES Some, to Sing and Play to the
Base- Violl alone: Others, to be sung to the Lute and Base Violl. 1612.
S & B edition by E.H. Fellowes, 1926. Out of print.

(3) Two lovers sat lamenting. Coll 19.
      G major. f °-g', [g°-e']. 2/2. 1'. 3 St. V/me, P/e.
For: *Sop, Ten*; Cont, C-Ten. See Comment.
Subject: Two rejected lovers find comfort in each other.
Voice: Steps, small skips; varied rhythms with one melisma.
Piano: Coll 19 gives only the original single line part for bass viol;
      Fellowes added upper parts in simple contrapuntal style for
      use with lute or piano.
Comment: Voice originally printed in alto clef; Fellowes prints it 8ve
      higher. St. 1, line 5: bewray = reveal; line 7: coth = quoth; line
      9: *bewraying* may well be an error for some other rhyming
      word, such.as *betraying*, on the other hand, the last words of
      lines 5 and 6 seem to have been transposed, *delaying,*
      bewraying (Doughtie); line 13: set looking by = stop just
      looking. St. 2, line 9: descryed = made known.

(5) Dear, though your mind. C major. Coll 20, *A major*; Coll 21, *F major*.
      A major. d' #-f "#. [g' #-e"]. 4/4. 40". 3 St. V/me, P/e.
For: (Sop, Ten); *Mezzo, C-Ten, Bar*; *Cont, Bass*.
Subject: Stay and hear my pleas, or go, and leave me to despair.
Voice: Steps, scales, simple skips; free rhythm with some patter.

Piano: Chordal, with decoration, melodic bass.
Comment: Accompaniment and introduction to each stanza by Keel,
                though the bass to the refrain actually follows Corkine!
                Underlay and wording of the refrain is uncertain: St. 1/2, *But
                stay and hear me yet, sweet love, EMV* and Ault, Doughtie St.
                2; *But yet stay and hear me, sweet love,* Fellowes, Doughtie St.
                1; St. 3, *And now leave me to my despair, EMV,* Doughtie and
                Ault, *And to leave me now to my despair,* Fellowes. Keel's
                version for St. 1 follows Fellowes and seems right, but must
                also apply to St. 2. Bar 6 of each stanza, voice, notes 5-7:
                should be dotted crotchet and two semiquavers.

(7) Down, down, proud mind. Coll 7; Coll 8, *G major.*
                C major. d'-g", [g'-g"]. 2/2. 2 St. V/me, P/e.
For: Sop, Ten; *Cont, Bass.*
Subject: My heart has aimed too high; let me retire and have peace
                instead of anguish.
Voice: Steps, 3rds, scales; 6th drops, 8ve leap; three phrases start on
                g"; slow and sustained, in simple rhythm.
Piano: Chordal, in three parts.
Comment: A fine and dignified song. Accompaniment originally for viol
                alone; lute part added by Fellowes, and modified for the low
                key version. An alternative poem is given in *EMV.*

(16) Shall a smile or guileful glance? F major. Coll 22, *G major*; Coll 23,
    Eb major.
                G major. g'-g", [g'-e"]. 4/4. (Moderato). 30". 3 St. V/e, P/me.
For: *Ten*; (Bar); *C-Ten.*
Subject: Unless she is true I will regain my freedom.
Voice: Steps, 4ths, 5ths; rhythm simple but varied.
Piano: Chordal, with bass melody and LH jumps.
Comment: Accompaniment and introduction to each stanza by Keel. St.
                2, line 2: remised = released. St. 3. line 1: *I must = must I,*
                Fellowes and *EMV*; line 4: endue = endow; line 5: *I first = first
                I,* all other editions. Bar 12, all stanzas: delete tie, notes 1-2,
                slur notes 2-3.

JOHN DANYEL
1564 – after 1625

43 SONGS for the Lute, Viol and Voice. 1606. S & B edition by E.H.
    Fellowes, 1926. Revised by David Scott, 1970 (*LS* 10).

(1) Coy Daphne fled. Coll 26.
                D major. c'#-e", [d'-d"]. 3/4. 1'. 2 St. V/e, P/me.

For: Mezzo, C-Ten, Bar.

Subject: Phoebus (Apollo) pursued Daphne, who fled, and was transformed into a tree. The second stanza is called 'The Answer', and proves Daphne right, for her honour is still green.

Voice: Steps, skips, broken chords, sequences; 8ve leap; rhythms in simple 3/4,3/2 phrases.

Piano: Contrapuntal in three parts, with much imitation.

Comment: The volume is dedicated to Mrs Anne Greene, hence the complimentary pun in the last line of this song. Also set as a madrigal by Pilkington, *EM* 26 (8-9). St. 2, line 2: of course = a matter of habit. Coll 26: a few notes added to bass from viol part.

(2) Thou pretty bird. Coll 30.

G major. d'-f ", [e'-e"]. 4/4. 1'40", [1'10"]. V/me, P/e.

For: [Mezzo], Bar.

Subject: Pretty bird, both you and I sing to our loved ones; but you live and I die.

Voice: Steps, skips, sequences, some chromatics; some unexpected rhythms.

Piano: Chordal, with some imitation.

Comment: Repeat optional. In bars 10 and 13 *her* could be changed to *him* and *his* respectively. St. 1, line 2: silly = helpless. The words are a translation, probably by John Danyel's brother Samuel, of a poem by Guarini – 'O come se' gentile', *Rime*, 1698.

(3) He whose desires are still abroad.

G minor. d'-f ", [d'-e"b]. 3/4. 2'10". V/me, P/e.

For: Mezzo, Bar.

Subject: Ambition is foolishness; glory and fame come from imagination; power is nothing.

Voice: Mostly by step; some chromatics, imitation and sequence; some fairly complex rhythms.

Piano: Contrapuntal, mostly in two parts, sometimes in three.

Comment: Requires fairly good breath control.

(4) Like as the lute delights (Samuel Daniel, Sonnet 57, *Delia*, 1592). Coll 5.

C minor. c'-e"b, [d'-c"]. 4/4. 3'30", (3'). V/m, P/me.

For: [Mezzo], C-Ten, Bar.

Subject: A sonnet on the power of music when played by the beloved, which moves the listener with two beauties.

Voice: Steps, small skips, chromatic, melismas; irregular rhythms, some long phrases; scales and sequences.

Piano: Contrapuntal, in three parts much of the time; much
                imitation; chromatic sections.

Comment: Repeat optional. A fine song, with beautifully detailed word
                illustration, and a fair variety in spite of its length and
                serious approach. In *Delia* lines 11-12 of the song are
                printed before lines 9-10. Variants: line 8: *gives* = *give*; line
                14: *sweet* = *true*. Bar 7: dislikes = offends; bar 14: *my Muse it
                sounds according*, in music = *my Muse according*, in text;
                bar 26: wise = manner; bar 37: ground = ground bass *and
                basis*; reports – in music, notes or parts answering others;
                usual sense also intended; bar 49: relish – in music,
                ornamentation; usual sense also intended; bars 52-53: *judge
                then*, in music = *then judge*, in text.

(5) Dost thou withdraw thy grace? Colls 5, 30.

                G minor. g'-f ", [b'*b*-f "]. 4/4. 1'05". V/me, P/me.

For: Sop, Ten.

Subject: You are mistaken if you think leaving me will destroy my
                love.

Voice: Steps, small skips; fairly complex rhythms and long
                phrases.

Piano: Contrapuntal; three parts, with much imitation.

Comment: Bar 8: *because*, in music = *for that*, in text = so that. Lines
                11-12: Doughtie quotes an Elizabethan proverb: 'That Fire
                which lights at a distance will burn us when near.' Coll 5:
                bar 2, beat 1, RH: delete f'#. Coll 30: bar 12, beat 3, LH:
                crotchet rest missing.

(6) Why canst thou not? Colls 5, 28.

                G major. e'-f", [g'-e"]. 4/4. 40". 2 St. V/me, P/me.

For: Mezzo, Bar.

Subject: Either cease to attract me, or return my affection.

Voice: Steps, some simple skips, sequence; some fairly complex
                rhythms.

Piano: Semi-contrapuntal, with much imitation and some complex
                rhythms.

Comment: The irregular phrasing is effective. Coll 5: bar 7, beat 1, RH:
                delete c'. Coll 28: St. 2, line 3: *others'* = *other*, *LS* 10.

(7) Stay, cruel, stay. Coll 28.

                G major. d'-e", [e'-d"]. 4/4,3/4,4/4. 2'40", [2'10"]. V/me, P/me.

For: Mezzo, C-Ten, Bar.

Subject: Have pity and leave me not; if you will go, at least say
                farewell.

Voice: Steps, small skips, repeated notes; 8ve leap, sequence, imitation; much variety of rhythm, tempo and phrase-length.

Piano: Chordal; then contrapuntal in three parts, with much imitation.

Comment: Repeat optional. Tempo relationship given in both *LS* 10 and Coll 28 is satisfactory. An interesting song for both singer and audience. Coll 28: bar 5, voice: phrased 2 and 2, not 1 and 3 as in *LS* 10; bar 27, beat 2, voice: the f′ with editorial # has a natural in *LS* 10, bar 25, beat 6; first time bars at end: the two chords before the voice enters given in *LS* 10 are omitted.

(8) Time, cruel time (Samuel Daniel, Sonnet 23, *Delia*, 1592). Colls 19, 29.

C minor. e′b-e″b. 4/4. 3′25″. V/me, P/me.

For: C-Ten, Bar.

Subject: Cannot even Time subdue her, or does he admire her for being cruel, like him? Let him do so then, and pause, lest he should take her unawares.

Voice: Steps, skips, repeated notes; 6th leap, melismas; much rhythmic variety, some imitation, some chromatics.

Piano: Contrapuntal, in three parts with imitation and some chromatics.

Comment: One of the finest lute-songs, for both words and music. The first eight lines are from Sonnet 23, but the remainder is different. Variants from the sonnet: line 1: *canst thou* = *come and*; line 2: *That* = *Which*; line 4: *and* = *or*; line 6: *might* = *may*; line 7: *love her* = *spare her*. St. 1, line 3: exempt from scythe or bow – free from Time (aging and death) and Love. St. 2, line 2: *aid*, in music, *LS* 10 and Coll 29 = *help*, in text and Coll 19; line 4: weighs = can measure.

(9-11) Grief, keep within. Coll 31.

D minor. c′-f ″, [d′-e″]. 4/4. 7′45″. V/m, P/m.

For: Mezzo.

Subject: 'Mrs M.E. her Funerall teares for the death of her husband'. Mere tears cannot express my grief, since they can come from joy as well as sorrow; my heart, which knows the cause, must burst and die. I wept at our past meetings and farewells, and can I do no more now he is dead? Have all our feelings their proper means of expression except true sorrow? Then all I can do is die.

Voice: Steps, skips; 8ves, dim. 4ths, chromatics; great variety of rhythm and phrasing; climb up to sustained e″ at the end of each of the three stanzas, which are through composed,

though with repeated material at suitable points in the
verse.

Piano: Contrapuntal; chromatic; much imitation and rhythmic
                variety.

Comment: In many ways the greatest of all the lute-songs, not
                excepting those of Dowland. It is on a larger scale, and is
                formally more elaborate than any other; the emotion is
                deeply felt, the harmony highly expressive, and the climaxes
                convincing. Page 24, bar 8, and page 28, bar 8: B needs a
                natural. Page 27, line 2, bar 1: b° needs a natural. Page 31,
                bar 12: e°# should be f°#. Page 25, bar 12: *the*, in music =
                more, in text and Coll 31. Coll 31: part 1, bar 15, note 2,
                voice: a' for g' of *LS* 10; bar 19, beats 1-2, voice: crotchet
                crotchet, for dotted crotchet quaver of *LS* 10. Part 2, bar 6,
                RH, note 2: b'*b* for f' of *LS* 10 (bar 5); bar 30, RH, last note: c'
                needs a natural. Part 3, bar 4, beat 4, RH, and bar 7, beat 4,
                LH: quaver two semiquavers for two semiquavers quaver of
                LS 10; bar 10, beat 4, RH: a' for e' of *LS* 10; bar 18, beat 4,
                voice: c' has natural in *LS* 10, missing here.

(12) Let not Chloris think. Coll 30.
                D minor. c'-d", [d'-c"]. 3/4. 2'30". V/e, P/me.

For: C-Ten, Bar.

Subject: Chloris should not think that because I am her slave she can
                enslave others; I love her more than any of them, so why is
                she not satisfied to rule me alone?

Voice: Steps, skips; dance rhythms, slightly complicated at the
                end.

Piano: Contrapuntal, in dance rhythms, with some surprises.

Comment: Repeat of last section required for dance form; cheerful
                music in spite of minor key. Coll 30: bar 7, beats 2-3, voice:
                two crotchets for dotted crotchet quaver of *LS* 10 (bars 6 and
                13, beats 5-6); bar 12, beat 2, voice: g' for e' of *LS* 10 (bars 18
                and 31); bar 14, beat 1, voice: crotchet a' for quaver a'
                quaver b'*b* of *LS* 10 (bars 19 and 32).

(13-15) Can doleful notes?
                G minor. b°-d', [d'-d"]. 4/4. 6'. V/m, P/me.

For: Mezzo, C-Ten, Bar; Cont, Bass.

Subject: No ordinary tunes can express this grief; only chromatic
                tunes are appropriate.

Voice: Steps, some skips; highly chromatic; long sustained phrases,
                fairly free rhythms; much word illustration.

Piano: Contrapuntal, chromatic; much imitation.

Comment: Harmonically adventurous, as befits the words. Though perhaps a little long it is quite exceptional among lute-songs for its originality of musicianship. The last two lines of the poem are somewhat obscure; a possible reading might be: some musical turns of phrase (chromatics) are uncertain, and anticipating sad thoughts bring back grief; though the music then fades, the thoughts remain. *EMV* has a slightly different interpretation, suggesting *forecast* here means *forepast*: 'Certain uncertainly-remembered melodies, evoking past thoughts, bring back the grief, and then – though the music dies away again – the grief remains.' Doughtie suggests: 'Certain uncertain turns of anticipated thoughts (like uncertain chromatic tunes) occur and recur, then die; but having been set down in song, they will last.'

(16) Eyes, look no more. Coll 31.

	A minor. d'-e″, [e'-d″]. 4/4. 3′50″. V/me, P/me.
For:	Mezzo, C-Ten, Bar.
Subject:	Look no more for joys and delights, these insubstantial things; only sorrow and grief are real.
Voice:	Steps, skips, small sequences; fairly free rhythms.
Piano:	Contrapuntal, with some additional decoration.
Comment:	A fine sustained piece of music, with a good climax. Bar 16: *black dark*, in music (and Coll 31) = *dark black*, in text (and *LS* 10), *EMV*; bar 28, beat 2, RH: Coll 31 has c', missing in *LS* 10; bar 34: unappropried = not possessed; bar 38: imports = means.

(17) If I could shut the gate. Coll 30.

	A minor. e'-e″, [e'-d″]. 4/4. 1′50″, [1′20″]. V/me, P/me.
For:	Mezzo, C-Ten, Bar.
Subject:	I would that I could forget my sins, or set them apart; my Saviour is able to do this for me, and I may at length be free.
Voice:	Steps, a few skips; very free rhythms, longish phrases.
Piano:	Contrapuntal; three-part, with decorations.
Comment:	A good religious song, suitable for church use. St. 2, line 1: without = outside. Given in Earle, 1615, with many variants.

(18) I die whenas I do not see. Colls 5, 26.

	A minor. c'-e″, [e'-c″]. 4/4. 1′05″, [45″]. 2 St. V/me, P/e.
For:	C-Ten, Bar.
Subject:	The misery of being either with or away from a cruel mistress.
Voice:	Steps, small skips; some unexpected rhythms.
Piano:	Simple counterpoint.

Comment: Repeat optional. St. 2, line 2: silency = silence; line 4, rend = burst. The poem is based on two madrigals in Guarini's *Rime*, 1598: 'Io mi sento morir', and 'Parlo, misero, e taccio'.

(19) What delight can they enjoy?
    F major/D minor. d'-f ", [e'-e"]. 4/4. 1'10", [45"]. V/me, P/e.
For: Mezzo.
Subject: Falling in love is a fool's game, and I will leave it to others.
Voice: Steps, small skips; some unexpected rhythms.
Piano: Contrapuntal, mostly two-part.
Comment: Repeat optional. Line 5: seely = poor; line 7: who seldom make a habit of responding to us; line 10: *And let them pine that lovers prove*, in text = *And they must pine that lovers prove*, in soprano and alto = *Then pine that lovers be*, in tenor = *And they must pine that lovers be*, in bass (there is an alternative four-part version of this song). The editor's suggested 'quick time' must refer to crotchets, not minims.

(20) Now the earth, the skies, the air. Duet, outside the scope of this volume.

(21) Mrs Anne Grene her leaves be green. Lute solo.

JOHN DOWLAND
1563 – 1626

44 THE FIRST BOOKE OF SONGES OR AYRES of fowre partes with Tableture for the Lute: So made that all the partes together, or either of them severally may be song to the Lute, Orpharion or Viol de gambo. 1597. Reissued 1600, 1603, 1606 (revised), 1613. S & B edition by E.H. Fellowes, 1920; revised by Thurston Dart, 1965. Tablature included (*LS* 1). All the songs have four-part versions, given in *MB* VI.

(1) Unquiet thoughts. Coll 15, *A minor*; Coll 16, *F minor*.
    G minor. f'-e"b, [g'-d"]. 4/4. 1'25", [1'05"]. 3 St. V/e, P/e.
For: *Ten*; C-Ten, Bar; *Bass*.
Subject: An unhappy lover would like to keep silent, but if he does so his heart will break.
Voice: Steps, skips in last phrase; simple crotchet rhythms.
Piano: Mostly three-part counterpoint, some chordal phrases.
Comment: Repeat optional. Bar 5, beat 1: RH f' should be sharp, not natural. Colls 15, [16]: bar 3: minim b', [g'] should be dotted crotchet quaver. Coll 16: bar 4, beat 6, RH: b°b not c'. St. 3, line 4: *that* refers to *tongue*, in line 3.

(2) **Who ever thinks or hopes of love** (Fulke Greville, Lord Brooke,
Caelica, Sonnet V, 1633). Colls 15, 19; Coll 16, *D minor*; Imperial
(Mezzo) *F minor*.

G minor. f'-g", [a'-f "]. 4/4. 1'25", [1']. 2 St. V/me, P/e.

For: Sop, Ten; *Mezzo, C-Ten, Bar*; *Cont, Bass*.

Subject: A warning that love is a risky business, from someone
clearly recently disappointed.

Voice: Steps, some skips; mostly simple rhythms, but some
awkward moments.

Piano: Chordal, with contrapuntal touches.

Comment: Repeat optional. Some variants in *Caelica*. Another version
set by Peerson as a madrigal. Underlay needs some attention:
St. 1, line 4: *not– been– made* = *not– been made–*, Colls 15, 16;
not been– made–, MB; *not been made– –*, Coll 19.

St. 2, line 4: *Who thinks that change–* (rest) *is by entreaty–
charmed–* is best; line 4: *light-god* = *light god*, Colls 15, 16,
EMV; line 5: *him* could be changed to *her*.

Colls 15, [16]: bar 1, beat 4: delete b°, [f °]; bar 2, beat 1:
add d', [a°]; bar 4: add d° and g°, [A and d°]; bar 5: delete a's,
[e's] and d°s, [a°s] in first two chords, and add a°s [e°s] in all
three chords; bar 6, RH 2nd note: add natural; bar 7, beat 1,
LH: delete a°, [e°]; bar 11, 2nd half, RH: top notes should be
dotted crotchet quaver; bar 14, beat 5: add b°, [f °]; bar 18,
beat 4: a° not b°*b*, [e° not f °]; bar 21, 2nd half: top notes of
RH should be crotchet crotchet; bar 23, beat 3: add d', [a°].
Coll 15: bar 19, beat 1: g° not a°. Coll 16: bar 7: bass should
be E crotchet, F crotchet, E minim; bar 8, beat 3: LH should
be an 8ve down. Coll 19: bar 1, beat 1: d' not b°; bar 5, beat 4:
add a'. Bar 21: *son* = *sun*, all other editions. Many of these
errors are from Dowland's original 1597 edition, revised in
1606. Imperial: spacing of accompaniment slightly modified.

(3) **My thoughts are winged with hopes.** Coll 15; Coll 16, *G minor*.

C minor. g'-g", [b'-f"]. 3/4. 1'15", [55"]. 3 St. V/me, P/me.

For: Ten, *C-Ten, Bar*.

Subject: The lover's emotions are compared with the waning and
waxing moon; all will be well when his Cynthia shines once
more.

Voice: Steps, small skips; many rhythmic changes.

Piano: Simple counterpoint; some rhythmic complications.

Comment: Galliard form; the melody appears in *Lachrimae* as 'Sir John
Souch, his Galliard'; the repeat of the last section is
therefore needed. The words have been attributed at various
times to George, Earl of Cumberland, Fulke Greville, John
Lyly and Sir Walter Raleigh, who now appears the most

likely candidate. It is almost certainly a plea for favour from Queen Elizabeth, in her frequent guise as Cynthia, according to *MB* VI. Printed in *EH*, 1600. St. 2, line 6: suspect = suspicion. Colls 15, 16: delete repeats for first two sections; bar 2, beat 3: add f', [c']; bar 11, last RH quaver e' not a', [b° not e']. Coll 16: bars 16/17, St. 2: *in-fect*, not *in feat*.

(4) If my complaints could passions move. Colls 6, 15, 19; Coll 16, *E minor.*

                 G minor. f'#-f", [g'-d"]. 3/4. 1'45". 2 St. V/e, P/e.

For:	Sop, Ten; Mezzo, Bar; *Cont, C-Ten, Bass.*
Subject:	Complaint of rejected lover; who explains how unfair this is, and warns others. The Earl of Essex about Elizabeth?
Voice:	Steps, a few 3rds; simple regular rhythms.
Piano:	Contrapuntal, in three parts.
Comment:	Appears in *Lachrimae* as 'Captain Digorie Piper, his Galliard'. One of Dowland's most beautiful tunes, suited to any audience. Given in Earle, 1615. St. 2, line 7: *men's* could be changed to *our* if desired. St. 2, line 2: *am I*, in 1597 and 1600, changed in 1606 to *I am*; line 3: scant = keep in short supply; line 4: contemned = held in contempt; line 11: *here* = *hear*, in *EMV*, DP, *MB* VI, notes to Coll 6, and Doughtie, which improves the sense. Coll 19, bar 3: slur notes 2-3, not 1-2.

(5) Can she excuse my wrongs? Colls 16, 19; Coll 15, *F minor.*

                 D minor. d'-d". 3/4. 1'40", [1'20"]. 2 St. V/me, P/me.

For:	*Ten*; C-Ten, Bar, Bass.
Subject:	She is unkind, and unless she relents I must die; but I shall still be content.
Voice:	Steps, small skips, repeated notes; varied rhythms.
Piano:	Chordal in various rhythms; takes over melody for last section.
Comment:	Appears in *Lachrimae* as 'The Earl of Essex's Galliard'; repeat therefore required. It possibly concerns Essex and Elizabeth, and may even have been written by Essex. Given in Earle, 1615. The lute melody in the last section uses a quotation from a popular song, the first lines of which run: 'Shall I go walk the woods so wild, / Wandering here and there, / As I was once full sore beguiled? / What remedy though, / Alas for love I die with woe.' This may refer to Wanstead, see 45 (10). Colls 16, [15]: bars 2 and 8, RH, last beat: d' not f', [f' not a']. Coll 16: St. 1, bar 13: *where* = *when*, all other editions. Coll 19: St. 3, line 4: *thus be* = *be thus*, all

other editions; St. 6, line 2: *thus tormented* = *thus still tormented*, all other editions. See DP, pp. 224-30.

(6) Now, O now I needs must part. Coll 15, *A major*; Colls 6, 16, 23, *F major*.

	G major. e'-e". 3/4. 1'15". 3 St. V/e, P/me.
For:	*Sop, Ten*; Mezzo, C-Ten, Bar.
Subject:	The lover will die, driven from the beloved by despair; but love itself will not die.
Voice:	Steps, some 3rds; simple rhythms.
Piano:	Chordal, with elaborated cadences.
Comment:	Known as 'The Frog Galliard', though actually a coranto, according to *MB* VI, it may refer to the Duc D'Alençon, a suitor to Elizabeth whom she called her 'frog'. St. 2, line 1: *am from thee* = *from thee am*, *MB* VI, *EMV*. St. 3, line 8: *dieth* = *died*, Colls 6, 15, 16; line 12: *that* = *which*, *MB* VI, *EMV*. *MB* VI has repeat marks for last 8 bars. Colls 15, [6 and 16]: bar 19, beat 4, LH: A not c°, [F not A]. Colls 6, 16: bar 21: all b°s need naturals. Colls 22, 23: accompaniment and introduction to each stanza by Keel. The words are wrongly organised: lines 5-8 of St. 1 are a refrain, and should be lines 9-12 of all three stanzas; lines 5-8 of St. 1 are missing, and lines 5-8 of St. 2/3 should be sung to the same music as lines 1-4. Bars 19, 26 and 33 of each stanza should be twice as long, making the 8 bar balancing phrases of the dance. Printed in Forbes, 1662.

(7) Dear, if you change. Coll 19; Colls 15, 20, *B minor*; Colls 16, 21, *G minor*.

	A minor. d'-e", [e'-e"]. 2/2. 1'30", [1'10"]. 2 St. V/me, P/me.
For:	*Sop, Ten*; Mezzo, C-Ten, Bar; *Cont, Bass*.
Subject:	The virtues of the beloved guarantee the faith of the lover.
Voice:	Steps, a few skips; 8ve leap; two bars of repeated top notes; varied rhythms; short melisma.
Piano:	Contrapuntal, with elaborated cadence.
Comment:	Repeat optional. St. 1, line 4: moe = more, prove = test; line 6: And, on my faith = And, I swear. Coll 15, [16]: bar 6, beat 1: add a°, [f °]; bar 10, beat 1: add # to a°, [f °]; bar 11, beat 1: c' not d', [a° not b°]; bar 12, beats 1 and 3: add c', [a°]; bar 13, beat 3: add c', [a°]. Coll 16: bar 8, voice, last note b'*b*, not g'; bar 11, RH, last quaver: b°*b*, not a°. Colls 20, [21]: accompaniment and introduction to each stanza by Keel. St. 1, line 5: *not, nor be* = *nor be not*, all other editions, but Keel's emendation clarifies the sense. In each stanza, voice: bar 9, note 4: b' not f', [g' not d']; bar 11, notes 2-3 should be dotted minim crotchet; bar 22, note 2: c" not b', [a' not g'].

(8) Burst forth, my tears. Coll 16; Coll 15, *B minor*.

G minor, d'-d'', [d'-c'']. 2/2. 1'30'', [1'10'']. 3 St. V/me, P/me.

For: *Ten*; C-Ten, Bar; Bass.

Subject: Listen to my tears, my tender flocks; my beloved is as hard as rock, and I must die.

Voice: Steps, small skips; repeated bottom notes; rhythms fairly free, but simple except for last phrase.

Piano: Contrapuntal, two and three part.

Comment: Repeat optional. Printed in *EH*, 1600, with the title, 'To his Flocks'. St. 1, line 1: forward = chief. St. 2, line 3: *disdain* = *disdains*, *EH*; line 4: *locks*, in all modern editions = *yokes*, in all old editions; Diana Poulton is against this emendation, but overlooks the fact that *yokes* has clearly been transferred from St. 1, as is pointed out in *EMV*. St. 3, line 3: repineth at my teen = complains about my annoyance. Coll 15, [16]: bar 8, beat 1: add c', [a°]; bar 9, last beat: add f', [d'].

(9) Go crystal tears. Coll 19; Coll 15, *D minor*; Coll 16, *B minor*.

C minor. g'-e''b. 2/2. 1'25'', [1'05'']. 2 St. V/me, P/me.

For: *Ten*; C-Ten, Bar.

Subject: The unrequited lover sends his tears and sighs as messengers to his hard-hearted mistress.

Voice: Steps, small skips; very varied rhythms, including some triple-time in line 5 which is easily overlooked.

Piano: Chordal, with some decoration.

Comment: Repeat optional, better omitted. *MB* VI considers the four-part version basic, with the solo version as an alternative. St. 1, line 5, and St. 2, line 4: desert = worthiness (pronounce desart). St. 2, line 1: *restless* = *hapless*, 1599, Doughtie and Coll 19; line 2: indurate = hardened; line 3: *whose* = *while*, *MB* VI. Colls 15, [16]: bar 7, LH, beat 1: quaver A, [F], not quaver rest; bar 16, beat 3: add a°, [f °]; beat 4: add a', [f'], delete d', [b°]; bar 17, beat 1: add crotchet a', [f']; 2nd quaver delete a', [f'], 3rd quaver add d', [b°], 4th quaver add b° natural, [g°#], delete f', [d']. Compare 2nd stanza with **60 (2)**.

(10) Thinkst thou then by thy feigning.

G minor. d'-d'', [f'-d'']. 4/4. 50''. 3 St. V/me, P/me.

For: C-Ten, Bar, Bass.

Subject: If you feign sleep may I not kiss you? If you were truly unconscious I might do more, but no, kisses are harmless.

Voice: Steps, small skips; simple rhythms, but some problems in word accentuation.

Piano: Semi-contrapuntal, with a fair sprinkling of accidentals.

Comment: In the form of an Alman, according to *MB* VI. St. 2, line 1: *my* = *thy, EMV*, which makes better sense; line 9: *sweet* = *deep, EMV*, better, since *sweet* appeared in line 8; line 10: *so* = *too, MB*. St. 3, line 10: armless = unarmed.

(11) Come away, come sweet love. Colls 6, 15, 19; Coll 16, *E minor*; Coll 22, *A minor*; Coll 23, *F minor*.

G minor. f'#-f ", [g'-d"]. 4/4,3/4. 45". 3 St. V/me, P/me.

For: [Sop], Ten; [Mezzo], Bar; *C-Ten*.
Subject: It is a lovely day, let us make love.
Voice: Almost all by step; much rhythmic variety.
Piano: Chordal, care needed with decorated cadences.
Comment: Delightful. Women could omit stanza 3. The tempo relationships given by the editors seem unsatisfactory, crotchet = crotchet works much better. Appears in *EH*, 1600, with the title 'To his love'. In Alman form, according to *MB* VI. St. 1, line 9: *love's long, EH* and Ault, = *love long*, Coll 19 and Doughtie; *love-long, EMV*; *pain*, all modern editions and *EH* = *pains*, all original editions and Doughtie. St. 3, line 4: *river's side*, Ault = *river-side*, Colls 6, 15, 16; *river side*, 1600, 1603; *rivers side*, Coll 19, *EH*; line 5: Cyprian – the island of Cyprus was devoted to the worship of Venus.

Coll 19: bar 13, beat 1, RH: quaver rest crotchet g', not dotted crotchet g'. Colls 15, [16]: bar 5, beats 5/6: dotted crotchet d° [b°] quaver e° natural [c°], not minim d° [b°]; bar 14, beats 3/4: dotted crotchet d° [b°] quaver e° natural [c°#], not minim d° [b°]. Colls 22, 23: accompaniment and introduction to each stanza by Keel. St. 2, line 4: *fierce* = *fiery*, all other editions; St. 3, line 4: *like the* = *like to the*, all other editions; line 10: *wishes* = *wished*, all other editions. Coll 22: line 5: *flee* = *flie* (fly), all other editions.

(12) Rest awhile, you cruel cares. Coll 15, *Bb major/minor*; Coll 16, *F major/minor*.

G major/minor. f'#-d", [g'-d"]. 3/4. 1'15", [1']. 3 St. V/e, P/e.

For: *Ten*; C-Ten, Bar.
Subject: A plea to Laura to be kind, for he loves her; a lively song for all that.
Voice: Steps, small skips; fairly straightforward rhythm.
Piano: Chordal; some decorations and bass melodies.
Comment: Interesting contrast between the first, major, section, in a rather jerky rhythm, and the much smoother minor section which follows. St. 1, line 7: *EMV* suggests *ever* was added by Dowland, since it makes the line two syllables longer than the subsequent stanzas; this adds weight to the idea in *MB*

VI of adding *ever* before *feigned* in St. 2, and before *prove* in St. 3. St. 3, line 7: *prove* = *proves*, in 1597, 1600, 1603, 1606, Doughtie and *EMV*. Coll 13, [14]: bar 9, RH, last quaver: add natural; bars 13, 24: RH 1st top note crotchet, beat 2 add a'b', [e'f'] quavers; bar 18, bass: minim g°, [d°] crotchet e°, [B]; bar 19: add f', [c']; bar 21, bass: minim crotchet, not dotted minim.

(13) Sleep, wayward thoughts. Colls 9, 15, *A major*; Colls 6, 10, 16, *Eb major*.

G major. g'-e''. 3/4. 1'05'', [50'']. 3 St. V/e, P/e.

For: *[Sop], Ten*; [Mezzo], C-Ten, Bar; *[Cont], Bass*.

Subject: An extended pun based on the fact that his Love, the girl, is asleep, whereas his love, the emotion, is awake.

Voice: Steps, some simple skips; simple rhythm.

Piano: Chordal, a few bass melodies.

Comment: Repeat optional. One of Dowland's most charming songs, suited to any audience. Printed in Playford, 1660, and in Forbes 1662, 1666, 1682; see also **45 (11)**. In short Galliard form, it may have originated as a dance. St. 1, line 2: diseased = made ill at ease; it may well be that this word and *displeased* at the end of line 4 have been accidentally interchanged, as suggested in *EMV* and Doughtie, and thus printed by Playford. St. 2, line 4: Cupid's closed fires = her eyes. Coll 6: notes give original key as G minor, in error.

(14) All ye, whom love and fortune.

G minor. d'-d'', [e'-d'']. 2/2. 1'50'', [1'15'']. 2 St. V/me, P/me.

For: [Mezzo], C-Ten, Bar.

Subject: All who have sorrows, listen to mine, which are without end.

Voice: Steps, small skips; chromatic rising and descending scales; some long and some very short phrases.

Piano: Contrapuntal; chromatic; some fairly involved rhythms.

Comment: Repeat optional. St. 1, line 5: a woman could substitute *one* for *man* as the last word. St. 2, line 4: rue = regard with pity.

(15) Wilt thou, unkind, thus reave me. Coll 15, *B minor*; Coll 16, *F minor*.

A minor. e'-e''. 2/2. 50'', [25'']. 5 St. V/me, P/e.

For: *Sop, Ten*; Mezzo, C-Ten, Bar; *Cont, Bass*.

Subject: Farewell, if you must go; but give me a kiss first, since love will not be changed by absence.

Voice: Mostly by step; some chromatics; first half in upper fifth, second in lower; a fair variety of rhythms.

Piano: Essentially chordal.

Comment: Since both halves have repeat signs both or neither should be repeated. Colls 15, 16, suggest 'briskly' for the tempo, but it might well be more effective slow. They also omit stanzas 3 and 4. St. 1, line 1: reave = bereave; line 4: or ere = before; St. 5, line 2: desert = merit. Coll 15, [16]: bar 13, beat 1, LH: a° not b°, [e° not f°].

(16) Would my conceit.

A minor. c'-e", [d'-d"]. 2/2. 1'40", [1'10"]. 3 St. V/me, P/e.

For: Mezzo, C-Ten, Bar.

Subject: Would that I were released from my miseries by death, but even that hope is forbidden me, and I must yield to my sufferings.

Voice: Steps, skips; 6th and 8th leaps; repeated notes; small melisma; longish phrases in varying rhythms.

Piano: Fairly simple counterpoint, much of it in two parts.

Comment: Rather in the style of a song with viols, the voice being one of the contrapuntal parts. St. 1, line 6: eke = also. St. 3, line 1: free = freedom; lines 2, 4/5: hap = chance, fortune; line 4: sith = since; aslope = awry; line 6: thralls = troubles.

(17) Come again, sweet love doth now invite. Coll 21, Imperial (Baritone); Colls 9, 15, *Ab major*; Colls 6, 10, 16, *F major*; Colls 20, 32, *A major*.

G major. d'-e", [f'#-d"]. 2/2. 45". 6 St. V/me, P/me.

For: *[Sop]*, Ten; [Mezzo], C-Ten, Bar; *[Cont]*, *Bass*.

Subject: A lover's complaint, but made with energy.

Voice: First half by step, then a sequence of small skips to a held d", then falling by step; some rhythmic variety.

Piano: Basically chordal, with elaborated cadences.

Comment: Repeat essential. Masculine viewpoint, but could easily be reversed. There is much confusion over the punctuation and meaning of the opening lines: commas are given as follows: after *delight, MB* VI; *graces and delight, EMV*; *refrain*, and full stop after *delight*, Colls 20, 21; *invite, refrain*, and *delight*, Colls 6, 9, 10, 15, 16 and Doughtie; best might be *graces, refrain,* and full stop after *delight*. A paraphrase might be: Love invites your graces to give me pleasure once again, which they refrain from doing at the moment, so that I may see, hear, touch etc. 'Die', at the end of the stanza has its common Elizabethan meaning of making love, and should clearly not be followed by a comma; Dowland's rest at this point is a matter of emotion, not grammar.

St. 3, line 2: lends me shine = gives me light; line 3: *doth*, 1613 and *MB* VI, *do*, all other editions; *doth* makes clearer

sense; line 6: *winters* = *winter, MB* VI. St. 4, line 3: streams
= tears. St. 5, line 1: *Out* = *But, MB VI; line 3: rue* = *repent.
St. 6, line 4: to*, all modern music editions except Colls 20, 21
= *do*, all original editions, Doughtie and *EMV*; approve =
test. St. 3-6, line 6: two syllables appear to be missing in this
line, and have been supplied by some modern editors – those
in *MB* VI and Coll 6 (and *mighty* in the last stanza in Colls 9,
10, 15, 16) are found, except for St. 3, in Earle, 1615, though
this source has no less than 13 variants from Dowland. All
are unnecessary, since in St. 3 the first two words and in the
other stanzas the third and fourth words can be repeated
(better than carrying over, as given in Colls 20, 21, or
omitting two notes, as in Coll 32). Coll 6, bar 1: delete *p.*
Colls 10, 16: bar 12, beat 4, RH: c' not e'. Colls 9, 10, 15, 16,
20, 21, 32 all omit St. 3-5. Colls 20. 21: accompaniment and
introduction to each stanza by Keel. Coll 32: accompaniment
and introduction to each stanza by Michael Diack; last bar,
voice: the penultimate syllable should start on the two
quavers. Imperial: accompaniment slightly modified; first
two stanzas only given. Printed in Forbes, 1662.

(18) His golden locks. Coll 19; Coll 15, *Bb major*; Coll 16, *F major*.
          G major. f'#-d", [g'-d"]. 3/2,2/2. 1'15", [55"]. 3 St. V/e, P/e.

For:	*Sop, Ten*; Mezzo, C-Ten, Bar; *Cont, Bass.*
Subject:	A serious and heartfelt meditation on retirement forced by old age.
Voice:	Mostly by step, in crotchets; a few skips and tied notes.
Piano:	Chordal, with some decoration.
Comment:	Repeat optional. Dotted minim = minim is possible, but probably better crotchet = crotchet. Sir Henry Lee inaugurated, about 1570, a tilt to mark the Queen's Accession Day, and took part in it, as Queen's champion, every year till 1590; in that year this song was performed by Robert Hales, the royal lutenist, at the tilt, to mark Sir Henry's retirement. The poem was published in George Peele's *Polyhymnia*, 1590, but may well be by Sir Henry Lee himself. See **45** (6-8) and **48** (1).

St. 1, lines 3, 4: spurned = kicked at. St 2, line 4: prayers,
must be sung as two syllables. St. 2, line 6: saint = the
Queen. St. 3, line 6: beadsman = one who prays for the soul
of another. St. 2 and 3, line 5: the rhythm needs
modification, the note values for the second and third
syllables should be reversed.

Colls 15, [16]: bar 3, beat 3, add c', [g']; bar 10: *her* = *him*;

bar 12: *Goddess = Ye gods*; these two changes were made in the 1606 and 1613 editions, after Elizabeth's death. Coll 16: bar 4, beat 2: add b°; bar 10, voice: last two notes dotted crotchet quaver, not two crotchets. Coll 19: page 97, bar 1, LH: first f°# dotted minim not minim, following d° should be crotchet not minim; RH: f'# should be minim, delete d° on 4th crotchet. St. 2, line 3: man-at-arms should have hyphens.

(19) Awake sweet love. Colls 6, 11, 15. Colls 12, 16, *D major*.

F major. e'-f ", [g'-d"]. 3/2. 1'15". 2 St. V/e, P/e.

For: Ten; *C-Ten, Bar*.

Subject: Pure happiness, that love, after some despair, has now returned.

Voice: Steps, descending from f ", many small skips; simple rhythms with occasional adjustments.

Piano: Mostly contrapuntal; rhythmic changes need care.

Comment: Originally a lute solo, with the second note flat, it is in short Galliard form, and is one of Dowland's most delightful songs. St. 1, line 6: annoy = annoyance. St. 2, line 3: which so despair hath proved = either, which has proved to be despair, or, which has thus tested despair. Colls 11, 15: last bass note F, not D. Printed in Forbes, 1662, 1666, 1682.

(20) Come heavy sleep. Coll 19. Coll 15, *A major*; Coll 16, *Eb major*.

G major. d'-e", [f'#-d"]. 2/2. 1'40", [1'10"]. 2 St. V/me, P/me.

For: *Sop, Ten*; Mezzo, C-Ten, Bar; *Cont, Bass*.

Subject: A prayer that sleep will give relief from thoughts of sorrow; the alternative being death, sleep's ally.

Voice: Steps, some skips; long phrases and varied rhythms.

Piano: Mostly contrapuntal; rhythmic changes need care.

Comment: Repeat optional. Colls 15, [16]: bar 2, RH: 2nd chord crotchet, not minim, followed by crotchet a', [e']; bars 13 and 15, RH: last chord quaver, not crotchet, followed by b'a', [f'e'], semiquavers. Coll 16: St. 1, bar 12: *though-worn = thought-worn*, in all other modern editions except Coll 19, which has *thoughts-worne*: but note that all original editions have *thoughts, worn soul*, and this makes sense both verbally and musically – sleep should come and take over the tired thoughts and the worn soul, as Doughtie agrees; but see DP, pp. 242-5.

St. 2 raises major problems of underlay. *LS* 1 and Coll 19 print it separately, as in the original; *LS* 1 makes no comment on how it should be fitted to the music; Coll 19 advises following Colls 15 and 16 in rearranging the first line, and the latter also make considerable changes elsewhere. The original words are as follows, with suggested rhythms using the halved note values of Colls 15 and 16: 'Come, [minim] shadow [dotted crotchet quaver] of my [two quavers] end, [minim, quaver rest] and [three quavers] shape of [two crotchets] rest, [minim, quaver rest] / Allied to [three quavers] Death, [minim tied to quaver] child [two semiquavers quaver] to [quaver] his (*this* in 1697 only) [minim tied to quaver] black- [two quavers] -faced [quaver] Night', then as printed as far as double bar save that in line 4 *do* (*LS* 1 and *MB* VI) = *doth* in all other editions. '[Quaver rest] O [crotchet] come, sweet [two semiquavers] sleep, [crotchet] come [quaver] or [semiquaver] I [quaver] die [dotted quaver] for [semiquaver quaver] ever; [quaver dotted crotchet] / Come ere my [three quavers] last, [dotted quaver] my [semiquaver] last sleep [two quavers] comes, [dotted quaver] my [semiquaver] last sleep [two quavers] comes, [crotchet, quaver rest] or [quaver] come, [minim tied to dotted crotchet] or [quaver] come [minim] never [quaver dotted crotchet].' This is a fine song, and well worth the trouble involved. The first stanza was also set by Robert Johnson, 56 (2).

(21) **Away with these self-loving lads** (Fulke Greville, Lord Brooke, *Caelica*, 1633, No. 51). Coll 19. Coll 22, *A major*; Coll 23, *F major*.
G major. d'-e", [f'#-d"]. 1/1. 25", [20"]. 5 St. V/me, P/me.

For: *Ten*; C-Ten, Bar.

Subject: Away with those who will not love! It may or may not be returned, but Cupid is a God, and without love life is not worth living.

Voice: Steps, repeated notes, simple skips; three phrases, all in the same rhythm, but in different keys, separated by silences.

Piano: Chordal, with some decorations which need care.

Comment: A strange song, with some obscure words, but with a life of its own. Repeat optional, but advisable. Some stanzas could be omitted. The poem appears in *EH*, 1600. St. 2, line 1: desert = merit. St. 4, line 1: if Cynthia asks for her ring back. St. 4, line 6: Doughtie quotes from a sixteenth-century jest-book: 'On a time the men of Gotam would have penned the cuckoo, that she should sing all the year and in the midst of the town they did make a hedge – The cuckoo as soon as she was set within the hedge flew her way. A vengeance on her said they, we made not our hedge high enough.' St. 5, line 2: Love (Cupid's bow?) is the instrument of producing love (Doughtie); line 3: foster (for'ster) = forester.

Coll 19: bar 2, LH: minim not dotted minim, add crotchet
G beat 3; bar 14, beat 3, RH: delete a°. St. 2, line 4: *feet =
foot*, all other editions except Doughtie and Ault, though the
1633 edition of the poem has *wing*. Colls 20, 21:
accompaniment by Keel. St. 3, line 6: *these = there*, all other
editions. St. 4: omitted.

45 THE SECOND BOOKE OF SONGS OR AYRES of 2, 4 and 5 parts:
With Tableture for the Lute or Orpherion, with the Violl de Gamba.
1600. S & B edition by E.H. Fellowes, 1925. Revised by Thurston
Dart, 1970 (*LS* 2). Tablature included. Nos. 1-8 have no part-song
version, the remainder appear in *MB* VI.

(1) I saw my lady weep. Colls 19, 26; Colls 13, 15, *C minor*; Colls 6, 14,
16, *G minor*.

A minor. e'-e'', [g'-e'']. 4/4. 1'45''. 3 St. V/me, P/me.

For: *Sop, Ten*; Mezzo, C-Ten, Bar.

Subject: My lady in tears makes even sorrow beautiful.

Voice: Mostly by step, some chromatics; long sustained phrases in
varied rhythms.

Piano: Contrapuntal; chromatic; varied rhythms.

Comment: A great song in any company, it requires sustained intensity
and a feeling for words. Wilfred Mellers makes a good case
for omitting the third stanza in *Harmonious Meeting*
(London, 1965). Dedicated to 'The most famous, Anthony
Holborne', see **54**. See also Morley, **66 (5)**, for another setting
of the first stanza. The poem may be by John Lyly
(Doughtie). Underlay for stanzas 2 and 3 given in Colls 6
and 13-16 thus: line 3: repeat *beyond all speech* and *your
joyful looks*; line 4: repeat *sighs to sing*, and *kills the heart*
(after *believe*); in this last case it might be better to retain
the rhyme by repeating *believe*, giving the first syllable
three notes; line 6: repeat *at once*, and *only*. St. 1, line 2:
advanced = put forward, raised in status. St. 3, line 2:
Leave...grieve – cease grieving after a time.

(2) Flow, my tears. Colls 19, 29; Colls 7, 15, *C minor*; Colls 6, 8, 16, *G
minor*; Coll 25, *B minor*.

A minor. d'-e'', [e'-c'']. 4/4. 3'45''. V/me, P/me.

For: *Sop, Ten*; Mezzo, C-Ten, Bar; *Cont, Bass*.

Subject: Weep for ever and despair, since all hope is gone.

Voice: Steps, many skips; free rhythms; some long phrases.

Piano: Much counterpoint and imitation.

Comment: This famous song – *Lachrimae* – became widely known all
over Europe. It appears as *Lachrimae Antiquae* in

Dowland's collection for viols and lute called *Lachrimae, or Seven Teares*. There is a quotation from the song in Beaumont's *The Knight of the Burning Pestle* (1609) and at least six other plays. It was copied in Earle, 1615. Repeat essential, since this is a pavan. The second of the three sections can take a slightly faster tempo than the rest. St. 1: Doughtie has only one punctuation mark, a colon after *ever*. St. 2, line 3: last (altered to *lost* in *EMV* and Colls 19, 29) = latest, most recent. St. 4, line 3: deserts = rewards. St. 5, line 2: contemn = hold in contempt; line 4: despite = scorn. Last bar but 1, LH: e° E, two minims, Coll 19, not e° semibreve, *LS* 2; (Colls 9, 15: g° G, two crotchets; Colls 6, 10, 16: d° D, two crotchets). Coll 19: page 112, bar 1, RH: last note f'♯, not g'. Coll 25: underlay wrong throughout, partly because many words have been omitted. Introduction added, and accompaniment modified. Printed in Forbes, 1662, 1666, 1682.

(3) **Sorrow, stay**. Colls 23, 30; Colls 9, 15, 22, *B minor*; Colls 6, 10, 16, *F minor*.

	G minor. d'-d", [f'-d"]. 4/4. 3'. V/m, P/m.
For:	*Sop, Ten*; Mezzo, C-Ten, Bar; *Cont, Bass*.
Subject:	Repentant tears and pleas for pity are rejected, to the despair of the singer.
Voice:	A small range, but enormous variety: steps, skips, quick repeated notes, long descending scales, long held top notes; free rhythms.
Piano:	Elaborate three-part counterpoint most of the time.
Comment:	A magnificent song which will repay much study, it can be very moving. BL Add. MS 17786-90 has a version for voice and viols arranged by William Whigthorp, with six extra lines of verse to give a religious slant to the ending (DP, p. 259). Colls 22, 23: accompaniment by Keel, with occasional reference to Dowland. Bars 13/14 should read: crotchet rest quaver rest, dotted quaver three semiquavers two quavers, with three *pitys*, not two. Bars 16/18: one note for *end-*, two notes for *-less*. Bar 26 and similar: first two notes both semiquavers. Perhaps used in a masque or play (Doughtie). Coll 30: bar 3, voice, crotchet 2 should be g' not a'; bar 12, voice has *wretched-*, all other editions have *wret-ched*.

(4) **Die not before thy day.**

	G minor. d'-d", [f'♯-d"]. 4/2,3/2. 1'40". V/me, P/me.
For:	Mezzo, C-Ten, Bar.
Subject:	Hope bids a man not to despair.

Voice: Steps, small skips, repeated notes; fair variety in rhythm and phrase length.

Piano: First part chordal with considerable decoration, then two-part counterpoint.

Comment: Contrasting sections: sustained lines, then dance-like. St. 1, line 3: contemned = held in contempt; line 4: Despair only enjoys misery. This enigmatic poem must have come from a masque or play. Perhaps it was sung by a comforting spirit (Doughtie).

(5) Mourn! day is with darkness fled. Coll 15, *F major/minor*; Coll 16, *C major/minor*.

D major/minor. d'-d", [e'-d"]. 4/4,3/4,4/4. 2', [1'30"]. V/me, P/me.

For: *Sop, Ten*; Mezzo, C-Ten, Bar; *Cont, Bass.*

Subject: Intense pessimism; darkness covers all.

Voice: Steps, small skips; starts on top note; contrasts between compound and simple time sections.

Piano: First part decorated chordal, second in two-part counterpoint.

Comment: An unusual and interesting song. The time relationships given are no doubt correct in theory, but crotchet = minim (Colls 15, 16, quaver = quaver) and vice versa till the final section, then minim = crotchet (quaver = crotchet) seems more satisfactory in practice. Colls 15, 16: bar 5, RH, note 6: should have a flat. Coll 16: bar 4, voice, note 4: should have a flat.

(6-8) Time's eldest son, old age.

G major. d'-e". 4'30", [3'20"]. V/me, P/me.

For: C-Ten, Bar.

Subject: In old age prayer is better than jousting. He can only give love and affection, not action. He should now teach others to pray.

Voice: Steps, small skips, repeated notes; long phrases in varying rhythms.

Piano: Contrapuntal throughout.

Comment: In the style of a song with viols, the voice being one of the contrapuntal parts. Repeats optional. Three sections, one for each stanza. Probably by Sir Henry Lee, see **44 (18)** and **48 (1)**. St. 1, line 6: devises = devices, or coats of arms on shields, etc. St. 2, line 1: *Nunc dimittis* = Now lettest thou thy servant depart in peace (Luke 2:29); line 2: *De profundis* = Out of the depths have I cried unto thee (Psalm 130); line 3: *Miserere* = Lord, have mercy; line 4: *Paretum est cor* *meum* = My heart is fixed, O God, my heart is fixed (Psalm 57:7). St. 3, line 1: *Venite exultemus* = O come let us sing unto the Lord (Psalm 95); line 2: *Noli aemulari* = Fret not thyself because of the ungodly (Psalm 37); line 3: *Quare fremuerunt* = Why do the heathen rage (Psalm 2); *Oremus* = Let us pray; line 4: *Vivat Eliza* = Long live Elizabeth; *Ave Maria* = Hail Mary.

(9) Praise blindness, eyes.

              D minor. d'-d″, [e'-d″]. 3/2. 2'05″. V/e, P/e.

For:	Mezzo, C-Ten, Bar.
Subject:	Be blind and deaf to love, for true love is unattainable. Though I know this to be true I still love.
Voice:	Steps, small skips; some rhythmic variety.
Piano:	Chordal with decorations.
Comment:	The barring is misleading: most of the song should be thought of as in 4/2, starting from the second note. There are three stanzas to the first part, followed by a two-line Envoi to new music, with a repeat which should be made. The poem appears to be a sonnet.

(10) O sweet woods. Coll 19.

              D minor. f'-g″, [g'-e″]. 4/4. 1'45″, [1'15″]. 4 St. V/me, P/me.

For:	[Sop], Ten.
Subject:	I love to be alone in the woods, retired from all false hopes of love.
Voice:	Steps, small skips; varied phrase-lengths and rhythms.
Piano:	Chordal with much decoration.
Comment:	Rondo form, the opening couplet is repeated after each stanza. This refrain is from Sir Philip Sidney's *Arcadia* (1580), but the rest of the poem is different. Dedicated to 'Master Hugh Holland', who wrote prefatory poems to Shakespeare's *First Folio*, 1623, *Parthenia*, 1611, and Farnaby's *Canzonets*, 1598, *EM* 20.

         St. 2, line 3: *their* = there, *EMV, MB* VI; *ther*, Coll 19 and source: DP prefers *their*, referring back to Kings, line 5, though admitting *there* is justifiable, see DP, pp. 264-5. Line 6: *die* = lie, *MB* VI, *die* all other editions. St. 3, line 3: *procure* in source, corrected to *prove* all modern editions. The following adjustments will be needed in underlay: St. 2-4, lines 1/5: rests within the line should be eliminated; line 4: word repetition thus: St. 2, *and apt*, St. 3, *you strive*, St. 4, *a place*. St. 2, line 4: *placed* must be two syllables. St. 3, line 5: Sisyphus – a character in Greek mythology who was condemned after death to roll a stone up a steep slope, but never to succeed in reaching the top. St. 4, line 7: Wanstead – the Earl of Leicester had a house at Wanstead, and Sidney's *Lady of the May* was presented there before the Queen in 1578. These two lines could be paraphrased: My mistress says it is Wanstead's fate to be the birthplace, nursery, and tomb of love. The poem may be by Sidney, or more probably by Robert, Earl of Essex, who is known to have stayed at Wanstead in 1597 and 1598 when out of favour with the Queen. See DP, pp. 262-3.

(11) If floods of tears.

	A minor. e'-e". 3/2,4/4,3/2. 1'20", [1']. 2 St. V/e, P/e.
For:	Mezzo, C-Ten, Bar.
Subject:	I would weep for my follies, but I have no hopes.
Voice:	Steps, small skips, some repeated notes; fairly simple rhythms.
Piano:	Chordal with decoration, some imitation.
Comment:	The poem is printed at the end of the 'Sonnets of Divers Noblemen and Gentlemen' in Sidney's *Astrophel and Stella*, 1591, and has been ascribed by some to Thomas Nash. The first stanza was set as a madrigal by Bateson, *EM* 22 (12). In Forbes, 1662, 1666, 1682, these words are given to **44 (13)**, with a third stanza, given in DP, p. 266. St. 1, line 3: salve = heal. St. 2, line 4: lightening but at hours – making light or alleviating sorrow only temporarily (Doughtie).

(12) Fine knacks for ladies. Colls 6, 13, 15, 20; Colls 14, 16, *D major*; Coll 21, 33, *Eb major*.

	F major. e'-f ", [f'-f "]. 4/4. 50". 3 St. V/me, P/me.
For:	Ten; *C-Ten, Bar.*
Subject:	Gay; a salesman's pitch, suited to Autolycus, but really referring to love.
Voice:	Many skips, and much rhythmic variety.
Comment:	The most extrovert of all Dowland's songs. The repeat is essential. St. 2, line 4: *the Orient's = th'orienst,* in source and *EMV*, which considers it a misprint for *th'orient's; the orient's*, Colls 19, 20, 21, 33; *th'orient, MB* VI. DP says *orienst* is the superlative form of *orient* – of superlative value or brilliance, but though the *OED* gives orient as an adjective meaning 'of superlative brilliance' it gives no example of a superlative form of the word. Ault gives *orient'st*, and Doughtie suggests *orienst* could be a contracted superlative. St. 3, line 3: *in* = missing in source; line 4: Turtles – turtle-doves, symbols of affection; a heavenly pair – Castor and Pollux, the twin sons of Leda by

Zeus, noted for their brotherly love, and children of the Court of Olympus. There is some confusion about the LH beneath *the* in the 3rd line, *for the fair to view*: LS 2 gives d°, with f °# in small print, implying that it comes from the viol part; *MB* VI gives f °# only, with a note 'D for F#'; Colls 6, 13, [14], 17, give d°, [B] only; Coll 15 gives both d° and f °#, while Coll 16 gives B and d°, but omits the #! Colls 20, 21: accompaniment by Keel. St. 3, line 3: *but my heart, wherein* = *but in my heart, where*, all other editions except Bullen, though see note above. Coll 33: accompaniment and introduction by Michael Diack.

(13) Now cease my wandering eyes. Coll 15; Coll 16, *D major*.
F major. f'-f ", [f'-d"]. 4/4. 45". 3 St. V/e, P/e.
For: Sop, Ten; *Mezzo, C-Ten, Bar.*
Subject: A happy day celebrating the rewards of faithfulness.
Voice: Steps, a few skips; rhythms essentially simple.
Piano: Chordal with some decoration.
Comment: The gap between the first two lines should be shortened, since the repeat was not written out in the original. The form is that of an Alman. St. 2, line 7: *spirits* should be pronounced *sprites*, to rhyme with *delights;* last line: hapless = unlucky, wretched. Colls 15, 16: St. 3, line 6: the repeat of *in us* is editorial, but perhaps the best solution. Coll 16: St. 3, bar 4: *import* = *impart*, all other editions.

(14) Come ye heavy states of night.
G minor. f'#-f ", [g'-d"]. 4/4. 1'10", [50"]. 2 St. V/e, P/e.
For: Sop, [Ten].
Subject: Elegy on a father's death.
Voice: Steps, two drops of 5th; rhythms fairly simple; the one f " is a semibreve starting a phrase.
Piano: Chordal with decorations.
Comment: Repeat optional. Seems suited to a scene from a play. Apparently sung by a daughter, but *her* in line 5 of each stanza could become *his.*

(15) White as lilies was her face. Coll 15; Coll 16, *E minor*.
G minor. g'-f ", [g'-d"]. 4/4. 35". 8 St. V/e, P/e.
For: Ten; *C-Ten, Bar.*
Subject: Anger at betrayal by faithless mistress.
Voice: Steps, many small skips; simple rhythm.
Piano: Mostly chordal; last phrase more elaborate.
Comment: The song being so short the repeat is necessary, though some stanzas could be omitted. The last line of words is

missing in Dowland, and has been added from an MS correction in the copy at St Michael's College, Tenbury; however, Forbes, 1662, 1666, 1682, gives 'To banish love with froward (unreasonable) scorn'. St. 1, line 3: quitting = requiting, repaying. St. 2, line 4: *grieving = groaning*, in source, an obvious misprint. St. 3, line 4: procured = induced. St. 6, line 4: envied = regarded with disapproval, to rhyme with denied. Coll 16, St. 2, bar 2: *my = her*, all other editions.

(16) Woeful heart.

G minor. d'-f '', [f'-d'']. 4/4. 45''. 2 St. V/me, P/me.

For: Bar.
Subject: Since my love has left me my heart may follow, it is of no more use to me.
Voice: Steps, skips; fairly regular rhythms and phrasing, last phrase long.
Piano: Chordal with decorations. Two bars of fairly involved rhythmic counterpoint.
Comment: Requires a sustained legato line. *MB* VI gives a repeat for the last section, optional. *Thy loss*, in the last line refers to the *woeful heart* of the first.

(17) A shepherd in a shade. Coll 16, 21; Coll 15, *B major/minor*; Coll 20, *Bb major/minor*.

G major/minor. d'-d''. 4/4. 1'45''. 2 St. V/e, P/e.

For: *Sop, Ten*; Mezzo, C-Ten, Bar.
Subject: A pastoral; a shepherd complains of his lover's cruelty.
Voice: Mostly by step, some simple skips; gentle rhythmic variety.
Piano: Simple counterpoint.
Comment: A sweet and gentle song. Note the instructions regarding repeats, but also that *EMV* prints the poem as three stanzas, using the last four lines of St. 1 for St. 2 as well. Doughtie considers this almost certainly correct; Colls 20, 21 give two eight-line stanzas, each with the four lines beginning *Restore, restore* added as a refrain, and using the two four-line musical phrases in the order AAB ABB. Either of these versions has some support from *LS* 2's note that the original has a repeat mark ('in error') for the last four lines rather than the last two. However in no other song is a second line of words printed beneath the music except where this line is intended for use in the repeat. *MB* VI considers this to be a madrigal, with the lute version as an alternative.

Colls 15, [16]: bar 16, beat 3: add crotchet c', [a°]. Coll 16: bar 14, RH: tie last two g°s. Colls 20, 21: accompaniment and

introductions by Keel. Page 16, bar 12, page 18, bar 14: one
note for *looks*, two for *hath*. Page 18, bar 5: make *I* a minim,
and delay the remaining syllables before *'ry* by one note.
Printed in Forbes, 1662.

(18) Faction that ever dwells (Fulke Greville, Lord Brooke, *Caelica*,
1633, Sonnet 28).

	G major. d'-d", [e'-c"]. 4/4. 35", [25"]. 5 St. V/e, P/e.
For:	[Mezzo], C-Ten, Bar.
Subject:	Good fortune and love cannot live together, for Fortune lives at Court, love in the woods. So to the woods I will go to live with my Joan.
Voice:	Steps, small skips, repeated notes; simple rhythm twice repeated.
Piano:	Chordal, a little decoration.
Comment:	A woman could omit the last stanza. Repeat optional. Dowland omits Greville's second stanza. St. 1, line 2: *wits* = *wit*, in *MB* VI; line 3: defiance – a quarrel, with the idea here of formal combat as in chivalric battles preceded by defiant speeches (Doughtie). St. 3, line 1: *begot* = *beget*, in source, but emended in all modern editions; line 2: *Atheist*, emended to *Atheists, EMV*. St. 4, line 3: *Fortune*, emended to *Fortune's, EMV*. A version of the poem was printed at the end of *Astrophel and Stella*, 1591.

(19) Shall I sue. Colls 6, 17; Colls 18, 23, *D minor*; Coll 22, *F# minor*.

	G minor. g'-g". 3/2. 55", [35"]. 4 St. V/me, P/me.
For:	[Sop], Ten; *[Mezzo], C-Ten, Bar*.
Subject:	Complaint of a rejected lover, sad and angry by turns.
Voice:	Steps, some skips; variable rhythm; fairly long phrases.
Piano:	Essentially simple counterpoint, if not taken too fast.
Comment:	Colls 17, 18, give 'Rather slow and smoothly'; ignoring barlines, the rhythm appears to be 2/2 starting with an upbeat crotchet, which suggests a fairly fast tempo; both are possible. If St. 3 is omitted *she* can be changed to *he* in St. 4, line 3, if desired. St. 1, line 1: sue = plead, woo; line 2: prove = strive, *and* test. St. 2, line 5: favour = beauty; fair = attractive, and even-handed; line 7: favour = exceptional kindness. St. 3, lines 1-4: to ask for pity is poor defence for a man dying of love, and will not be granted by ladies, who do not respect such moaning from one without merit. St. 3, line 7: but = yet. St. 4, line 7: fain = gladly. Some rhythmic modifications are needed in St. 2-4; suggestions are given in Colls 6, 17, 18. Colls 17, 18, omit St. 3. Colls 22, 23: accompaniment and introduction to each stanza by Keel. St.

2, line 3: *hopes require* = *hopes do require*, all other editions; line 4: *treasure* = *favour*, all other editions. St. 4, line 4: *faire* (4th word) = *fain*, all other editions.

(20) Toss not my soul. Coll 6.

	G minor. f'#-f ", [g'-e"]. 4/4. 1'45", [1'15"]. 2 St. V/me, P/me.
For:	Sop, Ten.
Subject:	A serious plea for certainty, whether for good or ill.
Voice:	Mostly by step; a few unexpected rhythms and underlay.
Piano:	Contrapuntal, with some rhythmic complications.
Comment:	Repeat optional. *MB* VI indicates that the first part should be repeated, with the second stanza, before singing the 'Envoi'; this seems good advice, see also **45 (9)**. St. 1, line 3: surely = with certainty; line 4: certain band = secure chain. First line of L'envoi: *of ill the uttermost*, in music = *the uttermost of ill*, in text. Coll 6, bar 2, LH: leger line missing from d'.

(21) Clear or cloudy. Coll 17, *Bb major*; Colls 6, 18, *F major*.

	G major. d'-e", [g'-d"]. 4/4. 1'10", [50"]. 3 St. V/me, P/me.
For:	*Ten*; C-Ten, Bar; *Bass*.
Subject:	Her moods may vary, but he loves them all, and trusts his love will be rewarded.
Voice:	Mostly by step; skips and 8ve drop in 2nd half; varied rhythms.
Piano:	Contrapuntal, much of it in three parts.
Comment:	Repeat optional. A fresh and delightful melody. Though the poem is a little obscure in places the general drift of meaning is clear enough. In the refrain Dowland provided an optional descant for treble viol, given in *MB* VI as Tenor I. The rhythmic alternatives given in Colls 6, 17, 18, for bars 1/4 in St. 2/3 are interchangeable. St. 1, line 6: a comma after *who*, as given in *OB 16* clarifies the sense – the night-bird, thought to be all sweetness, even so can produce jarring notes. St. 2, lines 1/3: *trimm'd, dimm'd*, *LS* 2 and *MB* VI = *trimmed, dimmed*, all other editions. All editions except *LS* 2 have a hyphen for *be-dimmed*, which seems essential; line 2: *height* would be pronounced to rhyme with *faith* at this time (Doughtie). St. 3, line 2: this line is two syllables short; *healing*, given in all modern music editions is editorial, and does not appear in *EMV*. *OB 16* gives *as well as into herbs*, Ault *as much as into herbs*. These emendations need not be used – *herbs* can easily take three notes. St. 3, line 3: *sees* = *seeds*, *OB 16*, which improves the sense; divers = various; line 4: haply seeming = perhaps only appearing to be, not truly 'being yours'.

(22) **Humour say what mak'st thou here**. A duet, beyond the scope of this book.

46 THE THIRD AND LAST BOOKE OF SONGS OR AIRES Newly composed to sing to the Lute, Orpharion, or viols. 1603. S & B edition by E.H. Fellowes, 1923. Revised by Thurston Dart, 1970 (*LS* 3). Tablature included. Nos. 1-4 have no four-part version, the remainder appear in *MB* VI.

(1) **Farewell too fair**.
> A minor. g'-e". 4/4. 1'15". 2 St. V/me, P/me.

For:	Mezzo, C-Ten, Bar.
Subject:	Farewell, you have destroyed my love by your neglect.
Voice:	Steps, small skips, repeated notes; rhythms simple, but very varied phrase-lengths.
Piano:	Chordal with decorations; some contrapuntal passages.
Comment:	Good legato essential.

(2) **Time stands still**. Coll 28; Coll 17, *Bb major*; Colls 6, 18, *F major*.
> G major. g'-d". 2/2. 1'45", [1'25"]. 2 St. V/e, P/me.

For:	*Ten*; C-Ten, Bar.
Subject:	Even Time waits upon my beloved, to whom I will always be faithful.
Voice:	Steps, small skips; short descending sequences.
Piano:	Chordal with decorations, then contrapuntal, with a somewhat complicated cadence.
Comment:	Repeat optional. A beautiful song. St. 1, line 6: contemned = held in contempt. St. 2: DP, pp. 276-7, describes this as being extremely obscure and fitting the words very badly. However, Scott's suggestion, Colls 6, 17, 18, of adding *her* at the end of the first line clarifies the sense, though admittedly destroying the rather weak rhyme, and enables the words to fit quite well. St. 2, line 3: desert = reward; line 4: Envy herself knows Duty's faithful heart; line 6: try = ascertain. Doughtie quotes Oliphant (1837): 'These lines must surely have been addressed to Queen Elizabeth. The flattery is too gross for anybody but her to have swallowed.' None the less, as a song it succeeds wonderfully. Coll 28: bar 20, LH: passing note G added from viol part.

(3) **Behold a wonder here**. Coll 28.
> G major. g'-e", [g'-d"]. 3/2. 45", [30"]. 5 St. V/e, P/e.

For:	Mezzo, C-Ten, Bar.
Subject:	Cynthia's beauty is so great that Love has recovered his sight and become wise.

Voice: Steps, small skips; simple though varied rhythm and phrases.
Piano: Chordal with decorations.
Comment: Repeat optional. St. 3/4 could be omitted. Care must be taken with the underlay of line 3 of each stanza, where two syllables require repetition: try *made him, for them, is turn'd,* and *his sight.* A nice cheerful song. St. 5, line 1: *Thus* in *LS* 3 = *This* in source and all other editions; the emendation is unnecessary – *this Beauty* is Cynthia herself. Coll 28: repeats *many hundred* once instead of *hundred* twice as in *LS* 3; though this works well here it cannot be applied to the other stanzas and is therefore probably a mistake.

(4) Daphne was not so chaste. Colls 6, 31.
         F major. e'-f ″, [f'-f ″]. 4/4. 45″. 2 St. V/me, P/e.
For: Sop, Ten; Mezzo, Bar.
Subject: A lively denunciation of promiscuity; only true love is truly free.
Voice: Steps, many repeated notes; rhythmic complication at end.
Piano: Chordal, with a little counterpoint.
Comment: A dance, but see Coll 6 for rebarring of last phrase. St. 1, line 2: *soon begun = soon-begun, EMV.* Repeat of second half not marked in source, but given in Coll 31 and advised in *LS* 3.

(5) Me, me, and none but me. Coll 17, *Bb major*; Coll 18, *F major*.
         G major. g'-e″. 4/4. 1'15″, [50″]. 2 St. V/me, P/e.
For: *Sop, Ten*; Mezzo, C-Ten, Bar.
Subject: A prayer for death, wishing to join the beloved in heaven.
Voice: Almost all by step; quite a variety of rhythm.
Piano: Chordal, then simple three-part counterpoint.
Comment: Repeat optional. There may be some difficulty in fitting in the occasional quick-note patter phrases to the essentially calm framework, but it is worth the effort. The repeated words needed in the last line of St. 2 can be either *He never happy,* or *never happy lived. MB* VI has *happier* for *happy,* and a different underlay: *Un-* [dotted minim tied to quaver] *-to my* [two quavers] *faithful* [two quavers] *dove,* [minim] *un-* [quaver] *-to my* [two semiquavers] etc. This would make the second stanza *He never happy lived, he never* to the same note values (half note values used by all but *LS* 3).

(6) When Phoebus first did Daphne love. Coll 6.
         G major. g'-e″. 3/2. 35″. 2 St. V/e, P/e.
For: Ten; C-Ten, Bar.

Subject: Since Phoebus has sworn that there should be no virgins
               over fifteen, girls should not be blamed for their behaviour!
Voice: Mostly by step; simple rhythm.
Piano: Chordal.
Comment: An entertaining song for the right performer and audience.
               A coranto. Though included in *Poems, Written by the Right
               Honourable William, Earl of Pembroke*, 1660, attributions
               in this collection are considered unreliable. This source
               gives a 3rd stanza: 'Yet silly they, when all is done, /
               Complain our wits their hearts have won, / When 'tis for fear
               that they should be / Like Daphne, turned into a tree; / And
               who herself would so abuse / To be a tree, if she could
               choose.'

               St. 1, line 6: *none but one* – these words appear to have
               been added by Dowland in defence against the possible
               wrath of Queen Elizabeth. They appear in none of the five
               MS sources of the poem, nor in the 1660 version mentioned
               above; they cause some problems in subsequent verses since
               the last line becomes three syllables short, and they upset
               the form of the dance. They could well be omitted, with notes
               and accompaniment, as given in Coll 6, which relegates this
               half bar to the Notes.

(7) Say love if ever thou didst find. Colls 8, 18; Colls 7, 17, *Bb major*.
               G major. f'#-d", [g'-d"]. 4/4. 30". 4 St. V/e, P/e.
For: *Sop, Ten*; Mezzo, C-Ten, Bar.
Subject: There is only one constant woman, and she, not being
               subject to Love, which she rejects, must be Queen of love.
Voice: Steps, simple rhythm; then four single off-beat notes and
               five bars of repeated g's.
Piano: Chordal.
Comment: Stanza 3 omitted in all Colls. Probably in praise of
               Elizabeth.

(8) Flow not so fast, ye fountains. Colls 6, 17; Coll 18, *D minor*; Coll 20,
     F# minor; Coll 21, *E minor*.
               G minor. g'-g", [b'-f"]. 2/2. 1'25", [1']. 3 St. V/me, P/e.
For: Sop, Ten; *Mezzo, C-Ten, Bar*.
Subject: My tears must continue; ordinary sorrows will abate, but
               true grief remains.
Voice: Mostly by step; it lies high, and needs long phrasing.
Piano: Chordal, with melodic bass; simple counterpoint.
Comment: Repeat optional, and best omitted. A similar song to **46 (15)**,
               both are beautiful, but not for the same programme. Last
               word in each stanza: spheres = eyeballs. St. 2, lines 3-4:

Neither passage of time (season) nor anything else can appease my sorrow (Doughtie). Colls 6, 17, [18]: bar 14, 1st half: a° and a´, [e° and e´] need flats. Colls 20, 21: accompaniment and introduction to each stanza by Keel.

(9) What if I never speed? Colls 6, 17; Coll 18, *F minor*; Coll 22, *B minor*; Coll 23, *G minor*.

             A minor. e´-f ˝, [g´-e˝]. 4/4. 1´. 2 St. V/me, P/me.

For:	*Sop, Ten*; Mezzo, Bar; *Cont, C-Ten, Bass*.
Subject:	Let me not despair, for love may be returned, and I must either love or admire you.
Voice:	First part by step in regular rhythms; then leaps, single notes, short runs, and cross-rhythms.
Piano:	Chordal, then contrapuntal.
Comment:	A slightly gloomy opening leads to a cheerful and confident ending. *MB* VI considers this a four-part canzonet, with lute as an alternative. The 'Moderate speed' of Colls 17, 18, applies to minim, not crotchet, for the basic mood is optimistic. St. 2, line 3: annoy = annoyance; line 6: forlorn = abandoned; line 7: scope = target. *MB* VI marks a repeat for the 2nd half. Colls 22, 23: accompaniment and introduction to each stanza by Keel. St. 2, line 4: *soon = still*, all other editions.

(10) Love stood amazed.

             G minor. a´-g˝, [a´-f ˝]. 4/4. 1´15˝, [45˝]. 6 St. V/me, P/e.

For:	Sop, Ten.
Subject:	Loves sees Beauty must die, and complains bitterly to the Gods; he tries to kill himself, and the Gods change him into a Phoenix.
Voice:	Steps, skips, many repeated notes; much variety in rhythm and phrase-length.
Piano:	Chordal with some decoration.
Comment:	Repeat optional. The words are closely matched to the music in the first stanza, but subsequent stanzas have different accentuation and will prove hard to fit convincingly; the last line, needing two syllables repeated, creates particular problems. St. 5, line 6: *forbade = forbid*, in source, with the same meaning.

(11) Lend your ears to my sorrow.

             A minor. e´-e˝, [g´-e˝]. 4/4,3/2,4/4. 1´05˝. 3 St. V/me, P/me.

For:	Mezzo, C-Ten, Bar.
Subject:	Listen to my grief; once I was happy in love; cold is the heart without love, for true love is like heaven.

Voice: Steps, small skips; 6th leap; much rhythmic variety.
Piano: Contrapuntal.
Comment: Note that the last three lines of St. 1 fail to rhyme, thus
              illustrating the sense. Problems arise in fitting the words of
              later stanzas: try repeating the first two words of line 6,
              giving the pairs of quavers in bars 5/7 one syllable each, and
              ending with 2 minims. Minim = dotted crotchet is right in
              theory, but crotchet = crotchet is better in practice.

(12) **By a fountain where I lay**. Coll 17; Coll 18, *E minor*.
              G minor. f'#-f ", [g'-f "]. 4/4. 55". 3 St. V/me, P/me.
For: Ten, *C-Ten, Bar*.
Subject: A shepherd celebrates his true love as Queen of the May.
Voice: By step, with many repeated notes in second part; some
              rhythmic traps in first part.
Piano: Three-part counterpoint; chordal passage in middle.
Comment: Be careful of accentuation in the last line: in St. 1/3 the
              accent comes on the second syllable, not the first, and in St.
              2/3 one syllable goes to the pair of quavers. *MB* VI marks a
              repeat for the second half. St. 2, line 6: cheer = countenance.
              St. 3, line 3: ground = ground bass. Colls 17, 18: delete
              repeat mark at end of first page.

(13) **O what hath overwrought**. Coll 17; Coll 18, *E minor*.
              G minor. f'#-f ", [g'-e"b]. 4/4. 1'05". V/e, P/e.
For: Sop, Ten; *Mezzo, C-Ten, Bar*.
Subject: Why be so pessimistic? The sun will shine again.
Voice: Steps, small skips; simple rhythm.
Piano: Chordal with a little decoration.
Comment: Repeats essential. A bright, straight-forward song, possibly
              written for a masque (DP, p. 282). St. 2, line 2: ne'er the near
              = not any nearer; line 11: can nothing hear – this probably
              means 'know nothing here' (Doughtie).

(14) **Farewell, unkind, farewell**. Colls 6, 17, *Bb major*; Colls 18, 23,
       F major; Coll 22, *A major*.
              G major. f'#-e", [g'-d"]. 4/4. 1'10", [55"]. 2 St. V/me, P/me.
For: *Sop, Ten*; Mezzo, C-Ten, Bar; *Cont, Bass*.
Subject: Farewell, father, even though you disinherit me love is a
              stronger tie than blood.
Voice: Steps; many dropping 3rds; repetitive rhythms.
Piano: Chordal, then contrapuntal.
Comment: Repeat essential. As DP suggests (p. 282), this could well be
              from a play, and would fit Jessica in *The Merchant of Venice*
              very well, though there is no record of such use. St. 1, line 4:

my = *thy*, in source, *EMV*, DP, Coll 23, and makes much better sense – the father's heart is in his wealth. St. 2, line 2: means = wealth; line 4: the underlay is debatable, Coll 6 gives one solution, Colls 17, 18, another, and Colls 22, 23, a third! A good song, particularly suited to women. Colls 22, 23: accompaniment and introduction to each stanza by Keel. Coll 22: St 1. line 5 (= line 4 above): both *the* and *thy* in music, *my* in text!

(15) Weep you no more, sad fountains. Colls 6, 11, 17, 19; Colls 12, 18, 23, *E minor*; Coll 22, *F# minor*.

	G minor. d'-g", [f'-e"b]. 4/4. 2'20", (1'30"). 2 St. V/me, P/me.
For:	[Sop], Ten; *[Mezzo], C-Ten, Bar; [Cont], Bass.*
Subject:	Do not weep, since your love will be reconciled on waking.
Voice:	Mostly by step; last phrase a chain of descending 4ths from the top note to the bottom, requiring good breath control.
Piano:	Gently contrapuntal, with some fairly confusing overlapping rhythms in the last phrase.
Comment:	Repeat optional. Similar to **46 (8)**, and better known. St. 1, line 4: *waste* would have rhymed with *fast*; lines 7-8: *lie* and *lies* appear in different voices in source and *MB* VI; *lie* gives better sense, since it is the eyes that are sleeping. See DP, pp. 283-4. Doughtie agrees it is the eyes that are sleeping, but prefers *lies* as a rhyme with *eyes* 'which could be considered a unit'. Ault gives *lies*. Colls 22, 23: accompaniment and introduction to each stanza by Keel. All other editions underlay the last two lines: That now lies sleeping, that now lies sleeping, softly, softly, now softly lies sleeping. Second stanza omitted.

(16) Fie on this feigning. Coll 6.

	F major. f'-g", [a'-f"]. 4/4. 45". 3 St. V/e, P/e.
For:	Sop, Ten.
Subject:	A lively insistence that everyone is capable of love.
Voice:	Many small skips; very simple rhythm.
Piano:	Chordal with decorations.
Comment:	A curiosity in that starting in F the song ends in D. St. 2, line 2: *now* – perhaps this should be *not* (Doughtie).

(17) I must complain (Thomas Campion).

	G minor. g'-g", [f'-g"]. 4/4,3/2,4/4. 1'20", [1'05"]. 2 St. V/me, P/me.
For:	Ten.
Subject:	Resigned acceptance that a beautiful mistress will not also be a faithful one.

Voice: Steps, small skips, repeated notes; varied phrase- lengths
                and rhythms; the only g″ is the first long note of a slow
                descent over four notes.
Piano: Contrapuntal, becoming chordal.
Comment: Repeat optional. A much more serious setting than
                Campion's own, **33 (17)**. The indicated minim = dotted
                minim is possible, but crotchet = crotchet seems better,
                continuing the rhythm of the previous bar. Variants in
                Campion: St. 1, line 2: *beauty's = lovely*; St. 2, line 2: *my =
                mine*; line 3: *suitors = lovers*. For further notes on words, see
                33 (17).

(18) It was a time when silly bees. Coll 17, *E minor*; Coll 18, *C minor*.
        D minor. d′-e″b, [d′-d″]. 4/4. 1′05″, [50″]. 3 St. V/e, P/e.
For: *Sop, Ten*; Mezzo, C-Ten, Bar; *Cont, Bass.*
Subject: A complaint that service has not been rewarded.
Voice: Steps, with a sequence of small skips in the last phrase;
                rhythms fairly simple.
Piano: Simple counterpoint, most movement in the bass.
Comment: Repeat optional. The poem being based on the words Thyme
                and Time, it is almost impossible to follow by ear rather
                than eye. An MS copy describes this poem as 'The Earl of
                Essex his Buzze, which he made upon some discontentment'
                1598. Several MSS ascribe the poem to Essex, some to his
                secretary, Henry Cuffe, and one to John Lyly. St. 1, lines 1/2:
                silly = simple. St. 2, line 3: sith = since. St. 3, line 4: atomies
                = small insignificant creatures. Colls 17, 18: bar 6, voice:
                dotted minim, not minim and crotchet rest; bar 13, voice:
                slur notes 1-2, not 2-3. Printed in Forbes, 1662, 1666, 1682
                (first word *There* for *It*).

(19) The lowest trees have tops. Coll 19; Coll 17, *B minor*; Coll 18,
        F# minor.
        G minor. d′-d″, [f′-d″]. 4/4. 1′15″, [55″]. 2 St. V/e, P/e.
For: *Sop, Ten*; Mezzo, C-Ten, Bar; *Cont, Bass.*
Subject: All things have hidden virtues; true hearts may also be
                hidden, and so suffer.
Voice: Steps, many small skips; some rhythmic variety.
Piano: Chordal with decorations.
Comment: Repeat optional. Printed in Davison, 1602, author 'Incerto',
                though a Bodleian MS, Rawl. Poet. 148, gives the poem to
                Sir Edward Dyer. Davison has the following variants, given
                by Ault: St. 1, line 2: *spark his = sparks their*; line 3: *And =
                The*; line 6: *and in = as in*. St. 2, line 1: *waters = rivers*; line
                4: turtles are turtle-doves; line 5: replace the rest with a dot,

so that the comma comes after ears, not eyes. Colls 17, [18]:
bar 17, RH, beat 1: c′ not f′, [g° not c′]. Coll 19: page 132, last
bar, note 1, RH: a° not d′; page 133, bar 1, LH, note 2: e°b, not
Bb. Printed in Forbes 1662, 1666, 1682.

(20) What poor astronomers are they.
G major. d′-e″, [g′-d″]. 4/4. 35″, [25″]. 4 St. V/me, P/e.

For:	Mezzo, C-Ten, Bar.
Subject:	Men are fools to fall in love and worship women; but it is fun to watch, and they never learn!
Voice:	Steps, skips; 8ve leap, very bouncy with varied rhythms.
Piano:	Chordal with decoration, and some runs in bass.
Comment:	Repeat optional, but recommended, as is the song. St. 3 could be omitted. St. 1, line 5: approve = demonstrate. St. 2, line 4: *it* – perhaps a misprint for *them, EMV* and Doughtie; line 6: *fledg'd* = *flidge*, in source, with same meaning. St. 3, line 3: *will* = *wit*, in source, emended by all modern editors except Doughtie, who merely notes *EMV*'s emendation without comment.

(21) Come when I call. A duet, beyond the scope of this volume.

47 A PILGRIM'S SOLACE Wherein is contained Musical Harmonie of 3,
4 and 5 parts, to be sung and plaid with the Lute and Viols. 1612. S & B
edition by E.H. Fellowes, 1924. Revised by Thurston Dart, 1969 (*LS* 4).
Tablature included. All the songs are given in their partsong version in
MB VI.

(1) Disdain me still. Coll 17, *Bb major*; Coll 18, *F major*.
G major. d′-e″, [e′-e″]. 4/4. 1′50″, [1′15″]. 2 St. V/me, P/e.

For:	*Ten*; C-Ten, Bar; *Bass*.
Subject:	Success in love destroys love, so still refuse me, that I may continue to love you in vain.
Voice:	Mostly by step; some complications in rhythm and underlay.
Piano:	Simple counterpoint.
Comment:	Repeat better omitted. Adjustments must be made to fit the words of St. 2: Colls 17, 18, give one of several possible solutions. Poem printed in *Poems, Written by the Right Honourable William, Earl of Pembroke,* 1660, but see Comment on **46 (6)**. Colls 17, 18: bar 14, voice: slur notes 3-4, not 2-3. St. 2, bar 27: *rewards*, Ault = *reward*, all other editions.

(2) Sweet stay awhile. Coll 17, *C minor*; Colls 6, 18, *G minor*.
A minor. e′-e″. 4/4. 1′40″, [1′10″]. 2 St. V/me, P/e.

For:	*Sop, Ten*; Mezzo, C-Ten, Bar.

Subject: Do not leave now, it is not yet dawn.
Voice: Steps, small skips; 8ve leap; varied rhythms and phrase-lengths.
Piano: Simple counterpoint.
Comment: Repeat optional. The first stanza, but beginning 'Stay, O sweet, and do not rise' appeared in the 1669 edition of Donne's poems, as a prologue to ''Tis true, 'tis day'. Neither Chambers nor Grierson consider it authentic, though Quiller-Couch accepted it in *OB*. There are some twenty versions of the poem in one form or another: 'Lie still, my dear', Coll 25; 'Ah, dear heart, why do you rise', set as a madrigal by Gibbons, *EM* 5 (15); see also **21**. Dotted semibreve [dotted minim] = minim is theoretically correct, but minim [crotchet] = crotchet might well be more effective in practice. A tender and affecting love-song. St. 2, line 2: the nest of the Phoenix was supposedly made of spices (Doughtie).

(3) To ask for all thy love. Coll 6.

G minor. e'-g'', [g'-f '']. 4/4. 1'05'', [40'']. 4 St. V/me, P/me.

For: Sop, Ten.
Subject: If you give me your whole heart you will have nothing left to give; I could give you mine to replace it, but better still, let them be joined in one.
Voice: Mostly by step; much rhythmic interest.
Piano: Contrapuntal, mostly simple.
Comment: Repeat optional, best omitted. St. 2 could also be omitted, since it is not essential to the argument, which is beautifully worked out in the other stanzas. Some care must be taken in fitting the words in later stanzas; Coll 6 offers one solution. The poem is an imitation of Donne's 'Lover's Infiniteness', and is ascribed to him in one MS. A fine song. St. 1, line 6: *EMV* has a full stop and Ault a colon after *yet*; neither has a comma after *all*, where *MB* VI has a semi-colon; *EMV* version is better musically and verbally. St. 3, line 7: *LS* 4 and *MB* VI have *doth [hence de-]part*; this helps the metre but not the sense, and the original is not hard to fit to the music.

(4) Love those beams. Coll 17; Coll 18, *E minor*.

G minor. f' #-g'', [g'-e'']. 4/4. 55''. 3 St. V/e, P/e.

For: Sop, Ten; *Mezzo, C-Ten, Bar.*
Subject: It is vain to try to escape from love; therefore, love, be kind to my misery.
Voice: Very smooth, rhythms fairly simple.
Piano: Simple counterpoint, in three parts.

Comment: Colls 17, [18]: bar 16, RH, last quaver d' not c', [b° not a°].

(5) Shall I strive with words to move? Coll 18; Coll 17, *A minor.*
         E minor. e'-d″, [e'-c″]. 3/2. 2'20″. V/me, P/me.

For: *Ten*; C-Ten, Bar.
Subject: If I tell her I love her maybe she will be kinder.
Voice: Mostly by step; varied rhythms and some unexpected underlay.
Piano: Contrapuntal, with a few rather involved rhythms.
Comment: A curiously attractive song. It appears in *Lachrimae* as 'Mr Henry Noel, his Galliard'. The 'Moderate speed' of Colls 17, 18, would seem to make it too sad, unless a dotted minim is thought of as the pulse unit. The last repeat, though editorial according to *LS* 4, is essential to the dance-form. At the beginning of the second section the underlay of 'delayed' as given in *LS* 4 and *MB* VI appears very clumsy, and giving three notes to the first syllable and one to the second, as in Colls 17, 18, seems preferable.

(6) Were every thought an eye. Coll 17; Coll 18, *G minor.*
         C minor. g'-g″, [g'-f ″]. 3/2. 2 '. V/me, P/me.

For: [Sop], Ten; *[Mezzo], C-Ten, Bar.*
Subject: The motives and moods of a clever and attractive woman are beyond men's understanding, and therefore more worthy of their attention.
Voice: Steps, small skips; many small rhythmic variations.
Piano: Contrapuntal, with considerable rhythmic independence of parts.
Comment: A strange song, which may be found irritating or attractive according to temperament; the final cadence is not the least of its oddities. The repeat of the third section, though editorial according to *LS* 4, is essential to the dance form – a coranto. St. 4, line 4: *but how none knows* – *EMV* states the source has *but none knows how*, but DP and Doughtie deny this. St. 5 lines 2/4: it seems that in both *conceit* and *sleight* the *ei* could be pronounced as a long *a* (Doughtie). Colls 17, 18: bar 5, last quaver, RH: b° not d', [f ° not a°]. Coll 17: bar 20, last quaver, RH: add c'.

(7) Stay time awhile thy flying. Coll 23; Coll 22, *C minor.*
         A minor. e'-d″. 3/2. 50″. 3 St. V/me, P/e.

For: *Sop, Ten*; Mezzo, C-Ten, Bar.
Subject: Let me die now, rather than live distressed and friendless.
Voice: Steps, a few small skips; simple note values, but

considerable variety in accentuation, and care is needed to make it convincing.

Piano: Chordal with some decoration.

Comment: Much of this is in 4/2 rather than 3/2, an interesting rhythmic exercise in what appears a simple song. A problem in the last line: where *LS* 4 and *MB* VI have two crotchet g's the source has one; DP, p. 298, makes it a minim, omitting the extra *than*; St. 3: using DP's note values put *here* on the two crotchets (g' f'), followed by *live*, then *here to live distressed*. Colls 22, 23: accompaniment and introduction to each stanza by Keel. St. 3, last line: the same as stanzas 1/2.

(8) **Tell me, true love**. Coll 18; Coll 17, *B minor*.
                G minor. d'-d". 4/4. 2'20", [1'40"]. 4 St. V/m, P/e.

For: *Sop, Ten*; Mezzo, C-Ten, Bar.

Subject: Where can true love be found in this day and age? If it can be found, happy the finder.

Voice: Recit. style, with much variety; repeated notes, leaps, melismas; smooth legato phrases in long notes.

Piano: Simple chords with some decoration.

Comment: An example of the new style being introduced by Johnson and Ferrabosco in their masque songs. The first stanza is very effective, but major problems arise in the fitting of stanzas 2/3, avoided by Colls 17, 18, which omit them; stanza 4 causes less trouble. The second section should be sung by four voices on its repeat, see *MB* VI. St. 2, line 2: debt = binding. St. 3, line 5: One only she = only one woman.

(9) **Go, nightly cares.** ⎫ These songs require obbligato
(10) **From silent night.** ⎬ treble and bass viols, and are
(11) **Lasso! vita mia mi fa morire.** ⎭ therefore beyond the scope of this
                                          volume.

(12) **In this trembling shadow cast.**
                G minor. f'#-e"b, [g'-d"]. 4/4. 2'35", [1'40"]. 3 St. V/me, P/me.

For: Mezzo, C-Ten, Bar.

Subject: I would sing to the Lord, praising him for all that he has made, though I have not power to praise him enough.

Voice: Steps, small skips, repeated notes; slightly chromatic; long phrases in free rhythms; two melismas.

Piano: Contrapuntal and chromatic.

Comment: Repeat optional. St. 1, line 2: lower voices have *winds* for *wings*. Considerable problems arise in fitting St. 2/3 to the music.

(13) If that a sinner's sighs. Coll 17; Coll 18, *D minor*.

	G minor. f'#-g", [g'-f"]. 4/4. 2'30", [1'50"]. V/me, P/me.
For:	Sop, Ten; *Mezzo, C-Ten, Bar*.
Subject:	A serious prayer of repentance.
Voice:	Mostly by step; considerable rhythmic variety.
Piano:	Contrapuntal throughout.
Comment:	Repeat optional. Conservative style, with the voice one of several contrapuntal parts. The tempo relationship given does not seem practical, crotchet = crotchet is better. Set by Byrd, *EM* 14 (30), with four more stanzas, and some variants: line 4: *doleful plaints = faithful tears*; line 6: *as Peter did, weep = with Peter wept most*. See *EMV*, p. 52. Colls 17, [18]: bar 13, beat 5, RH: add e'*b*, [b°*b*]; bar 18, beat 1: b° not a°, [f° not e°].

(14) Thou mighty God.
(15) When David's life.
(16) When the poor cripple.

(Nicolas Breton, *The Soul's Harmony*, 1602). Three parts, one song.

	A minor. d'-e", [e'-e"]. 4/4, 2/2, 4/4. 7', [4'30"]. V/m, P/m.
For:	Mezzo, C-Ten, Bar.
Subject:	(i) When Job suffered, Patience comforted him. (ii) When David was pursued by King Saul, Hope saved him (I Samuel 19). (iii) When the cripple lay by the Pool of Bethesda, Christ cured him (John 5). My sufferings are as great, may I be saved too.
Voice:	Steps, some skips up to 6th, 8ve leap; long phrases in free rhythms; some chromatics.
Piano:	Highly contrapuntal, with much chromaticism.
Comment:	Repeats optional. A major religious song. The texture is that of a song with viols, with the voice joining in the imitation; the harmony is complex, and wholly individual to Dowland. However, there is little contrast between the sections, and given its length the result is perhaps not fully successful. The words, apart from the first couplet which is borrowed and adapted from St. 9 of a poem by the Earl of Essex (the first two stanzas of which were set by Dowland as **46 (18)**), are adapted from Breton's sonnet. Part iii, bar 1, bass: notes 2-3 should probably be e°s, as given in the tenor part in *MB* VI.

(17) Where sin sore wounding. Coll 17, *F minor*; Coll 18, *D minor*.

	G minor. a'-a", [a'-g"]. 4/4. 2'05", [1'30"]. 4 St. V/me, P/me.
For:	Sop, Ten; *Mezzo, C-Ten, Bar*.
Subject:	A prayer of thanks for mercy on sins.

Voice: Steps, small skips; much rhythmic variety.
Piano: Contrapuntal throughout.
Comment: Repeat optional. Voice one of several contrapuntal parts. St.
                4, line 2: amated = confounded, cast down; line 3: related =
                described. Some rhythmic adjustments will be needed to fit
                the words of stanzas 2-4. Colls 17, [18]: only the first stanza
                is given; bar 8, beat 4, RH: add crotchet c′, [a°]. Coll 17: bar
                10, beat 1, RH: e′b, not d′.

(18) **My heart and tongue were twins.** Coll 17, *B minor*; Coll 18,
     G minor.
                D minor. f′-a″, [a′-g″]. 3/2. 2′30″. V/me, P/me.
For: Sop, Ten; *Mezzo, C-Ten, Bar*; *Cont, Bass*.
Subject: A serious philosophical poem, somewhat difficult to follow
                in places, which concludes that not even Gods can force
                affection.
Voice: Steps, small skips; a long climb to the top note; some
                awkward rhythms.
Piano: Chordal, then contrapuntal.
Comment: Printed in *EH*, 1600, with the title: 'Apollo's Love-song for
                faire Daphne', and a note: 'This Dittie was sung before her
                Majestie, at the right honourable Lord Chandos', at Sudley
                Castell.' The Sudeley Masque was presented in 1592. The
                description of the Masque has the following: 'Her Majesty
                saw Apollo with the tree, having on the one side one that
                sang, on the other one that played: "Sing you, play you, but
                sing and play my truth; / This tree my lute, these sighs my
                notes of ruth (pity): / The Laurel leaf for ever shall be green, /
                And Chastity shall be Apollo's Queen. / If gods may die, here
                shall my tomb be placed, / And this engraven, 'Fond
                Phoebus, Daphne chaste' ". After the Verses, the Song.'
                    The song is as here, save for line 10: *words nor deeds =
                deeds nor words*, and the final couplet, which reads:
                'Engrave upon this tree, Daphne's perfection, / "That neither
                men nor gods, can force affection".' Daphne was pursued by
                Apollo, and to escape was changed into a laurel-tree; but the
                name of Daphne was also used for Queen Elizabeth, famed
                for her chastity. Dowland no doubt changed the end when
                preparing the song for publication, after the Queen's death.
                Some minor adjustments, shown in Colls 17, 18, are needed
                to fit the words in St. 2/3. St. 2, line 2: discover = reveal.
                Colls 17, [18]: bar 9, bass: 2nd A, [F], from viol part; bar 13,
                voice: slur notes 3-4, not 2-3; bar 21, voice: 1st two notes
                quavers. Coll 15: bar 13: tie first two f′s. Ignore the
                instruction in *LS* 4 about *twinnes* being two syllables; it is
                printed as *twins* in all other editions, including text of *LS* 4.

(19) **Up, merry mates.**

(20) **Welcome, black night.**

(21) **Cease these false sports.**

Songs with chorus, outside the scope of this volume.

48 THREE SONGS FROM 'A MUSICAL BANQUET'. Coll 1 and *LS* 4. See **75**.

(1) **Far from triumphing court** (Sir Henry Lee). Coll 29; Coll 17, *A major*; Coll 6, 18, *F major*.

G major. d'-e″, [e'-e″]. 4/4. 1′45″, [1′10″]. 4 St. V/m, P/me.

For: *Sop, Ten*; Mezzo, C-Ten, Bar; *Cont, Bass*.

Subject: Describes Sir Henry Lee's life in retirement, and the visit he received from Queen Anne. See Comment.

Voice: Recit. style; steps, repeated notes, leaps; varied rhythms.

Piano: Chordal, then contrapuntal, in two parts.

Comment: In 1708 Queen Anne, consort of James I, visited Sir Henry Lee and his mistress, Mrs Anne Vavasour, to whom the Queen made a present of 'a very fayre jewell'. This poem commemorates that visit. For further information on Sir Henry Lee see **44** (**18**) and **45** (**6-8**). A dramatic setting. There are problems of underlay in St. 2-4; one solution is offered in Coll 6.

St. 1, line 1: wonted = accustomed; line 3: he...story – he told stories to pass the time, *and* he told stories of his former pastimes, tilting etc; line 4: erst-afforded = once provided; (*erst-affording*, in Colls 6, 17, 18); line 5: that goddess = Queen Elizabeth. St. 2, line 1: *from* – should probably read *on, from* having been copied in error from line 2; line 3: referring to Queen Anne, whose children, particularly Prince Henry, were much admired; line 5: a star – perhaps refers to the 'fayre jewell' mentioned above. St. 3, line 2: denaid = denied. St. 4, line 2: in sort most meet = in the most suitable manner; line 3: *with* – the sense demands *which* (Doughtie). Coll 6: St. 4, line 2: *dreams* = *dream*, all other editions; line 6: *life's* = *Time's*, all other editions. 2nd phrase of second half, under *is* in St. 1, Coll 1 has d', missing in *LS* 4, though in the tablature; in Coll 17 add e', in Colls 6, 18, add c'. Coll 29: some bass notes added from viol part.

(2) **Lady, if you so spite me.** Colls 6, 17, 26; Coll 18, *A minor*.

C minor. g'-f″. 4/4. 2′40″, [1′45″]. V/me, P/me.

For: Ten; *C-Ten, Bar*.

Subject: Lady, if you dislike me, why do you kiss me? But if you wish to make love...!

Voice: Steps, some skips; varied rhythms and phrase-lengths; melismas.

Piano: Chordal with decorations, becoming fairly contrapuntal.

Comment: The usual complaining lover, in this case loaded with double meanings (spill, die), and a highly original setting. Words from Yonge's *Musica Transalpina*, 1588, set by Ferrabosco the elder, translated from Rinaldi's 'Donna si voi m'adiate', with the following variants: line 3: *overcloyed = overjoyed*; line 4: *thus overjoyed = and be destroyed*; another translation was used by Wilbye, *EM* 6 (18). Line 1: spite = regard with contempt; line 5: spill = destroy, *and* deprive of chastity; line 6: kill = overwhelm; line 8: die = reach consummation.

(3) **In darkness let me dwell.** Colls 19, 26; Coll 17, *C minor*; Colls 6, 18, *G minor*.

A minor. c'-e", [e'-d"]. 4/4. 3'15". V/md, P/me.

For: *Sop, Ten*; Mezzo, C-Ten, Bar; *Cont, Bass*.

Subject: An embracing of black despair that even music cannot cure.

Voice: Mostly by step, some skips, some chromatics; an immense variety of rhythm and phrase-length.

Piano: Contrapuntal throughout.

Comment: One of the great songs of all time, it offers many possibilities to a singer of imagination. The poem was also set, with a second stanza, by Coprario, **37** (4). Coll 1, bar 28, Coll 19, page 124, bar 13, Coll 26, page 24, bar 12, RH, note 2: all other editions give g' not d', correcting a misprint in the tablature. Coll 19: page 121, bar 7, 2nd half, RH: quaver crotchet quaver, not quaver quaver crotchet; page 123, line 4, bar 2, beat 2, LH: f°, not g°. Colls 17, (6, 18): bar 29, 5th crotchet beat: add minim d', (a°). Coll 26 includes a number of notes from the viol part.

ALFONSO FERRABOSCO
before 1578 – 1628

49 AYRES. 1609. S & B edition by E.H. Fellowes, 1927. Out of print.

(1) **Like hermit poor.** Colls 5, 27.

G minor. d'-e"*b*, [d'-d"]. 4/4. 1'20". V/me, P/me.

For: Mezzo, C-Ten, Bar.

Subject: A sombre piece, desiring retirement from active life.

Voice: Repeated slow d's, gradually developing in range and rhythmic variety; some chromatics.

Piano: Contrapuntal and chromatic.

Comment: Gloomy but surprisingly haunting song. A translation from
            Desportes' 'Je me veux rendre hermite et faire penitence',
            Amours de Diane, II, 8, probably by Sir Walter Raleigh.
            Printed in *BD*, 1591, and in *PN*, 1593. Ault uses the MS in
            Rawl. Poet. 85, and *OB 16* gives *BD* as source but disagrees
            with Rollins in several places. Line 1: *Like hermit = Like to a
            hermit (PN, OB 16), Like to an hermit (BD,* Ault); line 2: *of =
            in (BD,* Ault); line 3: recure = cure; line 4: *Love = death (OB
            16); shall find = shall ever find (BD, PN,* Ault, *OB 16*); line 6:
            gates = gate (BD, PN, Ault, *OB 16*).

    Both sources give two more stanzas before the final
            couplet: 'My food shall be of care and sorrow made / My drink
            nought else but tears fall'n from mine eyes; / And for my light
            in such obscured shade / The flames shall serve that (which
            [*PN*]) from my heart arise. // A gown of grief (gray [*PN*]) my
            body shall attire, / my staff of broken hope whereon I'll stay,
            (And broken hope the staff of all my stay, [*BD*, Ault]) / Of late
            repentance linked with long desire / The couch is made
            (framed, [*PN, OB 16*]) whereon (wherein, [Ault]) my limbs I'll
            lay (bones to lay [*BD*]). These variants and extra lines could
            easily be fitted to Ferrabosco's music, treating the final
            couplet as a refrain. Also set by Lanier (published Playford
            1652, 1653, 1659), with many variants, S & B, B 448, where it
            is set complete as three six-line stanzas, as also given in five
            MS versions of the poem. Rollins, in *PN*, gives numerous
            mentions of the poem in seventeenth-century writings,
            demonstrating its immense popularity; he also refers to the
            music, but seems to assume all the references to be to
            Ferrabosco's setting rather than Lanier's without adducing
            any evidence to this effect.

(5) Fain I would. Colls 5, 27.

    G major. d'-f ", [g'-e"]. 2/2. 45". V/me, P/e.

For: Bar.

Subject: Happiness; the girl's merits are beyond description.

Voice: Steps, skips; an awkward rising phrase to the one f " on
            higher; one or two odd rhythms.

Piano: Chordal.

Comment: Short and sweet; simple but not too obvious. Line 2: at full =
            fully. Line 5: *thoughts are = thought is*, in Christ Church MS
            of poem, which has a second rather weak stanza, given in
            Doughtie. Coll 5: bar 5, beat 4, LH: delete small print # to f °.

(6) Come, my Celia (Ben Jonson, *Volpone*, 1607. Act III, Scene vii). Colls
19, 27.

F major. c'-e''b, [f'-d'']. 2/2. 1'50". V/me, P/me.

For: C-Ten, Bar.

Subject: A seducer's song: Let us enjoy ourselves while we have the
chance, it will be no crime if not discovered.

Voice: Steps, and skips; dim 4th; much rhythmic variety.

Piano: Chordal, with occasional decoration.

Comment: Sung by Volpone himself in the play, probably to this
setting, in an attempt to seduce Celia, Corvino's wife. An
effective piece with excellent words, a translation from
Catullus. See **29** (1). Jonson reprinted the poem in *The
Forest*, 1616. Line 10: toys = trifles; lines 13-14: if we are
quiet no one will hear us. Line 2: *may the sweets = can the
sports*, in *Volpone*; *may the sports*, in *The Forest*; line 7: *We
once = once we*, in *Volpone* and *The Forest*; line 14: *Thus =
So*, in *The Forest*; line 15: *fruits = fruit*, in *The Forest*; line
16: *theft = thefts*, in *Volpone*. Coll 27: much of the bass 8ve
lower, from viol part; bar 10, last quaver, RH: flat added to
e'; bar 29: from here to end marked as repeat.

(7) So, so, leave off this last lamenting kiss (John Donne, 'The
Expiration', *Poems*, 1633). Colls 19, 27.

G major. d'-f ", [g'-d'']. 2/2. 1'30". V/me, P/me.

For: Mezzo, Bar.

Subject: Lover's parting.

Voice: 3rds and steps; slightly chromatic; varied rhythms.

Piano: Chordal, with patches of counterpoint; many accidentals.

Comment: A contemporary setting of this complex and beautiful poem,
this was, in fact, the first publication of any of Donne's verse.
St. 1, line 1: *So, so = So, go*, according to 1669 edition of
poems; *leave = breake*, according to all printed editions,
though most MSS have *leave*; line 2: vapours = evaporates;
line 4: *selves = soules*, according to some MSS; benight = to
cloud, *OED*; *happy = happiest*, all editions; line 5: *aske =
ask'd*, according to many MSS and Gardner. St. 2, line 3: *O =
Or*, according to 1635-1669 editions and several MSS; line 5:
Except = unless.

(8) Young and simple though I am (Thomas Campion). Coll 5.

G major. g'-g", [a'-e'']. 2/2. 30", [20"]. 5 St. V/me, P/e.

For: Sop.

Subject: Cheerful thoughts of a young girl about men and love.

Voice: A lot of words for a fairly high-pitched song, but melodically
and rhythmically quite straight-forward.

Piano:　　　Chordal, a few passing notes.
Comment:　Repeat optional; some stanzas could be omitted. A delightful
　　　　　little song. St. 2, line 5: use to do = are in the habit of doing. St.
　　　　　3, line 3: thirst longing = either thirst for drink, or any
　　　　　passionate desire (Davis). St. 5, line 1: gull = fool, fop.
　　　　　Campion's own setting is **33 (9)**, with these variants: St. 2,
　　　　　line 2: *or to* = *nor to*; St. 4, line 3: *'tis* = *'twere*. Vivian gives a
　　　　　6th MS stanza: 'Married wives may take or leave, / When they
　　　　　list, refuse, receive: / We poor maids may not do so, / We must
　　　　　answer Ay with No. / We must seem strange, coy, and curst, /
　　　　　Yet do we would fain if we durst.' Doughtie gives three more
　　　　　MS stanzas, which become rather bawdy. Set by Lanier in
　　　　　Playford, 1652, 1673. First stanza in Earle, 1615. Several
　　　　　other MS versions also exist.

(9) Drown not with tears. Coll 5.
　　　　　G major. d'-f ″, [g'-e″]. 3/2,2/2. 2'30″, [1'50″]. V/me, P/me.
For:　　　Mezzo, Bar.
Subject:　Loving reminder at sad parting that reunion will be joyful.
Voice:　　Steps, small skips; modulates to Bb major!
Piano:　　Chordal, some passing notes, many accidentals.
Comment:　Repeat of second part optional. A wonderfully romantic song.
　　　　　First eight lines set by Pilkington as a madrigal: *EM* 26 (20).
　　　　　Line 3, lights = eyes.

(21) So beautie on the waters stood (Ben Jonson, *The Masque of Beautie*,
1608). Coll 19.
　　　　　C major. g°-g', [g°-e']. 2/2. 1'. V/e, P/e.
For:　　　*Sop*, Ten; Cont, C-Ten; *Bass*.
Subject:　Love and Concord.
Voice:　　Steps, a few skips; 7th drop; rhythms fairly simple.
Piano:　　Chordal.
Comment:　Original in Alto clef, but could be sung an 8ve higher. Repeat
　　　　　at end advisable. At this point in the masque, the dancers,
　　　　　'standing still, were by the *Musicians* with a Second *Song*
　　　　　(sung by a loud *Tenor*) celebrated'. Line 2: 'As in the creation
　　　　　he is said by the ancients to have done'. Jonson's note. Jonson
　　　　　wrote two Epigrams in praise of Ferrabosco and his music.

(24) Unconstant love. Colls 5, 27.
　　　　　C minor. g'-g″, [b'b-g″]. 4/4. 1'25″. V/me, P/me.
For:　　　Sop, Ten.
Subject:　Sad farewell to a faithless partner.
Voice:　　Many skips in first part, then by step; some high-lying
　　　　　phrases.
Piano:　　Moderately contrapuntal, with a sprinkling of accidentals.

Comment: Some lovely phrases for a singer with a comfortable upper
              register. Coll 27 has several bass passages 8ve lower, from
              viol part.

THOMAS FORD
d. 1648

50 MUSICKE OF SUNDRIE KINDS Aries (sic) for 4. Voices to the Lute,
    Orphorion, or Basse-Viol. 1607. S & B edition by E.H. Fellowes, 1921.
    Revised by Thurston Dart, 1966 (*LS* 11). Tablature given.

(1) **Not full twelve years**. Coll 13, *C# minor*; Colls 5, 14, *A minor*.
              D minor. d'-a", [g'-f "]. 4/4. 2'20". V/m, P/me.
For: Sop, Ten; *Mezzo, C-Ten, Bar*; *Cont, Bass*.
Subject: A meditation on death by a young man who may have
              committed suicide shortly afterwards.
Voice: Many repeated notes, skips, long off-beat descending scale;
              both ends of the wide range need good control; a big climax
              for this type of song.
Piano: Contrapuntal, mostly two-part; some tricky rhythms.
Comment: A great song, dignified and powerful, needing a singer who
              can sustain emotional intensity through long phrases. In
              Folger MS V.a. 345 this poem is entitled 'A young man's
              Epitaph'. And below: 'These verses above written, were
              made by one mr. Henry Morrice, sone to mr. morrice,
              Attorney to the Court of awards, who dyed sudenly in
              milford Lane having these verses in his pocket.'

(2) **What then is love, sings Corydon**. Coll 19. Coll 7, *E minor*; Coll 8,
     C minor.
              D minor. d'-e". 3/2. 1'10", [55"]. 3 St. V/e, P/e.
For: *Sop, Ten*; Mezzo, C-Ten, Bar; *Cont, Bass*.
Subject: Corydon will no longer love; Phillida has grown coy, and love
              is shown to be unreliable.
Voice: Steps, some skips; 3/4,3/2 changes with some quicker notes.
Piano: Chordal, some passing notes.
Comment: Repeat optional. Corydon is clearly not very worried by his
              change in fortune, this is an essentially cheerful song. St. 1,
              line 6: scanty dearth = great scarcity; line 9: 'chill = I will. St.
              2, line 7: salveless = incurable; line 8: erring scope = wander-
              ing target. St. 3, line 3: thrall = enslave. Coll 19: page 145, bar
              14, beat 2: add semibreve e°. Line 7, St. 2/3: underlay needs
              adjustment; Colls 7, 8: start on the previous upbeat, and give
              the third syllable two notes; an alternative would be to change
              the rhythm to three equal notes, without adding an upbeat.
              Coll 19: page 145, bars 7/10, slur notes 2 and 3, not 1 and 2.

(3) **Unto the temple of thy beauty.** Coll 5.

	G minor. d'-f ", [g'-f "]. 4/4. 1'. 3 St. V/me, P/me.
For:	Bar.
Subject:	An elaborate ode on the funeral of Pity, slain by the singer's mistress.
Voice:	Mostly by step, one small melisma; unusual basic rhythm needs care in phrasing.
Piano:	Chordal, with elaborated cadences.
Comment:	An original and beautiful song, rebarred in Coll 5 to make the phrasing clearer. St. 2, line 6: suffer = allow.

(4) **Now I see thy looks were feigned** (Thomas Lodge, 'An Ode', *Phillis*, 1593). Coll 11, *A minor*; Colls 5, 12, *E minor*.

	G minor. d'-f ", [g'-d"]. 4/4. 30". 5 St. V/e, P/e.
For:	*Ten*; Bar; C-Ten, Bass.
Subject:	Lively and imaginative curse on an unfaithful woman.
Voice:	Mostly by step, some simple skips; rhythms fairly simple.
Piano:	Chordal, some short runs in bass.
Comment:	Repeat optional. Some stanzas could be omitted. Copied in Earle, 1615, and printed in *PN*, 1593, which agrees with *Phillis* in giving the following variants. St. 1, line 1: *see = find*; line 3: wethers = sheep; line 4: *unconstant = unstable*; light = not heavy, *and* immoral; line 5: subtle sighted = with cunning glances; line 7: Siren – a sea-nymph who lures sailors to their destruction; line 8: *thy = this* (except in final stanza, according to Ault and *OB 16*, but not Rollins, who only prints the first two words of each refrain after the first). St. 2, line 1: *eye = eyes*; line 2: *my = mine*; line 4: *sighs = smiles*. St. 3, line 5: pretty winking = archly conniving. St. 4, line 1: seemly cruel = cruel beauty; line 3: durance = imprisonment. St. 5, line 2: *those = these*; line 4: acquaint = become familiar to; line 5: date = set an end to. Rollins mentions three variants in *Phillis*, all of which are clearly misprints.

(5) **Go, passions, to the cruel fair.**

	G minor. f'#-g", [g'-d"]. 4/4. 1'. 3 St. V/me, P/me.
For:	[Sop], Ten.
Subject:	A lover asks for pity, but this is a more interesting poem than usual.
Voice:	Steps, skips; 8ve leap to g"; broken phrases; chromatics.
Piano:	Contrapuntal, mostly in three parts.
Comment:	Repeat advisable. *Her* in St. 1, 2, could be changed to *his* and *him* if desired. Many small rhythmic adjustments needed for St. 2/3. St. 1, line 6: date = end. St. 2, line 1: urge = charge; line 2: wrack = breaking. St. 3, line 1: importune = beg.

(6) Come Phyllis, come into these bowers. Colls 13, 20, *A minor*; Coll 14, *E minor*; Coll 21, *F minor*.

G minor. f'#-f ", [g'-d"]. 4/4,3/2. 45", [35"]. 2 St. V/e, P/e.

For: *Ten*; Bar; C-Ten.

Subject: Come to this sheltered place, where the birds will plead my love, and all nature praise you.

Voice: Steps, small skips; rhythms fairly simple, though varied; small melisma.

Piano: Chordal with some decorations.

Comment: The tempo relationship given is possible, but crotchet = minim [Colls 13, 14, crotchet = crotchet] might well be better. Colls 20, 21: accompaniment and introduction to each stanza by Keel. Penultimate bar of each stanza, voice should have: dotted quaver two demisemiquavers dotted minim crotchet.

(7) Fair, sweet, cruel. Coll 20; Coll 9, *A minor*; Colls 5, 10, *E minor*; Coll 21, *F minor*.

G minor. d'-f ", [g'-d"]. 4/4. 45", [30"]. 2 St. V/me, P/me.

For: *Sop, Ten*; Mezzo, Bar; *C-Ten, Cont, Bass*.

Subject: A pursuit song: wait for me, I love you.

Voice: Steps, broken chords; many rests to create breathless effect; varied rhythms.

Piano: Chordal, some imitation; some awkward moments at speed.

Comment: Repeat recommended. Scope for a variety of interpretations and therefore of tempi; time given is for a fairly fast version. Colls 20, 21: accompaniment by Keel. Bar 12, voice, note 1: should be flat, not natural, which means changing the accompaniment.

(8) Since first I saw your face. Colls 5, 19; Coll 33, *Eb major*.

C major. c'-c", [c'-a']. 4/4. 45". 3 St. V/e, P/e.

For: Mezzo, C-Ten, Bar; Cont, Bass.

Subject: I have loved you since I first saw you, you cannot reject me now.

Voice: Steps, broken chords; very simple rhythms.

Piano: Chordal, occasional imitation.

Comment: Second repeat optional. Perhaps the best known of all the lute songs, it has attained the status of a folk song. Printed in *Golden Garland,* 1620, and Cotgrave, 1662, which has extra stanzas: 'If I have wronged you, tell me wherein, / And I will soon amend it, / In recompense of such a sin, / Here is my heart, I'll send it. // If that will not your mercy move, / Then for my life I care not; / Then, O then torment me still, / And take my life and spare not.' 'Answer to the Third Stave':

'Art thou so mad to love a lass / And leave thy heart behind thee? / Go learn more wit, greenheaded ass / For Cupid's rules will bind thee. // A young wench loves a lad that's bold / And not a simpering noddy; / Therefore before thou leave thy hold / Be sure thou bounce her body.'

Coll 33: accompaniment and introduction by Michael Diack; St. 1, bars 8/12: *you* = *ye* all other editions; bar 14, beat 4, voice: e'*b* not b'*b*; bar 17, voice: half bar's rest omitted.

(9) There is a lady sweet and kind. Coll 19.

G major. d'-e", [g'-e"]. 4/4. 30", [20"]. 6 St. V/e, P/e.

For: C-Ten, Bar.
Subject: Dreams about a women once seen, and loved ever since.
Voice: Steps, some slightly odd skips; very simple rhythm.
Piano: Chordal, some simple decoration.
Comment: Repeat optional. A famous lyric, but the setting is a little disappointing; however, Ford does include the whole poem, which is more than most of the later settings do. Poem printed in *Golden Garland*, 1620. St. 5, line 2: Phoebus – Apollo, the Sun-God. St. 6, lines 1-2: Cupid wanders around, so does my beloved. Coll 19: St. 6, line 3: *the...the* = *she...she*, all other editions.

(10) How shall I then describe my love?

C major. c'-c". 4/4. 1', [40"]. 3 St. V/e, P/e.

For: C-Ten, Bar; Bass.
Subject: A lover attempts to describe the graces and virtues of his beloved, and his fortune in possessing her.
Voice: Mostly by step; some rhythmic variety; folk-song style.
Piano: Chordal, with occasional decoration.
Comment: Repeat optional. Similar to, though not as memorable as **50** (8) above. St. 2, line 1: Philome = the nightingale (Philomela).

THOMAS GILES
fl. 1607

51 (THE MASKE FOR LORD HAYS. 1607. See **34**.)

(4) Triumph now with joy and mirth (Thomas Campion). Coll 4.

G major. d'-d". 4/4. 55". V/e, P/e.

For: Mezzo, C-Ten, Bar.
Subject: A celebration of peace and good fortune.
Voice: Steps, small skips, quaver pairs; fairly regular rhythms, but words not very well fitted to the music.
Piano: Chordal with decoration.

Comment: Repeat essential. Used solely as a dance in the masque, the
             words being added later for publication.

THOMAS GREAVES
fl. 1604

52 SONGES OF SUNDRIE KINDES Aires To Be Sung To the Lute, and
Base Violl. S & B edition by Ian Spink, 1962. Out of print.

(1) Shaded with olive trees. Colls 20, 28; Coll 21, *Eb major.*
             F major. d′-f ″, [f′-d″]. 2/2. 1′15″. V/me, P/me.
For: *Sop, Ten*; Mezzo, Bar; *C-Ten.*
Subject: Celestina played and sang more sweetly than the birds.
Voice: Short scales, 3rds, sequences; much rhythmic variety, some
             patter.
Piano: Chordal, with some imitation and melodic bass.
Comment: Colls 20, 21: accompaniment and introductions by Keel.
             Keel has misunderstood the notation of triple time in this
             period; the 3/2 sections should be in crotchets, not minims,
             with crotchet = crotchet throughout. The first 3/2 section
             should probably end halfway through bar 23, as altered in
             the BL copy and given in Spink, though not in Coll 28. (In
             this change bars 31-33 into 2 bars of 3/4, halving the note
             values.) Bars 30/31: there should be twice as many *prettys*,
             each crotchet being two quavers, running into what will now
             be the quavers of bar 32. Line 4 (3-4, *EMV*): with careful
             spending of labour, and adorned with gold. Line 8 (10,
             EMV): time − used in both musical and temporal senses.
             Line 9 (11, *EMV*): Apaid = satisfied. Bar 6: comma not
             semicolon after *singing*, all other editions, see Subject,
             above; bars 6-9: *then = than*, all other editions. Bar 19: *duty*
             = *duly*, all other editions; bar 24: *duly = truly*, all other
             editions. Bar 15: *and = that, EMV*. Col 28: Title: Celestina.

(3) Ye bubbling springs. Coll 5.
             G minor. d′-f ″, [f′-d″]. 4/4,3/4. 1′20″, [1′05″]. V/me, P/me.
For: [Mezzo], Bar.
Subject: Asks nature to report his love to the beloved, but in the
             contrasting section says he will not die for her!
Voice: Steps, small skips, in crotchets; then downward scales in
             dotted rhythms followed by broken chords in quavers; final
             section by step in minims and crotchets.
Piano: Chordal with some decoration; much imitation in places.
Comment: Repeat optional. Pleasant song with nice contrasts and

surprise sentiment at the end. Words from masculine viewpoint, but could be reversed. Line 5: Philomel = the nightingale. Also set by Pilkington as a madrigal, *EM* 26 (5).

(7) What is beauty but a breath? Colls 19, 30.

	G minor. f'#-f ", [g'-e"]. 2/2. 1'10". V/me, P/me.
For:	Sop, Ten.
Subject:	Beauty does not last, but it is free to all.
Voice:	Steps, small skips; some rhythmic variety.
Piano:	Chordal and contrapuntal by turns.
Comment:	Simple but pleasant. Line 6: *to*, Coll 19 = *that*, all other editions; the emendation seems unnecessary – those that are truly beautiful do not realise what they possess.

ROBERT HALES
fl. 1583; d. before 1616

53 O eyes, leave off your weeping. Colls 1, 30.

	C minor. e'*b*-e"*b*. 4/4. 50", [35"]. 4 St. V/e, P/me.
For:	Mezzo, C-Ten, Bar.
Subject:	I should not weep, it may only be a misunderstanding which time will put right, but I will die if this hope proves an illusion.
Voice:	Steps, small skips; simple four-square rhythm with last phrase extended.
Piano:	Chordal, a fair amount of decoration.
Comment:	Repeat optional. See **44** (18) for note on Hales. St. 2, line 4: attended = waited for. St 4, line 2: hap = chance. Bar 6, voice, note 5: should have flat, not natural. The poem appears in BL Add. MS 34064 in a group of poems known to be by Nicholas Breton, and is given in Grosart's edition of Breton's works, with a fifth stanza: 'But if I be that lover / That never shall recover / But spite shall spill me; / Then let this much suffice me / That heaven this death denyest me / That love should kill me.'

ANTHONY HOLBORNE
fl. 1584; d. 1602

54 My heavy sprite (George Clifford, Earl of Cumberland). Coll 1.

	G minor. f'#-g", [g'-f "]. 4/4. 2'. V/e, P/me.
For:	Sop, Ten.
Subject:	I am oppressed by sorrow, having lost my beloved.

Voice: Steps, small skips, broken chords; many separate short
                phrases; good climax.
Piano: Chordal, with considerable decoration.
Comment: Rather old-fashioned viol-song style, as might be expected
                from the early date, but has charm. Line 4: Life's despite =
                scorned by life. Clifford succeeded Sir Henry Lee as Queen
                Elizabeth's Champion. See **44 (18)**. See **16** for another song
                which may be by Holborne.

TOBIAS HUME
c. 1569 – 1645

55 THE FIRST PART OF AYRES Songes to bee sung to the Viole, with
the Lute, or better with the Viole alone. (Running title: *Musicall
Humors*.) 1605.
    Although designed to be sung with the lyra viol rather than the
lute, the following songs are printed in Coll 4.

(1) The soldier's song: I sing the praise of honoured wars.
                C major. g°-g″, [c′-g″]. 4/4. 1′40″. V/m, P/me.
For: Bar.
Subject: The glory and excitement of battle.
Voice: Mostly by step; trumpet calls and excited shouts break up
                the basically simple music.
Piano: Chordal with decoration; some trumpet and drum effects.
Comment: Certainly different! It would show off a wide-ranging voice
                to good effect.

(3) Tobacco, tobacco. Colls 19, 28; Imperial (Bass), *Bb minor*.
                D minor. d′-f″. 4/4,6/8,4/4. 1′10″. V/me, P/e.
For: Mezzo, Bar.
Subject: Tobacco is proved to have the same effects as love.
Voice: 4/4 section wide-ranging broken chords and scale; 6/8
                section steps and simple skips; simple rhythms.
Piano: Chordal with some decoration.
Comment: The opening section is repeated at the end, the argument
                having been triumphantly proved. Line 5: tumour =
                swelling. John Gerard says that tobacco dries up humours,
                and is good for tumours when applied in a poultice
                (Doughtie). The tempo relationship in Coll 19 is probably
                correct, but crotchet = crotchet is more effective. Imperial
                has modified the layout of the accompaniment.

(112) Fain would I change that note. Colls 11, 19, 29. Coll 12, *D major*;
Coll 20, *F major*; Coll 21, *Eb major*.

G major. d'-g", [g'-g"]. 6/8. 40". 2 st. V/e, P/e.

For: Sop, Ten; *Mezzo, C-Ten, Bar; Cont, Bass.*

Subject: I can sing of nothing but love.

Voice: Steps, small skips; sequence; simple rhythms.

Piano: Mostly chordal.

Comment: The first sentence is often misunderstood. A free paraphrase would run: 'I do not wish to sing songs of love, I would rather work at vocal exercises, for singing lovesongs is harmful.' Coll 19: the notation appears complicated, but is not so in practice, with minim = dotted minim throughout. Colls 20, 21: accompaniment and introduction to each stanza by Keel. Major errors in the rhythms can be easily corrected: in all bars not in 6/4 dotted minims have been written as crotchets, thus tripling the tempo for these bars! Note, the sixth bar from the end should be 2/4, in Keel's notation, i.e. two dotted minims in the correct notation. First bar of voice in each stanza: slur notes 5-6, not 4-5.

(113) What greater grief.

G minor. d'-f ", [d'-d"]. 4/4. 1'10". 2 St. V/me, P/e.

For: Mezzo, Bar.

Subject: The greatest grief is to despair and yet live; but if death comes not I may yet hope.

Voice: Steps, a few skips. 8ve drop; fairly free rhythms.

Piano: Chordal, with contrapuntal moments.

Comment: Musically more ambitious than the rest of Hume's songs. St. 1, line 5: sith = since.

ROBERT JOHNSON
1583 – 1633

56 AYRES, SONGS, AND DIALOGUES. Manuscript sources. S & B edition by Ian Spink, 1961, 1974 (*LS* 12).

(1) As I walked forth. Coll 24, *F minor.*

G minor. d'-g", [g'-f "]. 4/4. 45". 4 St. V/e, P/e.

For: Sop, Ten; *Mezzo, Bar.*

Subject: The singer overhears the complaint of a girl who has lost her lover and is preparing for death.

Voice: Mostly by step, some skips; 8ve leap; simple but varied rhythms with many paired quavers.

Piano: Chordal, occasional decoration. Printed in *Wit and Mirth* 1, *Songs Compleat* 3.

Comment: The editor's marking of 'slower' for bar 15 seems strange, though a pause on the last note of the bar is certainly possible. St. 3, line 2: bents = reeds. Coll 24: accompaniment modified throughout, and an introduction added to each stanza, but the bass agrees with *LS* 12. St. 2/3, line 6: *as I = like me*, LS 12. St. 3, line 1: *scent = scents*, *LS* 12; line 4: *and she wrong = she wrung*, *LS* 12. St. 4, line 3: *things = leaves*, LS 12; line 4: *pillows = pillow*, *LS* 12; line 5: *Then down she laid, ne'er more did speak*, *LS* 12. Printed in Playford, 1652, 1659.

(2) **Come heavy sleep**.

G minor. d'-e"*b*, [d'-d"]. 4/4. 1'20". V/e, P/e.

For: Mezzo, C-Ten, Bar.
Subject: A prayer for sleep to overcome sorrow.
Voice: Mostly by step, sequences of 3rds, scales; simple speech rhythms.
Piano: Chordal, then simple counterpoint.
Comment: Also set, with second stanza, by Dowland, **42 (20)**. There are a few minor variations of text between the two settings.

(3) **Dear, do not your fair beauty wrong**. Coll 5.

F major. c'-g", f'-f "]. 4/4. 1'10". V/me, P/e.

For: Sop, Ten.
Subject: Conversational, encouraging a young girl to feel ready for love, and not to leave it too late.
Voice: Recit. style; irregular rhythms, broken chords, a few melismas.
Piano: Chordal, occasional decoration.
Comment: A very attractive song in the new Jacobean style. It is quoted in Thomas May's play *The Old Couple*, 1636. Bar 24: toy = play.

(4) **With endless tears**.

A minor. g'-g", [g'-f "]. 4/4. 1'. 2 St. V/e, P/e.

For: Sop, Ten.
Subject: I saw a maid weeping bitterly for lost love.
Voice: Many simple skips, some broken chords; simple rhythms.
Piano: Chordal, with some decoration.
Comment: Tune better than the words. St. 1, bars 13-14: amain = violently.

(5) **For ever let thy heav'nly tapers**.

D minor. f'-a", [a'-f "]. 4/4. 1'05". V/me, P/e.

For: Sop, Ten.
Subject: An Epithalamium: let us praise Hymen (God of Marriage).
Voice: Steps, small skips; scale down from the only a" to a'; many

f″s; simple rhythms, with many brief interludes for accompaniment.

Piano: Gently contrapuntal.

Comment: It may be difficult to carry the sense across the empty bars. It may well be that the second part should be for chorus.

(6) Shall I like a hermit dwell?

G minor. f′#-g″, [g′-g″]. 4/4. 35″. 4 St. V/me, P/e.

For: Ten.

Subject: If my love is too free with her favours I will leave her, whatever her charms.

Voice: Many skips and broken chords; 8ve leaps and drops; simple rhythms.

Piano: Chordal with decoration.

Comment: Quite an entertaining piece. St 4. line 4: fire – treat as two syllables.

(7) Woods, rocks, and mountains.

C minor. c′-e″b, [e′b-e″b]. 4/4. 1′20″. 2 St. V/me, P/e.

For: Mezzo.

Subject: A deserted maid curses her fortune.

Voice: Steps, skips, many repeated notes; 6th leap; very free rhythm with many crotchet rests.

Piano: Chordal, with occasional counterpoint.

Comment: Words printed in *The Academy of Compliments*, 1650. St 2. bar 18: the minim minim rest must become a semibreve, to complete the sense.

(8) How wretched is the state.

C minor. e′b-g″. 4/4. 1′40″. V/m, P/e.

For: Sop, Ten.

Subject: A call to sinners for repentance, for no one knows when death will come.

Voice: Steps, broken chords; 8ve leap; sustained g″ for climax; free rhythms.

Piano: Chordal, with occasional decoration.

Comment: A fine dramatic song, well worth performing. A lute version of the accompaniment is provided as an alternative.

(9) Arm, arm (Beaumont and Fletcher, *The Mad Lover*, c. 1616. Act V, Scene iv).

G major. d′-g″, [d′-e″]. 4/4,3/4. 2′15″. V/me, P/e.

For: Ten, high Bar.

Subject: A description of the battle of Pelusium sung by Stremnon ('a soldier that can sing'), in which Memnon ('the Mad Lover'),

Eumenes ('a general'), and Polybius ('his captain') have taken part.

Voice: Steps, broken chords, repeated notes, trumpet calls; speech rhythm till final page, which is regular 3/4.

Piano: Recit. chords, with occasional trumpet calls.

Comment: A much more successful piece than Hume's *Soldier's Song*, 55 (1). Pelusium lay west of modern Port Said, on the easternmost mouth of the Nile. Bar 8: bill – a kind of concave axe with a spike at the back and its shaft terminating in a spear-head; glaves – halberds, weapons with a sharp-edged blade ending in a point and a spear-head, mounted on a handle five to seven feet long. Bar 11: *or a* = *or*, in play; bar 21: *batalia* = *battle*, in play.

(10) Full fathom five (Shakespeare, *The Tempest*, 1611. Act I, Scene ii).
        G major. f'#-f ", [g'-e"]. 4/4. 1'20". V/e, P/e.

For: Sop, Ten.

Subject: The fate of a father lost at sea.

Voice: Steps, small skips; sequences of 3rds; slow descending scales.

Piano: Simple counterpoint.

Comment: Effective pealing of bells in last section. Printed in *Cheerful Ayres*, 1660.

(11) Where the bee sucks (Shakespeare, *The Tempest*, 1611. Act V, Scene i).
        G major. d'-e". 4/4,6/4. 35". V/e, P/e.

For: Mezzo, C-Ten, Bar.

Subject: Ariel's song.

Voice: Steps, broken chords, three-note sequences; simple rhythms.

Piano: Chordal.

Comment: Dance-like, in two distinct sections. Printed in *Cheerful Ayres*, 1660, and in a setting by Wilson in Playford, 1659, 1667, 1673.

(12) Away delights (Beaumont and Fletcher, *The Captain*, c. 1612. Act III, Scene iv).
        F minor. e'-f ", f'-e"b. 4/4. 1'. 2 St. V/me, P/e.

For: Mezzo.

Subject: Let me reject hopeless love; let maids die rather than be mocked by men.

Voice: Steps, skips; 8ve leap; chromatic melisma; simple rhythm.

Piano: Chordal, with flowing bass.

Comment: More like an old style lute-song. Lelia ('a cunning wanton widow') causes this sad song to be sung in order to soften her estranged lover, Julio. Variants in the play: St. 1, bar 4: *will* =

must; bar 6: *hope = Love*; bar 12: *smart = smarts*; bar 13: *stay = go*. St. 2, bars 7-8: *overflow = overgrow*; bar 11: *rest whilst = sleep while*; bar 18: *clay = day* in sources, emended by Seward in 1750 and many other editors.

(13) Come hither you that love (Beaumont and Fletcher, *The Captain*, c. 1612. Act IV, Scene iv).

G major. d'-e″, [g'-e″]. 4/4. 50″. 2 St. V/e, P/e.

For:	Mezzo.
Subject:	My song shall make boys men, and old men young.
Voice:	Mostly by step; some skips; 8ve leap, 6th leap; paired quavers, dotted rhythms; speech rhythms.
Piano:	Chordal with decoration.
Comment:	Sung by Lelia (see (12) above) to assist in the seduction of an old man, who to her consternation reveals himself to be her father! Printed in *Cheerful Ayres*, 1660.

(14) Oh, let us howl (John Webster, *The Duchess of Malfi*, c. 1613. Act IV, Scene ii).

F minor. c'-f″, [e'b-e″b]. 4/4. 1'05″. V/me, P/e.

For:	Bar.
Subject:	Let us make dreadful sounds till we run out of breath, then sing like swans and die.
Voice:	Steps, many broken chords; 8ve leaps, 6th drops; recit. style.
Piano:	Chordal.
Comment:	'Here by a Madman this song is sung to a dismal kind of music'. Designed to terrify the Duchess before she is murdered. Bar 16: *bell = bill* (make bird noises?) in first edition of play, altered to *bell* in second edition. Bar 25: *corrosived = corroded*. Bars 23/26: *our = your*, in play. The last sentence in Ian Spink's note might well be followed in performance.

(15) Care-charming sleep (Beaumont and Fletcher, *Valentinian*, c. 1614. Act V, Scene ii).

D minor. c'-f″, [d'-f″]. 4/4. 2'. V/me, P/e.

For:	Mezzo, Bar.
Subject:	O sleep, come and give rest to this afflicted man.
Voice:	Steps, broken chords; 8ve leap and fall; free speech rhythms.
Piano:	Chordal, with hints of counterpoint.
Comment:	A beautiful song, with or without ornaments. Sung to the dying Valentinian. Variants in play: bar 9: *wight* (person) = *Prince*; bar 12: *to it = that is*; bar 15: *slumber = slumbers*; bar 28: *thyself = this prince*.

(16) **Come away, thou lady gay!** (Beaumont and Fletcher, *The Chances*,
c. 1617. Act V, Scene iii).

F major. c'-a", [f'-f "]. 4/4. 1'05". V/m, P/e.

For: Ten; [Bar].
Subject: A mock incantation.
Voice: Steps, broken chords; 8ves; recit. style leading to patter-song.
Piano: Chordal.
Comment: Sung by Vecchio, 'a teacher of Latin and Musick, a reputed
Wizard'. For an actor rather than a singer. The only a" comes
at the final cadence, and could be sung down the 8ve; in any
case this phrase really belongs to an answering voice, after
the conjuration is concluded. It could be made an effective
comic song. Bars 14-16: metheglin was mead, a drink made
from honey; Peter is Peter-sameene, a rich and delicate
Malaga wine.

(17) **From the famous peak of Derby** (Ben Jonson, *The Gypsies Meta-
morphosed*, 1621).

G major. e'-e", [g'-d"]. 3/2,3/4. 45". 2 St. V/e, P/e.

For: C-Ten, Bar.
Subject: Don't be afraid of us gypsies; give us some presents and we
will tell your fortunes.
Voice: Mostly by step; simple rhythm.
Piano: Chordal.
Comment: A cheerful dance-like piece, which could be sung in duet with
a bass. Music for the whole masque was composed by Lanier.
Variants from the masque given below: St. 1, bar 3: the
Devil's Arse – a cave in Castleton, Derbyshire, now politely
called Peak Cavern; *that's* = *there*; bar 5: *make* = *keep*; bar 7:
There = *Thus*; *Gipsies* = *Egyptians*; bar 27: *Ribbons* =
Ribands; bar 29: *saffron* = *saffroned*, dyed orange-yellow; bar
31: *And* – missing in masque. St. 2, bars 7-8: *And not cause
you quit your places* – for the performance at Windsor this
line replaced the original: *And not cause you cut your laces*,
meaning 'Will not make the ladies faint', which would mean
that the laces of their bodices would be cut to allow the blood
to flow more freely; bar 9: *futures* = *fortunes*; bar 12: *your* =
the; bar 30: Burleigh was where the first performance took
place; bar 33: hurly = a disturbance, affray. Notes from
Parfitt. The phrase 'hurly-burly' was already common.
Printed in Playford, 1673.

(18) **'Tis late and cold** (Beaumont and Fletcher, *The Lover's Progress*,
1623. Act III, Scene i).

G minor. F-d', [G-b°*b*]. 4/4,6/8,4/4. 1'20". V/m, P/e.

For: Bass.
Subject: Sit by the fire, order what drinks you like, food will come
            later.
Voice: Dramatic recit. almost Purcellian in style; wide leaps, dotted
            rhythms, melisma; dance section.
Piano: Chordal.
Comment: Original copy headed 'For a Base alone. / Myne Osts songe. /
            Sung in ye Mad-lover'; it may have been unaccompanied in
            the play. A good dramatic piece for a bass with reasonable
            flexibility of voice. The Host is a ghost, he died three weeks
            previously but has appeared to meet important guests!
            Variants in play: bar 7: *good* omitted; bar 8: *the = a*; bar 9:
            beds = bed; bar 10: *down = down's*; bar 11: *may = shall*; bar
            13: *well* omitted; bar 23; *drinking = drink*; bar 28: *a = the*; bar
            31: *the = your*.

(19) Charon, Oh Charon. Dialogue for Mezzo and Baritone, beyond the
scope of this volume.

Note: Songs (20)-(26) are probably, but not certainly, by Johnson.

(20) Hark hark! the lark (Shakespeare, *Cymbeline*, c. 1609. Act II, Scene
iii).
            F major. f'-a", [f'-f "]. 4/4. 40". V/me, P/e.
For: Sop, Ten.
Subject: Arise, 'tis morning.
Voice: Steps, broken chords, melismas; free rhythm, suggestions of
            dance.
Piano: Chordal, some bass melody.
Comment: Two lines from the lyric as it appears in the play are omitted,
            but could be included by repeating bars 3-9: 'His steeds to
            water at those springs / On chaliced flowers that lies. / And'.
            Bar 8: Phoebus – Apollo, the Sun-God. Bar 10: winking =
            closed. Bar 11, Marybuds = marigolds.

(21) Adieu, fond love (Beaumont and Fletcher, *The Lover's Progress*,
1623. Act III, Scene i).
            G minor. b°b-d". 4/4. 2". V/me, P/me.
For: Mezzo, C-Ten, Bar; Cont, Bass.
Subject: I will forsake earthly love for heavenly.
Voice: Steps, skips, short scale, melismas; speech rhythm.
Piano: Chordal, but considerable movement in bass.
Comment: The supposedly dead Lidian is reported to have written this
            'his long and last farewell to Love and Women'. Though the
            source needed much correction it was well worth transcrib-

ing; in spite of some clumsy moments it has much beauty. Variants in play: bar 16/17: *heaven = heaven doth*; bars 27-28: *by eternity and joy*; bar 30/32: *thoughts = love*.

(22) **Come away, Hecate.**   ⎫ Dialogues, beyond the scope of
(23) **Get you hence.**   ⎬ this volume.
                                        ⎭

(24) **Have you seen but the bright lily grow?** (Ben Jonson, *The Devil is an Ass*, 1616. Act II, Scene vi). Coll 24.

      F major. e'-f ", [f'-f "]. 4/4. 1'10". V/me, P/e.

For: [Sop], Ten; [Mezzo], high Bar.
Subject: She is whiter than snow, softer than wool, sweeter than honey.
Voice: Steps, skips, broken chords, short melismas; speech rhythms.
Piano: Chordal.
Comment: An alternative lute accompaniment is provided. There are six different sources for this famous song, and the one followed here differs considerably from the version given in Coll 24. Line 1: *bright* – Dolmetsch mentions one source giving *white* instead of *bright*, 'the last line of the poem shows *white* to be correct'. However, Parfitt, *New OB* and Ault give *bright*, in giving the three stanza version of the poem from Jonson's collection of verse called *Underwoods*, 1640. The first stanza (not the last, as stated by Dolmetsch) does not appear in the play. Line 8: nard = spikenard, an aromatic ointment. It would require considerable modification of the music to fit the missing first and second stanzas, but the result would make a remarkable song. They run as follows:

      'See the chariot at hand here of Love, / Wherein my lady rideth! / Each that draws is a swan or a dove, / And well the car Love guideth. / As she goes, all hearts do duty / Unto her beauty; / And enamoured do wish, so they might / But enjoy such a sight, / That they still were to run by her side, / Through swords, through seas, whither she would ride. // Do but look on her eyes, they do light / All that Love's world compriseth! / Do but look on her hair, it is bright / As Love's star when it riseth! / Do but mark, her forehead's smoother / Than words that soothe her; / And from her arched brows such a grace / Sheds itself through the face, / As alone there triumphs to the life / All the gain, all the good of the elements' strife.'

(25) **Orpheus I am** (Beaumont and Fletcher, *The Mad Lover*, c. 1616. Act IV, Scene i).

	C minor. c'-f ", [g'-e"b]. 4/4,6/4. 2'. V/me, P/e.
For:	Bar.
Subject:	Orpheus warns man of the perils of love, and of the greater perils of failing to love.
Voice:	Mostly by step, some skips; 6th leaps and drops, melismas; recit. and (6/4) aria, with short concluding recit. phrase. Some additional melismas given above the stave.
Piano:	Chordal.
Comment:	Sung by Stremnon, in the guise of Orpheus, attempting to calm Memnon's madness; it is followed almost at once by **56 (19)**. See also **56 (9)**. Variants in play: bar 33: *Those = They*; bar 34: *died = die*; bar 43: *their = these*. Dramatic, it could be made effective.

(26) **Tell me, dearest** (Beaumont and Fletcher; *The Captain*, c. 1612. Act II, Scene ii).

	G minor. g'-f ", [g'-e"b]. 4/4. 30". 3 St. V/me, P/e.
For:	Sop, Ten.
Subject:	Questions and answers on love and women.
Voice:	Steps, skips, short sequences, melismas; rhythms fairly simple.
Piano:	Chordal.
Comment:	Sung in the play by Frank ('a lady passionately in love') and Clora ('a witty companion to Frank'). In spite of question and answer form it can be performed satisfactorily as a solo. Spink prints two versions, one for solo voice and one dialogue; strangely, although the play has two singers it is the solo version that shows the words as given in the play, with the following exceptions. St. 3, line 1: *can women = yet can they*; line 3: *too and allay = and delay*.

ROBERT JONES
fl. 1600 – 1610

57 THE FIRST BOOK OF SONGES & AYRES Of foure parts with Tableture for the Lute. So made that all the parts together, or either of them severally may be sung to the Lute, Opherian or Viol de Gambo. 1600. S & B edition by E.H. Fellowes, 1925; revised by Thurston Dart, 1959. Out of print. The partsong versions are given in *MB* LIII.

(9) When love on time and measure makes his ground. Coll 19.

A minor. e′-e″, [g′-d″]. 2/2. 1′15″, [1′05″]. 2 St. V/me, P/me.

For: Mezzo, C-Ten, Bar.

Subject: It is easy to make a pretence of love.

Voice: Steps, small skips; some rhythmic variety.

Piano: Chordal, with occasional decoration.

Comment: Repeat advisable. The poem appears in the commonplace book of John Lilliat (Rawl. Poet. 148) and may be by him. Tempo relationship has caused problems: Coll 19 has semibreve = bar, Dart has minim = bar; crotchet = crotchet [crotchet = minim Coll 19] works very well. Line 1: *on = and* in Jones; makes his ground = bases his argument. Coll 19: second bar of the first time bars should be deleted.

(18) What if I seek for love of thee? Coll 6; Coll 20, *A minor*; Coll 21, *F# minor*.

G minor. d′-f″, [f′-d″]. 4/4. 1′, [40″]. 2 St. V/e, P/e.

For: *Sop, Ten*; Mezzo, Bar; *C-Ten*.

Subject: I could easily fall in love with you; reject or encourage me without delay.

Voice: Steps, small skips; many short sequences, rising scales; simple but varied rhythms.

Piano: Chordal with decorations; some simple counterpoint.

Comment: Repeat optional. A lively song. St. 1, line 3: desert = merit; line 4: sue = plead; line 11: remove = depart. St. 2, line 5: beguile = cheat. Colls 20, 21: accompaniment and introduction to each stanza by Keel.

58 THE SECOND BOOK OF SONGS AND AYRES Set out to the Lute, the base Violl the playne way, or the Base by tableture after the leero fashion. 1601. S & B edition by E.H. Fellowes, 1926. Out of print.

(4) Dreames and imaginations. Colls 19, 28.

G minor. f′#-a″, [g′-d″]. 2/2. 1′30″, [1′]. 3 St. V/me, P/me.

For: Ten.

Subject: I have nothing left but useless dreams, since she has betrayed me.

Voice: Steps, skips, sequences; slightly chromatic; varied rhythms.

Piano: Moderately contrapuntal.

Comment: Repeat optional. An interesting song, though some of the verse is a little obscure. The violent false relations in bar 18 are unconvincing, though given in both Colls; it is better to sing f′ natural. The underlay of stanzas 2/3 will need care. St. 2, line 2: stand to = abide by; lines 5-6: he (?the blind child Cupid) is not wrong in thinking he has pierced me to the heart. Coll 28: bar 17, beat 1, RH: f′ has a sharp not given other editions.

(7) Fie, what a coil is here. Colls 6, 28.

G major. d′-g″, [g′-e″]. 2/2,3/4. 1′10″, [50″]. 2 St. V/me, P/me.

For: Sop.

Subject: Don't you dare kiss me – till I am ready!

Voice: Steps, small skips; legato phrases mixed with broken up passages; varied rhythms.

Piano: Chords and a little counterpoint.

Comment: Repeat optional. An excellent song for a soprano with a sense of humour. Bars 19-26: proportion suggests minim = dotted minim, though crotchet = crotchet is equally possible; rhythm is that of a Lavolta. St. 1, line 1: coil = turmoil; line 4: ne'er the near = never any nearer (to a target); line 6: billing = kissing. An MS copy has a third stanza, given by Doughtie: 'Tush, tush, tush, now leave for shame / My mother comes, I pray forbear. / Hark, hark, hark how she calls; / Ay me, here's much to do. / Think you with kisses / To win love's blisses / O no, no, no, there's more to do. / Whoe: quicke dispatch, I shall be shent (punished) / Now since 'tis done I needs must be content.' Coll 28: bar 35, beat 1, RH: g′ for d′ of other editions (bar 34).

(9) Now what is love? Colls 19, 26; Coll 9, *Bb major*; Coll 10, *F major*.

G major. d′-d″, [g′-d″]. 3/4. 55″, [40″]. 5 St. V/e, P/e.

For: *Sop, Ten*; Mezzo, C-Ten, Bar; *Cont, Bar.*

Subject: An attempt to describe the many sides of love.

Voice: Mostly by step, one or two skips; simple rhythm.

Piano: Chordal, some simple counterpoint.

Comment: Repeat optional. A pleasant dance tune, with some imitation between voice and accompaniment. Colls 9, 10, omit St. 2/4. The poem is printed in Davison, 1602, *PN*, 1593, and *EH*, 1600, in which an ascription to Raleigh was cancelled and *ignoto* substituted. Though Latham is doubtful whether it is by Raleigh, both Ault and *OB 16* accept it as his, and print the text as in *PN*, which Rollins considers the superior version. Variants as follows: St. 1, line 3: *pleasures = pleasure*; line 4: *sauncing = sanctus.* St. 2: omitted in Coll 26; line 1: *Now = Yet*; line 4: *blood = bloods*; line 5: *their = the.* St. 3, line 1: *Now = Yet*; *faine* (Colls 19, 26, and *EMV*) = *saine [sayen]*, all other editions; lines 3-5: *It is a tooth-ache, or like pain, / It is a game where none doth gain, / The lass saith no, and would full fain*; full fain = gladly enjoy. St. 4, lines 2-3: *It is a yea, it is a nay, / A pretty kind of sporting fray*; line 4: *decaie* = *away*;. line 5: *whilst* = *while*. St. 5, line 1: *Now* = *Yet*; line 4: moe = more; line 5: proves = tries it; *shall* = *must*; line 6: *as I well know* (*as well I know*, Coll 26) = *sweet friend I trow*. Doughtie gives no less than 14 more stanzas, from various MS versions. Stanzas 1 and 5 appear as the third song in Thomas Heywood's *The Rape of Lucrece*, 1608, and probably used this setting, since the play version uses the same word repetitions as in this song.

(10) Love's god is a boy. Colls 13, 26; Coll 14, *C major*.
G major. g'-g". 4/4,3/4,4/4. 1'05", [45"]. 3 St. V/me, P/me.

For:	Sop, Ten; *Mezzo, C-Ten, Bar*; *Cont, Bass*.
Subject:	Cupid is but a boy, who must be kept in his place.
Voice:	Steps, small skips; sequences, patter; simple but varied rhythms.
Piano:	Contrapuntal and somewhat unexpectedly chromatic.
Comment:	Could be fun. If the tempo relationship given seems rushed try crotchet = crotchet. St 1, line 2: cowherds = cowards, and thus given in Coll 26. Coll 14: spacing of accompaniment much modified. Coll 26: bar 10, beat 1, RH: f' for c' of other editions (bar 10, beat 3); bar 5 of refrain, beat 1, RH: g° for b° of other editions.

(17) Love is a bable. Colls 11, 19; Coll 12, *G major*.
C major. d'-g", [g'-g"]. 4/4,3/4,4/4. 35". 4 St. V/me, P/e.

For:	Ten; *C-Ten, Bar*; *Bass*.
Subject:	Love is many things, mostly bad, and not worth the trouble.
Voice:	Steps, broken chords, sequences; some rhythmic variety.
Piano:	Simple counterpoint.
Comment:	An excellent setting, full of life and humour. The tempo relationships suggested differ: Colls 11, 12, have minim = dotted minim, Coll 19 has semibreve = dotted minim; crotchet = crotchet works well. The typical Jones false relation near the end is unavoidable. St. 2, line 2: sable = mourning garments, but Doughtie suggests this is an error for *saddle*. St. 3, line 2: yellow – a colour associated with jealousy; line 4: privy = secret. St. 4, line 3: moe = more. In *Wit and Mirth* 5 and 6, set by Leveridge.

59 ULTIMUM VALE Whereof The first part is for the Lute, the Voyce, and the Viole Degambo. 1605. S & B edition by E.H. Fellowes, 1926. Out of print.

(2) Beauty sat bathing (Anthony Munday). Colls 19, 28.
G minor. d'-f ", [g'-d"]. 2/2. 1'05", [45"]. 2 St. V/me, P/me.

For: Bar.
Subject: Beauty was bathing, but I forbore to look.
Voice: Mostly by step; simple but varied rhythms.
Piano: Chordal, slightly chromatic.
Comment: Repeat optional. Also set by Corkine, 41 (9), and Pilkington, 70 (18), who includes the 'hey nonny no' ending of the original poem. The words are printed in *EH*, headed 'To Colin Cloute', and stated to be by 'Sheepheard Tony'. From the prose romance *Primaleon of Greece*, Book II, chapter 27, translated by Munday, 1596. Variants below are from *EH*: St. 1, line 5: intiste = enticed; line 7: *cried = said*; line 8: *delights were = desire was*; chidden = rebuked. St. 2, line 2: *But = When*; line 7: *the = this*. Coll 28: bar 3, last note, voice: b′ for c′ of other editions.

(3) **Go to bed sweet muse**. Colls 6, 19, 26, 32; Coll 20, *A minor*; Coll 21, *F minor*.

G minor. d′-f ″, [g′-e″b]. 4/4. 40″, [25″]. 3 St. V/e, P/e.
For: *Sop, Ten*; Mezzo, Bar; *C-Ten*.
Subject: Advice to a young man not to worry about the problems of love.
Voice: Mostly by step; simple rhythm.
Piano: Chordal, with slight decoration.
Comment: Repeat optional. A little gem of a song. The f′ natural in bar 8 of the voice could be an error for f′ sharp, Jones's songs are notorious for their misprints. St. 1, line 1: muse = poet. St. 2, line 4: franzy = frenzy, as given in Earle, 1615; line 5: toy = caress; line 6: annoy = annoyance; line 6: leave = cease. Note the change of accentuation in the second part of stanza 3, which requires a break after *beguile* to recover. Colls 20, 21: accompaniment and introduction to each stanza by Keel. The accidental in bar 8 of the voice referred to above is taken as a misprint, as it is in Coll 32, where the introduction and accompaniment are by Michael Diack and the repeat of the last 8 bars is ignored. Coll 26: bar 7, beats 3-4, voice: crotchet crotchet, for dotted crotched quaver of all other editions.

(5) **What if I speed**. Colls 19, 28. Coll 22, *A minor*; Coll 23, *F minor*.
G minor. d′-f ″, [g′-d″]. 2/2. 55″. 3 St. V/me, P/me.
For: *Tenor*; Bar.
Subject: Whether I succeed or fail love is a good game, and is always worth a try.
Voice: Steps, short scales, sequence of 4ths; varied rhythms.
Piano: Chordal with some decoration.

Comment: Lively and effective. Given in Earle, 1615. The two violent
            false relations pointed out in Coll 19 as 'original' are almost
            certainly misprints, though agreed in Coll 28. Bar 15, beat 1,
            RH: make e′ natural into e′ flat; bar 21, beat 3, RH: make f′
            sharp into f′ natural; bar 20, beat 2, voice: the f′ natural
            should probably be f′ sharp. In St. 2 and 3 many of the quaver
            pairs carry only one syllable, and in the first two lines of St. 2
            the final *ed*s must be pronounced. St. 1, line 2: affected =
            fancied; line 3: have at = have a go at; line 5: meaning close =
            intention secret; line 6: hit = succeed. St. 2, line 2: leathe =
            Lethe, the river of forgetfulness. St. 3, line 2: chance of =
            chance on, happen to find; line 9: Vulcan set a net to catch his
            wife Venus making love to Mars; line 10: wot = knows. Colls
            22, 23: accompaniment and introduction to each stanza by
            Keel. Only the first stanza given. Line 6: *It's* = *'Tis*, all other
            editions; line 8: *speede* = *hit*, all other editions. Page 110, bar
            11, voice: delete slur over notes 4-5, add tie to notes 3-4; bars
            13-15: the accidentals in the voice fit Keel's harmony, and are
            a possible solution to the misprints of the original.

(6) **Sweet if you like and love me still** (Francis Davison, *A Poetical
      Rhapsody*, 1602). Colls 19, 26.
                G minor. d′-f ″, [g′-d″]. 2/2. 50″. 2 St. V/me, P/me.
For: Mezzo, Bar.
Subject: If you are faithful I will love you always, but if not I shall hate
            you equally.
Voice: Steps, some 3rds, many repeated notes; simple rhythm.
Piano: Chordal with some decoration.
Comment: One of Jones's best serious songs. Davison, 1602, has the
            following variants: St. 1, line 8: *No* = *Nor*. St. 2, line 1: *one*
            (Coll 26 and *EMV*) = *me* (Coll 19 and *EMV* note); line 2: *loves*
            = *love*; line 5: *Yet* = *If*. St. 1, line 3: from your promise start =
            withdraw from your promise.

60 **A MUSICALL DREAME** Or The Fourth Booke Of Ayres; The Third
      part is for one Voyce alone, or to the Lute, the Basse Viole, or to both if
      you please, Whereof, two are Italian Ayres. 1609. S & B edition by E.H.
      Fellowes, 1927. Out of print.

(19) **In Sherwood lived stout Robin Hood.** Colls 7, 19, 29; Coll 8,
       Eb major.
                G major. d′-g″, [g′-e″]. 3/4. 45″. 4 St. V/me, P/me.
For: [Sop], Ten; *[Mezzo], C-Ten, Bar.*
Subject: Even Robin Hood was defeated by love, as are we all.
Voice: Steps, skips, broken chords; 8ve drops; rhythms fairly
            simple.

Piano: Chordal.

Comment: A lively dance number. *EMV* suggests this may be the original of 'For bonny sweet Robin is all my joy', sung by Ophelia in *Hamlet*, Act IV, Scene v. St. 1, lines 5-6: note pun on *heart* and *hart*. St. 2, line 6: logde = lodged. St. 3, line 6: obeydness = ?obedience. Coll 19: St. 4, line 1: *end* = *wend*, all other editions. Fellowes prints the song in F major, without comment, though his notes on misprints appear to refer to a version in G major! Coll 19: bar 29, voice, beat 3: all other editions add #; bar 34: all other editions have repeat from here to the end.

(20) Ite caldi sospiri (Francesco Petrarch). Coll 19.

                    G minor. d'-d″, [f'-d″]. 2/2. 1'40″. V/m, P/me.

For: Mezzo, C-Ten, Bar.

Subject: Let me die, since there is no pity.

Voice: Steps, small skips; many melismas, some quite long.

Piano: Chordal, somewhat chromatic.

Comment: Italianate in style. The first four lines of Petrarch's Sonnet CLIII, according to *EMV*. Coll 19 has an English version by Chester Kallman, if this is used *she* may be changed to *he* in line 3.

61 THE MUSES GARDIN FOR DELIGHTS Or the fift Booke of Ayres, onely for the Lute, the Base-vyoll, and the Voyce. 1610. S & B edition by E.H. Fellowes, 1927. Out of print.

(14) There was a wyly ladde. Colls 19, 27.

                    G minor. f'-g″, [g'-d″]. 2/2. 30″. 6 St. V/me, P/me.

For: Sop, Ten.

Subject: Description of the progress of a flirtation.

Voice: Steps, and skips; simple but broken up rhythms.

Piano: Chordal with decorations.

Comment: Fun. Some stanzas could be omitted. St. 2, line 1: tearms = terms, periods. St. 3, line 1: nice = reluctant. St. 4, line 3: bane = curse. Coll 19: bar 8: for the original c' sharp here changed to a° Coll 27 offers c' natural and f' sharp, and Fellowes has c' natural and f' natural, which seems the best solution. Bar 17, beat 2, RH: the b'*b* should probably be a crotchet g', as given in Fellowes. Coll 27 omits stanzas 2 and 6.

(15) My father fain would have me take. Colls 6, 27.

                    G major. g'-g″, [g'-e″]. 3/4. 35″. 5 St. V/e, P/e.

For: Sop.

Subject: Father wants me to marry, and so do I, whatever mother says!

Voice: Steps; simple rhythm.
Piano: Chordal with decorations.
Comment: Effective song, the rhythm being that of a Lavolta. Some
              stanzas could be omitted – it might well be worth replacing
              the last two lines of St. 4 with those of St. 3, and omitting the
              rest of St. 3. Coll 27 omits stanzas 3 and 4. St. 1, line 1: fain =
              gladly; line 4: *afeared* = *afraid,* in source and Coll 27; line 6:
              goodly stuff = real rubbish; lines 7 and 8 = *marry* and *bury*
              have surely been interchanged in error, though neither *EMV*
              nor Doughtie make any comment (Coll 27 has: *Faith! let some
              young man marry me / Or let my mother bury me,* which seems
              a little ruthless in the way of emendation!) St. 2, lines 7 and 8
              = I would be mad to refuse to marry simply because I could
              not choose my husband, though it would be nice to do so. St. 3,
              line 4: suck a dug = return to the breast (like a baby). Bar 3,
              beat 3, RH: g° Coll 6 and Fellowes, b° source and Coll 27 (bar
              2, beat 3); bar 5, beat 3, RH: g′ of Coll 6 and Fellowes not given
              in source or Coll 27 (bar 3, beat 3); bar 15, beat 1, RH: add g′ in
              Coll 6; bar 25, beat 1, RH: source has b° and g′, Coll 27 offers
              b° and d′, other editions offer a° and a′.

(16) My love hath her true love betrayed. Coll 6.
              G major. g′-f″, [g′-e″]. 2/2,6/4. 45″. 3 St. V/e, P/e.
For: Bar.
Subject: My love may have been unfaithful, but why complain?
              Women are like that, and cannot help it.
Voice: Steps, small skips; some rhythmic variety; varied phrase-
              lengths.
Piano: Chordal with decorations.
Comment: A nice change from the usual lover's complaints. St. 1, line 5:
              aught – missing in source, added in *EMV.*

NICHOLAS LANIER
1588 – 1666

62 (THE MASKE OF SQUIRES. 1614. See **39.** Coll 4)

(1) Bring away this sacred tree (Thomas Campion).
              G major. d′-f″, [g′-e″]. 2/2. 1′20″, [55″]. V/me, P/e.
For: Mezzo, Bar.
Subject: Bring this sacred tree to Bel-Anna (Queen Anne, present at
              the performance) who can break the spells upon you.
Voice: Steps, skips, broken chords, quick repeated notes; 6th drops,
              8ve leap; great rhythmic variety.

Piano: Chordal, as for recit.
Comment: Repeat optional. A song in the new Italian style, which would
                   lead to Purcell. This song is sung by 'Eternitie'; towards the
                   end of it 'the three Destinies set the Tree of Gold before the
                   Queen'.

THOMAS LUPO
1571 – 1628

63 (THE MASKE FOR LORD HAYS. 1607. See 34. Coll 4.)

(3) Shows and nightly revels (Thomas Campion).
                   G minor. d'-e''b, [f'-d'']. 4/4. 1'15''. V/e, P/e.
For: Mezzo, C-Ten, Bar.
Subject: Britain can now celebrate friendship between once divided
                   kingdoms.
Voice: Steps, skips; 8ve leap; simple rhythms, many paired
                   quavers.
Piano: Chordal, some decoration.
Comment: The divided kingdoms were England and Scotland, the
                   marriage being between Lord Hays of Scotland and the
                   daughter of Lord Denny of England. Written as a dance, the
                   words were added for publication. Line 8: an allusion to the
                   'Gunpowder Plot' of 1605, a fitting contrast to the unity
                   which the masque celebrates (Davis).

(5) Time, that leads the fatal round (Thomas Campion).
                   G major. d'-e'', [g'-e'']. 4/4. 45''. V/e, P/e.
For: Mezzo, C-Ten, Bar.
Subject: Time has here stayed, and Venus and her Cupids celebrate
                   our feast.
Voice: Steps, skips, repeated notes; 8ve drop; quaver pairs, fairly
                   regular rhythms and phrase-lengths.
Piano: Chordal.
Comment: A dance, words added for publication.

RICHARD MARTIN
?1517 – ?1618

64 Change thy mind since she doth change (Robert Devereux, Earl of Essex). Colls 1, 6, 28.
                   G minor. g'-g''. 2/2. 45'', [35'']. 5 St. V/e, P/e.
For: Ten.
Subject: A bitter denunciation of his false love (Queen Elizabeth?).

Voice: Steps, small skips; very simple rhythm.
Piano: Chordal, some simple decoration.
Comment: Repeat of second half optional. Some stanzas could be omit-
           ted. St. 2, line 4: *deceived = betrayed, OB 16*, and Ault, which
           maintains the rhyme. St. 5, line 4: quite forgotten – not
           remembered, *and* replaced as begetter (of children). St. 5, line
           5: changed base – changed for the worse, *and* obtained a bad
           exchange; line 6: *vile = vilde, EMV, vild, OB 16*; vile and
           reviled, she is changed for the worse in allowing a worse lover
           the use of her body, now reviled as vile.
              Ault and Doughtie give an MS version of the poem from
           before 1600 (Rawl. Poet. 85), which is also used in Grosart's
           The Poems of Robert, Earl of Essex, 1872. It has many
           interesting differences: St. 1, line 3: *untruth = untruths*; line
           4: *excuse = accuse*. St. 2, line 2: *she hath still = still she did*;
           line 4: *that = which*; line 5: *although = but all*. St. 3 is given as
           stanza 5: line 3: *being once = having been*; line 4 = *Leave to
           love* (leave off loving) *and love no other*. St. 4 is given as St. 3:
           line 2: *preservest = preserved'st*; line 3: *all joys are = thy joy is*;
           line 4: *deservest = deserved'st*; lines 5-6: *They envy what's not
           their own* (Ault), *They enjoy what's just their own* (Doughtie) /
           Happier life to live alone. St. 5 is not given, but the following
           appears as St. 4: 'Yet this much to ease my mind: / Let her
           know what she hath gotten, / She, whom time hath proved
           unkind, / Having changed, is quite forgotten. / Fortune now
           hath done her worst; / Would she had done so at first.' In most
           places this is an improvement on the poem as given by
           Martin; in particular, the alternative stanza given above
           avoids the problems of the last two lines as they appear in the
           song. There are several other versions of the poem, mostly
           close to Martin but with minor variants.
              Coll 28: bar 7, beats 1-2, LH: B c° d° B, dotted quaver
           semiquaver two quavers, for two crotchet Bs of other editions;
           bar 8, beat 3, LH: d°, not given in other editions.

GEORGE MASON
fl. 1610 – 1617

**65 THE AYRES THAT WERE SUNG AND PLAYED AT BROUGHAM
CASTLE.** With John Earsden. 1618. S & B edition by Ian Spink, 1963.
Out of print.

(5) Dido was the Carthage Queen. Coll 6.
           C major. g'-g". 2/2. 40", [30"]. 3 St. V/me, P/e.

For: Ten.
Subject: Aeneas betrayed Dido, but it was on the orders of Jove, so, gentlemen, follow his example!
Voice: Steps, skips, up to 8ves; rhythm quite varied within four-square phrasing.
Piano: Chordal.
Comment: Repeat optional. The following note was omitted from Coll 6 in error: George Mason was in the service of Francis Clifford, Earl of Cumberland, in 1610. In 1617 there was an 'Entertainment' before James I at Brougham Castle, and in the following year the music was published, being 'composed by Mr George Mason and Mr John Earsden'. Little more is known of Mason and nothing of Earsden. It is probable but not certain that Mason was the composer of the song included here; it is also likely that Campion provided the words for the 'Entertainment'.

St. 1, line 4: *fight* = *sight*, *EMV*; line 5: *road* = *rode*, *EMV*. St. 2, line 1: Hymen – the God of marriage; line 6: Jove's winged son – Mercury, messenger of the Gods. An excellent song for a male audience!

JOHN MAYNARD
1517 – after 1614

66 THE XII WONDERS OF THE WORLD Set and composed for the Violl de Gambo, the Lute, and the Voyce to Sing the Verse, all three jointly, and none several. 1611. S & B edition by Anthony Rooley, 1985 (*LS* 20). Tablature provided.

A fascinating and quite original set of songs, though they do not strictly qualify for inclusion in this guide, since both lute and gamba are essential. However, with care a pianist could conflate the two parts, which are contrapuntal, fairly chromatic, with considerable rhythmic variety. The vocal lines. too, are immensely varied, scales, sequences, leaps of all kinds, including a diminished 8ve, long legato lines, broken phrases, imitation of the accompaniment, and variable rhythms. The complete set would be an interesting challenge for a group of singers, lasting about 25', or 17' without repeats. Five singers would be needed; Sop, Mezzo, Ten, Bar, Bass. The poems, by Sir John Davies, were written in January 1600, and published in *A Poetical Rhapsody* in 1608. They are, as Anthony Rooley says, pithy epigrams; satirical descriptions of twelve representative characters of the age. Performed with understanding and imagination they could be effective today.

(1) Long have I lived in court.
> G minor. c'-g″, f'-g″. 1'15″, [1'].

For: Ten.
Comment: 'The Courtier'. Bar 3: livde = lived; bar 7: suters = suitors; bar 8: smoake = smoke, that is, something of no real value; bar 9: a comma after *hate* clarifies the sense.

(2) My calling is divine.
> G minor. d'-f ″, [f'-d″]. 2', [1'25″].

For: Bar.
Comment: 'The Divine' (The Clergyman). Bar 4: chop-church = a dealer or trafficker in ecclesiastical benefices, *EMV*; bar 10: loose = lose; bars 8-13: see the story of the Judgment of Solomon, I Kings 3:16; bar 10, viol, note 3 should be a quaver.

(3) My occupation is the noble trade of kings.
> G major. g'-a″, [g'-f ″]. 1'15″, [50″].

For: Ten.
Comment: 'The Soldier'. Bar 5: try-all = trial; bar 7: Mars – God of war; Maister = Master; Bacchus – God of drink and revelry.

(4) The law my calling is.
> D minor. a°-c″, [d'-a″]. 1'40″, [1'10″].

For: Bass.
Comment: 'The Lawyer'. Bar 6: sutes = law-suits; bar 8: bewray = betray.

(5) I studie to uphold.
> G minor. a'-f ″, [d'-d″]. 2', [1'20″].

For: Bar.
Comment: 'The Physician'. Bar 15: 'pothecaries' = chemists'.

(6) My trade doth everything.
> G minor. c'#-d″, [f'#-c″]. 1'45″, [1'15″].

For: Bar or Bass.
Comment: 'The Merchant'. Bar 7: allye = join; bar 11: ingrose = engross, monopolise.

(7) Though strange outlandish spirits praise.
> G major. d'-g″, [g'-e″]. 1'50, [1'20″].

For: Ten.
Comment: 'The Country Gentleman'. Bar 13: pertake = partake; bar 16: haukes = hawks; bar 14: soul = sole, *and* soul; bars 27-28: abridge my charge or train – reduce my expenses and the size of my establishment; bar 26, lute, bass, note 2: e° not f °.

(8) **How many things.**

                    G major. d'-d'', [g'-d'']. 1'40'', [1'10''].

For: Bar or Bass.

Comment: 'The Bachelor'. Bar 19, lute, bass, note 3: g° natural, not g° sharp; bar 23, viol, note 3: f° sharp, not f° natural.

(9) **I onely am the man.**

                    G minor. d'-f'', [f'#-d'']. 1'40'', [1'15''].

For: Bar.

Comment: 'The Married Man'.

(10) **The first of all our sexe.**

                    G minor. c'-e''b, [f'#-d'']. 2', [1'25''].

For: Mezzo.

Comment: 'The Wife'. Bar 9: in counsaile = in counsel, in confidence.

(11) **My dying husband knew.**

                    G minor. d'-a'', [g'-g'']. 2'05'', [1'30''].

For: Sop.

Comment: 'The Widow'. Bar 17: lute, bass, note 1: b° should have a natural.

(12) **I marriage would forsweare.**

                    G minor. c'-e''b, [d'-d'']. 1'40'', [1'20''].

For: Mezzo.

Comment: 'The Maid'. Bar 13: ape in hell = see Comment to **29 (19)**; bar 28: wants = lacks.

THOMAS MORLEY
1557 – 1602

67 THE FIRST BOOKE OF AYRES Or Little Short Songs, To Sing And Play To The Lute, With The Base Viole. 1600. S & B edition by E.H. Fellowes, 1932. Revised by Thurston Dart, 1966 (*LS* 13). Tablature provided.

(1) **A painted tale.**

                    A minor. g'-g'', [a'-e'']. 2/2. 1'45'', [1'20'']. V/e, P/e.

For: Sop, Ten.

Subject: A good love poem shows skill in words rather than in love.

Voice: Steps, small skips; varied phrase-lengths; simple rhythm.

Piano: Chordal with decoration; simple counterpoint.

Comment: Repeat optional. Nice little climax at end; good legato needed throughout. Line 2: *profess* = *profest*, in source,

Doughtie notes emendation in *EMV*; line 5: *right = night*, in source, Doughtie prefers to emend as *might*.

(2, 3) Thyrsis and Milla.

G major. g'-g". 2/2. 2'50", [2'20"]. V/me, P/m.

For:	Sop, Ten.
Subject:	(2) Two lovers walk in the garden; the boy asks the girl for a posy. (3) The brings him one, laughs, and runs away.
Voice:	Steps, skips; considerable rhythmic variety and change of metre; a sequence of patter phrases in (3).
Piano:	Chordal and contrapuntal; (3) ends with fast broken chords and repeated notes.
Comment:	Repeat optional. A very enjoyable tale with scope for the imaginative performer. The tempo relationships given are satisfactory. St. 2, line 4: for an answer to the riddle see Richard Edwards' poem, 'When May is in his prime', published 1576, set by Ireland as 'The Sweet Season' – 'Take May in time, when May is gone the pleasant time is past'.

(4) With love my life was nestled (Robert Southwell, 'Mary Magdalen's complaint at Christ's Death', *Saint Peter's Complaint*, 1595). Coll 25, F major.

G major. g'-g". 2/2. 35". 3 St. V/me, P/e.

For:	Sop, Ten.
Subject:	I was happy with my true love; now it is death to live alone.
Voice:	Steps, many skips, broken chords; 8ve drop; very simple rhythm.
Piano:	Chordal, with short sequential runs in the bass.
Comment:	The second stanza is complicated, but could be omitted, as in Coll 25. Southwell's original poem has seven stanzas; Morley has set St. 5, 4, 3, in that order! Southwell's title makes the poem much more comprehensible, and should perhaps be given in a programme. St. 1, line 6: sith = since. Coll 25: Morley's St. 2 is omitted. Two bars of introduction are added to both verses, and the accompaniment is slightly modified in many places. Southwell's poem differs from Morley as follows: line 2: *sum = sonne* (4 MSS have *somme*); line 3: *was = is*; line 8: *vanities = vanitie*; line 10: *slaves = salves* (which makes much better sense); line 13: *love = life*; line 17: *and = or*; *with = to*. Printed in Forbes, 1662, 1666, 1682.

(5) I saw my lady weeping. Coll 6.

A minor. d'-e", [e'-d"]. 4/4. 2'35", [1'50"]. V/me, P/me.

For:	Mezzo, C-Ten, Bar.
Subject:	My lady in tears makes even sorrow beautiful.

Voice: Long phrases, mostly by step; one melisma; some rhythmic complexity.

Piano: Contrapuntal and decorative.

Comment: Repeat optional. See Dowland's setting, 45 (1); Morley only uses the first stanza. This is not as intense as Dowland, but is still very beautiful. Variants in Dowland: line 1: *weeping = weep*; line 3: *perfection kept = perfection keep*.

(6) **It was a lover and his lass** (Shakespeare, *As You Like It*, 1599. Act V, Scene iii). Coll 19; Colls 6, 32, *F major*.

G major. g'-g", [f'-g"]. 2/2. 55". 4 St. V/me, P/me.

For: Sop, Ten; *Mezzo, Bar.*

Subject: The pleasures of Spring.

Voice: Steps, skips; 8ve leap; downward runs; very rhythmic with some surprises.

Piano: Contrapuntal, in three parts.

Comment: It is worth remembering that the 'carol' of St. 3 would have been a cheerful song and dance on the subject of 'gather ye rosebuds while ye may', not a funeral dirge as implied by many settings. Though the play was not published till 1623, on August 4th, 1600 the Lord Chamberlain's Men entered in the Stationer's Register 'As you like it, a booke' to 'be staied', i.e. not published at that time. The coincidence of dates suggests that this was the setting used, in spite of a few verbal discrepancies noted below: All stanzas, line 2: *with a ho = and a ho*; line 5: *hey ding a ding a ding = hey ding a ding, ding*. St. 1, line 3: *fields = field*. St. 2, line 3: *fools = folks*. St. 4, line 1: *And therefore take the present time*. St. 1, line 4: ringtime = wedding season. St. 4, line 3: prime – spring of the year, and of life – youth. Coll 32: introduction and accompaniment by Michael Diack; St. 2 omitted; the repeat of the chorus, with its fascinating change of rhythms, is also omitted.

(7) **Who is it that this dark night?** (Sir Philip Sidney, Song 11 in *Astrophel and Stella*, 1598).

G minor g'-g". 2/2. 1'30", [1']. 9 St. V/me, P/me.

For: Sop, Ten.

Subject: Dialogue between a lover in the street and his mistress at the window, who tries to persuade him to give up and leave. He finally agrees, but only because she is afraid he will disturb the neighbours and harm her reputation!

Voice: Steps, skips; simple but varied rhythms; some long phrasing.

Piano: Contrapuntal.

Comment: Repeat optional. Voice is one of the contrapuntal parts,
             joining in the imitation. First two lines of each stanza belong
             to the girl, the other three to the man. Many stanzas could be
             omitted; in most of the later stanzas make the start of the
             third phrase two crotchets instead of a minim, and slur the
             two quavers in the last phrase; this solves most of the
             problems. Variants from *Astrophel and Stella*: St. 1, line 2:
             under = underneath; line 3: *that = who*. St. 2, line 2: *those
             fond = yet those*. St. 3, line 4: *now = how much*. St. 6, line 1: *the
             = your*. St. 7, line 3: *do = doth, EMV*, but no other edition. St.
             8, line 5: *there = thee*, 1598 and 1613, though *there* in 1629
             edition of the poem; 9, line 3: *unjustest = unjust is*. St. 1, line
             2: plaineth = complains. St. 3, 5, and 6, line 2: leave = cease.
             St. 4, line 3: Doughtie quotes Ringler, 'Things change in time
             in accordance with their own natures'. St. 8, line 2: anger =
             angry. St. 9, line 2: Argus – a many-eyed monster, slain by
             Hermes and changed into a peacock; line 5: louts = servants
             (Ault).

(8) Mistress mine, well may you fare. Coll 19.

             G minor. g'-g". 2/2. 30", [20"]. 4 St. V/e, P/e.
For: Ten.
Subject: 'Tis a lovely day – come and make love; there is no one here
             but the birds. Any child can say 'go away', true lovers should
             embrace.
Voice: Steps, small skips; quick downward scale in last phrase;
             four-square rhythm.
Piano: Chordal, a little decoration.
Comment: Repeat optional. A delightful little song. All stanzas, line 5:
             coll = hug, clip = embrace. St. 2, line 4: *out*, Coll 19, *but*, *LS* 13,
             our, *EMV*, but says source reads *out*; Doughtie says source
             has *our*, as also given in Earle, 1615. He also gives an
             alternative poem of 5 stanzas from an MS source.

(9) Can I forget what reason's force.

             C major. g'-g". 2/2,3/2,2/2. 1'. 4 St. V/me, P/me.
For: Sop, Ten.
Subject: A rather difficult poem, which seems to be contrasting true
             love with mere fancy.
Voice: Steps, small skips, broken chords; varied rhythms and
             meters; fairly regular phrase-lengths.
Piano: Chordal with decoration, some imitation.
Comment: The tempo relationship given is satisfactory. St. 4, line 1: *fool*
             should probably be *foul* (Doughtie).

(10) **Love winged my hopes**. Coll 25, F major.

> G major. f'-g", [g'-g"]. 2/2,3/2,2/2. 1'35", [1']. 3 St. V/me, P/m.

For: Sop, Ten.

Subject: Love gave me hope, but warned me not to fly too high; I did, and was burnt by the sun. Though my hopes lie drowned, it was for love of the purest light of heaven.

Voice: Steps, small skips, broken chords; short sequential phrases; quick rising scales right up to g".

Piano: Contrapuntal, with imitation and fast overlapping scale passages.

Comment: Repeat optional. Time relationship in *LS* 13, semibreve = dotted semibreve satisfactory, but crotchet = minim seems more likely, since *pleasure* and *measure* will then match. Some small problems of underlay: St. 2, line 2: either repeat *enamour'd sought* or *to woo the sun*; line 6: repeat *consumed* in second scale passage. St. 3, line 6: repeat *purest* in second scale passage. A song that well repays the study required. Also set by Jones, **58** (1), with the following variants: St. 2, line 1: *flight = light* in source, *flight* in Jones. St. 2, line 3: *doth = did*; line 3: *fates = fate*. St. 3, line 1: hap = luck, fortune. Coll 25: one bar introduction added, and repeat written out. Bar 4, voice: notes 3/4 should be two crotchets. Accompaniment slightly modified throughout. Only the first stanza given.

(11) **What if my mistress now**. Coll 25.

> G major. e'-g", [g'-e"]. 3/2. 30". 7 St. V/e, P/e.

For: Ten.

Subject: If my mistress is unfaithful I will still love her and not complain; but if time does not give my love its due reward, I will then bid her farewell.

Voice: Mostly by step; very simple rhythm.

Comment: Looks difficult on paper, but is actually very simple triple time throughout, if the tempo relationships given are followed. Coll 25 has modernised the notation to make this clear. Some stanzas could be omitted. St. 5, line 2: omit first note of this phrase. St. 6, line 3: *mistress' longs = mistress longs*, without possessive, in source. 'EMV makes *mistress* possessive, making *longs*, I suppose, mean "long notes". But the relation to the next stanza would be clearer if *or* were emended to *for*, and the line understood thus: I'll sing this song: "My mistress longs for change" ' (Doughtie). St. 7, line 3: hap = luck, fortune. Coll 25: St. 3, 5, and 6 omitted. Introduction and interludes added; and slight modifications to accompaniment throughout.

(12) Come sorrow, come.
        A minor. g'#-a", [a'-g"]. 2/2. 2'15", [1'35"]. 3 St. V/me, P/me.
For: Sop, Ten.
Subject: Come, sorrow, let us mourn our fate; weep, but speak not; live thus till heaven is sorry for us.
Voice: Steps, small skips, chromatics; very even note values; longish phrases; the a" is first note of last phrase.
Piano: Chordal, with many contrapuntal details; chromatic.
Comment: Repeat optional. Serious and sad, but a fine song, with some marvellous false relations and a good build-up. St. 2, line 5: Not a word but mum = keep silent.

(13) Fair in a morn (Nicholas Breton, 'Astrophell his song of Phillida and Coridon'). Coll 19.
        F major. f'-g", [f'-f "]. 2/2. 45". 4 St. V/me, P/me.
For: Sop, Ten.
Subject: On a lovely morning a fair face appeared; a happy man saw it; he asked for pity and it was granted; he was so joyful that Pan came out to hear him.
Voice: Steps, skips; 8ve leaps; fast crotchets throughout.
Piano: Chordal, with some imitation.
Comment: Must be taken quickly to make its effect. The poem is full of puns and puzzles, and the whole thing is a good joke. First printed in *EH*, 1600, it also appears in several MSS and Cotgrave, 1655. The words are a fascinating textual problem discussed in detail in Coll 19. Agreeing with the suggestion that the poem as set by Morley is a rather poorly memorised version of Breton it might well be better to return to the original words (given in Coll 19) as far as the music will allow, rather than emending just the worst pieces of nonsense, the procedure adopted by both editors, though with slightly different results. This would mean omitting two lines of the poem, probably lines 7 and 8, as in Morley, or just possibly using some of the sixteen additional lines to be found in *EH*.

(14) Absence, hear thou my protestation. Coll 6.
        G major. d'-f ", [g'-d"]. 2/2. 2'05", [1'25"]. 4 St. V/me, P/me.
For: Bar.
Subject: Absence cannot harm true love; a view put forward calmly and with conviction.
Voice: Long legato phrases, with occasional short quicker ones; mostly by step.
Piano: Contrapuntal, in 2 and 3 parts.
Comment: Repeat best omitted; St. 3 could also be left out without

spoiling the argument. Some problems of underlay; Coll 6 gives possible solutions, though making no use of the variants given below. The poem, though probably not by Donne, is worthy of him, and was accepted as his by Quiller-Couch in *OB*. Though long, a very beautiful song. St. 3, line 1: want = lack; line 4: notion = understanding.

Only St. 1 survives in the only copy of Morley still in existence. The remaining stanzas given in *LS* 13 and Coll 6 are from Grierson's edition of Donne's poems, though he and others consider it to be by John Hoskyns. Patrides does not mention it. Ault (A) and apparently Doughtie (D) favour Donne, but give many variants, some of which, that might well fit the music better, are given below: St. 1, line 4: *you dare = thou canst* (A). St. 2, line 1: *right = such* (A), *Whose mistress is of such a quality,* (D); line 2: *His mind = He soon* (A); line 4: *all = his* (D); line 6: *doth not = doth* (A). St. 3: line 1: *motion = motions* (A); line 4: *by = in* (A); *her = their* (D); *notion = notions* (A). St. 4, line 4: *my brain = my secret brain* (D); line 5: *and there kiss = and kiss* (A); line 6: *And so I both enjoy and miss her,* (A), *And so enjoy her and so miss her* (D). Doughtie's variants are taken from an MS signed by John Donne; Ault's come from Davison, 1602, and are also given by Doughtie.

(17) Will you buy a fine dog?

F major. f'-a", [g'-g"]. 6/2. 1'45". V/me, P/me.

For: Ten.
Subject: Sales patter, with many double meanings and suggestions, some of which are still recognisable.
Voice: Steps, skips, many repeated notes, quick scales; great variety of rhythm and phrase-length.
Piano: Chordal with decoration, some quite quick.
Comment: Restored by Dart from an MS copy of Morley's voice and bass. Good fun to sing if you dare! Tempo decided by last two lines; these should be fast, but imply a slower start than seems likely at first. Line 3: rebatoes – the stiff collars worn c. 1590 – 1630, *EMV*; sister's thread: sister = sewster, that is, seamstress, *EMV*. Line 8: potting-sticks = poking-sticks, for stiffening ruffs, *EMV*. Line 11: musk-cods – the bag or gland containing musk in animals, especially the musk deer, *EMV*.

(18) Sleep, slumb'ring eyes.

G minor. f'#-f ", [g'-f "]. 4/2. 1'20". 3 St. V/e, P/e.

For: [Sop], Ten.

Subject: Sleep will give rest to my troubles; since my eyes brought on
                  these sorrows let them close; but since the night banishes her
                  from me, wake eyes, and share my sorrow.
Voice: Steps, small skips; long legato phrases in fairly regular
                  rhythms but varying phrase-lengths.
Piano: Simple counterpoint; some repeated chords.
Comment: Restored by Dart from an MS copy of Morley's voice and bass.
                  Wholly contrapuntal in feeling, the voice one of the parts. The
                  last stanza is somewhat obscure, and might be omitted; in
                  this case the song is well suited to a woman.

68 O grief! e'en on the bud. Colls 4, 6. (Not in *LS* 13.)
                  F major. f'-e"b, [g'-d"]. 4/4. 1'20". V/me, P/me.
For: Mezzo, C-Ten, Bar.
Subject: Sorrow at the death of a loved child.
Voice: Steps, with some rhythmic complications.
Piano: Chordal with decorations.
Comment: An arrangement by Morley of his own madrigal, *EM* 3 (7), it
                  makes a beautiful and original solo. Line 2: low'red = frown-
                  ed; line 3: durst never venture = never dared risk entering.

ROBERT PARSONS
1530 – 1570

69 In youthly years (Richard Edwards). Coll 2.
                  D minor. c'-c", [d'-c"]. 4/4. 1'25". 2 St. V/e, P/e.
For: C-Ten, Bar.
Subject: The good advice my father gave when I first went to Court.
Voice: Steps, small skips; simple rhythm; slightly irregular
                  phrasing.
Piano: Simple counterpoint, in 3 parts.
Comment: Old-fashioned style, like an air for voice and viols. Copied
                  from BL Add. MS 15117. Also found in a Dublin MS with a
                  different tablature. Dublin ascribes the song to 'Mr Parsons'.
                  The second stanza, underlaid by the editor, has been added
                  from a four-stanza version printed in *The Paradise*, 1576.

FRANCIS PILKINGTON
c. 1570 – 1638

70 THE FIRST BOOKE OF SONGS OR AYRES OF 4 PARTS with
Tableture for the Lute or Orpherian, with the Violl de Gamba. 1605.
S & B edition by E.H. Fellowes, 1922. Revised by Thurston Dart, 1971
(*LS* 14). Tablature provided. Four-part versions printed in *MB* LIII.

(1) **Now peep, bo peep.** Coll 19; Coll 13, *A minor*; Coll 14, *E minor*.
> G minor. d'-f ″, [f′#-e″b]. 4/4,3/2. 1′35″, [1′10″]. 3 St. V/me, P/me.

For:	*Ten*; C-Ten, Bar; *Bass*.
Subject:	I have found where Phyllis lies and I must guard her; she is asleep so I will kiss her; she wakes so I must leave her.
Voice:	Steps, small skips; wide variety of rhythms and phrase-lengths.
Piano:	Chordal, with occasional fast decorations.
Comment:	Repeat optional. The suggested tempo relationship makes 'a little slower' for the last phrase (as given in Colls 13, 14) unnecessary. A cheerful song with lively rhythms.

(2) **My choice is made.**
> D minor. d'-f ″, [f′-e″]. 3/2. 1′50″. 3 St. V/e, P/me.

For:	Mezzo, Bar.
Subject:	I have made up my mind about my life; others may still wait upon fortune; friends may fear and foes hope I fail – whatever happens I shall not change.
Voice:	Steps, small skips, broken chords; fairly regular rhythms.
Piano:	Chordal, with some elaborate decoration in places.
Comment:	A serious philosophical statement.

(3) **Can she disdain.**
> G major. e'-e″, [g′-d″]. 4/4,3/2,4/4. 1′05″, [45″]. 3 St. V/e, P/me.

For:	C-Ten, Bar.
Subject:	A complaining lover points out that love is stronger and wiser than his proud mistress; since he wishes to unite minds, not bodies, she has no reason to refuse him.
Voice:	Steps, small skips; 4/4 sections with many repeated notes; 3/2 section of two legato phrases, almost all by step.
Piano:	Chordal, with some slightly awkward decoration.
Comment:	Repeat optional. The tempo relationship given is quite possible, as is crotchet = minim. The two c″s in bar 7 of voice will be tied in St. 2/3. St. 1, line 3: Time will prove my truthfulness, and compassion will prove hers (Doughtie); line 4: thralled = imprisoned; froward = unreasonable.

(4) **Alas fair face.**
> G major. f′#-e″, [g′-d″]. 3/2. 1′15″, [55″]. 3 St. V/e, P/e.

For:	C-Ten, Bar.
Subject:	Alas, why do you now scorn me? Is it perhaps only outward show, hiding inward affection? Be kind and renew my hopes.
Voice:	Steps, small skips; simple rhythm.
Piano:	Chordal with some decorations.

Comment: Repeat optional. The usual 3/2 3/1 alternation, despite the barring. A gentle song.

(5) **Whither so fast**.

G major. e'-e", [f'#-d"]. 3/2,4/4. 1'20", [55"]. 3 St. V/me, P/me.

For: C-Ten, Bar.

Subject: All nature invites us to love. The woodbind embraces you, the ground kisses your feet, the birds and fishes make music. Rest your head on my knee and I will kiss you.

Voice: Steps, small skips; short repeated phrases in lively rhythms, with much variety.

Piano: Chordal, with some imitation.

Comment: Repeat optional. The minim of the first two bars might well equal the crotchet of the rest. Underlay needs care in St. 2/3. St. 1, line 4: clips = clasps; line 5: 'Fortune my Foe' was a popular song of the day. St. 2, line 2: Philomela = the nightingale; line 4: strike crotchet time = make fast music (Doughtie); line 5: Zephyrus – God of the west wind. St. 3, line 1: *heliotrope = helitrope* in source (Doughtie); line 3: is not of force = has not the strength. Phoebe, in the refrain – Artemis, the moon Goddess who loved Endymion. The first stanza was set as a madrigal by Bateson, *EM* 21 (7), the second as a madrigal by Pilkington, *EM* 25 (4), starting: *Stay nymph* for *Fear not*. This alteration of two words is described as 'with some changes' in *EMV*!

(6) **Rest sweet nymphs**. Colls 6, 7, 19, Imperial (Tenor); Coll 8, *E minor*.

G minor. g'-f ", [g'-e"b]. 4/4,3/2,4/4. 1'05", [45"]. V/e, P/e.

For: Sop, Ten; *Mezzo, C-Ten, Bar*.

Subject: Lullaby for young ladies, wishing them sweet dreams of their true loves.

Voice: Mostly by step; simple rhythms, varied phrase-lengths.

Piano: Chordal with slight decoration.

Comment: A charmer. Repeat optional. The minim = dotted minim is best ignored; the semibreve = dotted minim of Coll 19 is possible but crotchet = crotchet is more effective, and indeed the only way of producing the right accentuation of the words. St. 1, line 4: sympathies = harmonies. Imperial: a few extra bass notes, and considerable invention over the move in and out of triple time, adding two extra beats at the beginning.

(7) **Ay me, she frowns**.

C minor. f'-g", [g'-g"]. 4/4,3/4,4/4. 1'20", [55"]. 3 St. V/me, P/me.

For: Ten.

Subject: If I have done wrong it was the fault of love, so be friends; do
            not cry over what has gone. Are you still angry? Ah no! So let
            us embrace.
Voice: Steps, small skips; broken chords in last line; phrases sepa-
            rated in first section, then a legato line.
Piano: Chordal with some decoration, which needs care.
Comment: Repeat optional. Minim = minim might be better for the 3/4
            section, judging by the return to 4/4 at the end. Some
            adjustments for underlay are needed in St. 2/3. St. 2, line 1:
            lowers = frowns; line 3: sith = since.

(8) Now let her change (Thomas Campion). Coll 6.
            F major. e'-f ", [f'-d"]. 4/4. 40", [30"]. 3 St. V/e, P/e.
For: Bar.
Subject: My false love has left me. Who cares! Her new love will have
            no better luck.
Voice: Almost all by step; some varied phrase-lengths, a short
            sequence.
Piano: Basically chordal; a short imitative sequence.
Comment: Repeat optional. A gay and easy song. For Campion's own
            setting see **32 (2)**; also set by Jones, **59 (17)**. Variants as
            follows: St. 1, line 2: *false = strange* (Campion, Jones); line 3:
            so bewitched = charmed so (C); line 5: *desires = joys* (C); line 6:
            deserts = desires (C) (deserts = merits). St. 2, line 3: *care did
            attend = heart did attend* (J), *cares served* (C); line 5: *till the
            day = to the day* (J), *to th'hour* (C). St. 3, line 1: *Then false =
            Thou false* (J), *False then* (C); line 2: *prove = proves* (C,J), and
            EMV, Notes! line 3: *now so triumphs in = boasts now* (C); line
            5: *I = he* (C,J) (that is, he who triumphs); *divine Adonis =
            Adonis* (J), *bright Adonis* (C); line 6: *Love = Faith* (C,J).

(9) Underneath a cypress shade.
            F major. f'-f ", [g'-d"]. 4/4. 1'10". 4 St. V/e, P/me.
For: Sop, Ten; Mezzo, Bar.
Subject: Describes the sorrows of Venus at the unkindness of
            Myrrha's son, Adonis, and says that he will later repent.
Voice: Steps, skips, repeated notes; 6th leap; simple rhythms; short
            phrases separated by rests.
Piano: Chordal, with some quite lively decoration.
Comment: The repeat, being written out in the original, should be sung.
            Strangely cheerful music for these words. St. 2, line 1:
            mourne = Although this could be a noun meaning *sadness*, it
            is probably a misprint for *bourne* (boundary) (Doughtie). St.
            3, line 1: *kindness = unkindness* in source (Doughtie).

(10) Sound, woeful plaints.

    D minor. d'-d", [d'-c"]. 4/4,3/2,4/4. 1'35", [1'30"]. 2 St. V/me,
    P/me.

For: Mezzo, C-Ten, Bar.
Subject: A lament over the death of a friend.
Voice: Steps, small skips; varied phrase-lengths, some quite long;
              one very strange phrase for the period: d' a' c"# d".
Piano: Mostly chordal, some decoration and simple counterpoint.
Comment: Repeat optional. The tempo relationship given is satisfac-
              tory, but minim = minim is also possible. St. 1, line 5: Time
              might recover friends, chance might recover goods. St. 2,
              line 5: hap = chance; line 7: my weel repine – grudges me my
              source of happiness. A long and not very interesting song.

(11) You that pine in long desire.

    A minor. e'-e", [a'-e"]. 4/4. 1'10", [40"]. 4 St. V/e, P/e.

For: [Mezzo], C-Ten, Bar.
Subject: You who love in vain, help me to call to my love for mercy;
              beauty should not be alone.
Voice: Steps, small skips; varied rhythms and phrase-lengths.
Piano: Chordal with some decoration.
Comment: Repeat optional. St. 4, line 1: *Her* could be changed to *His*,
              for women. St. 4, line 2: shrikes = shrieks.

(12) Look mistress mine.

    G major. f'#-f ", [g'-e"]. 3/2,4/4. 1'20", [1']. 2 St. V/me, P/me.

For: Ten; Bar.
Subject: Mistress, here in my breast is a Phoenix nest; pierced by
              your dart it asks a cure from you. O Phoenix, either end by
              burning your nest, or grant me my desires.
Voice: Steps, small skips, broken chords; short sequences; varied
              rhythms; fairly regular phrases.
Piano: Chordal, simple decoration; a few awkwardly placed
              overlapping chords.
Comment: Repeat optional. No time relationship is suggested, perhaps
              because minim = minim is satisfactory; however the dotted
              semibreve = semibreve given in all other cases also works
              here, and its absence may be an oversight. A rather difficult
              poem.

(13) Climb, O heart.

    G minor. d'-f ", [g'-d"]. 4/4. 55", [35"]. 6 St. V/e, P/e.

For: Bar.
Subject: Rise to her, my heart; love her for her virtue, and if she
              disdains you do not blame her.

Voice: Steps, small skips; some variation in rhythm and phrase-length.
Piano: Chordal with some decoration.
Comment: Repeat optional. Some stanzas could be omitted. St. 1, line 4: *fall'th, heart*, in source; *fall, th'heart, EMV* and Doughtie. St. 2, line 2: arrant = presumption.

(14) Thanks gentle moon.

A minor. d'-e″, [e'-e″]. 4/4,3/2,4/4. 1′25″, [1′]. 3 St. V/me, P/me.
For: C-Ten, Bar.
Subject: He thanks the moon and wind for saving him and his beloved, but curses the arbour where they made love, because it held his enemy, her brother, and nearly destroyed them.
Voice: Steps, some small skips; some variety of rhythm and phrase-length; a generally smooth line with some quicker moments.
Piano: Chordal with a little decoration; one passage of simple imitation.
Comment: Repeat optional. Time relationship given is best. This song would appear to belong to a play. St. 1, line 3: Zephyrus = God of the west wind. St. 2, line 5: missing in source; a possible replacement would be: 'And for their treachery deserve our ire'.

(15) I sigh as sure to wear the fruit.

E minor. e'-e″, [e'-d″]. 4/4. 1′45″, [1′10″]. 5 St. V/e, P/e.
For: C-Ten, Bar.
Subject: A rather long-winded lover's complaint.
Voice: Steps, small skips; not much rhythmic variety, but varied phrase-lengths, and one passage of short repeated phrases.
Piano: Chordal, occasional decoration.
Comment: Repeat optional. Several stanzas could be omitted, the music is more interesting than the poem. St. 1, line 1: a willow wreath is a sign of mourning. St. 2, line 2: *frid* – misprint for *frie* (fry)? *EMV*. Doughtie notes that an MS version has *feed*. St. 4, line 3: froward = unreasonable.

(16) Down a down, thus Phyllis sang (Thomas Lodge, *Rosalynde*, 1690).

Colls 6, 12, 23; Colls 11, 22, *Bb major*.
G major. d'-d″. 4/4. 2′40″. V/e, P/me.
For: *Sop, Ten*; Mezzo, C-Ten, Bar.
Subject: Love is a great invention of the Gods, but when accompanied by jealousy is best forgotten.
Voice: Steps, small skips; simple rhythms often repeated.
Piano: Semi-contrapuntal needing neat fingers in places.
Comment: Unusual in being in rondo form, ABACA. A gay piece, suited

to any audience. The poem appears in *EH*, 1600; there and
in Rosalynde *distressed* ends line 2 and *oppressed* line 4.
Line 7: did quicken man's conceit = brought man's
imagination to life. Colls 22, 23: accompaniment and
introduction to each stanza by Keel. Page 37, line 4, bar 1:
notes 3-4 dotted crotchet quaver; page 38, line 1, bar 3: notes
1-2, dotted crotchet quaver. The same in St. 2. Last note of
refrain a third too low each time.

(17) Diaphenia (Henry Chettle, or Henry Constable). Coll 21; Colls 9, 20,
Bb major; Colls 6, 10, *F major*.
> G major. d′-d″, [f′ #-d″]. 3/2. 45″, [30″]. 3 St. V/e, P/e.

For:	*Ten*; C-Ten, Bar; *Bass*.
Subject:	A contented lover, even though not yet accepted.
Voice:	Steps, small skips; simple rhythm.
Piano:	Chordal.
Comment:	Repeat optional. The poem appears in *EH*, 1600, with the initials H C; these may stand for either Henry Chettle or Henry Constable, see long note in *OB 16*. St. 1, line 6: prove = try. St. 3, line 6: requite = return.

(18) Beauty sat bathing (Anthony Munday).
> G minor. d′-f ″, [f′-e″*b*]. 4/4. 1′35″, [1′15″]. V/me, P/me.

For:	Bar.
Subject:	Beauty was bathing; I would have looked, but conscience prevented me; I then slept and dreamt of what I might have seen.
Voice:	Steps, small skips, a melisma; considerable rhythmic variety; some long sustained notes.
Piano:	Chordal and contrapuntal passages alternate.
Comment:	Repeat optional. Printed in *EH*, 1600, and given in Earle, 1615. Set by Corkine, 41 (**9**), and Jones, **59** (**2**) (see the latter for further details of the poem), but this is the only setting to include the 'hey nonny' refrain of the original poem. St. 2, line 3: *seemed* must take three notes.

(19) Music dear solace to my thoughts.
> G minor. d′-f ″, [g′-f ″]. 3/2. 1′20″, [1′]. 3 St. V/me, P/me.

For:	Mezzo, Bar.
Subject:	A hymn in praise of a woman singing and playing the lute; possibly St Cecilia is intended.
Voice:	Almost entirely by step; rhythmic contrast between sections simple in themselves.
Piano:	Chordal, occasional decoration.
Comment:	Repeat optional. Time relationships given are satisfactory,

and the continual change of metre adds interest. Fitting the words of St. 2/3 will need care, but should not prove difficult. St. 1, line 2: time sporter – music makes sport of time (or this might possibly read *time's porter*, Doughtie); line 5: secluse = secluded place. St. 3, line 6: attone = attune.

(20) With fragrant flowers (Thomas Watson, *The Honourable Entertainment given to the Queen's Majesty…at Elvetham… 1591*).

        G minor. d'-e"b. 4/4. 1', [40"]. 3 St. V/e, P/me.

For:	Mezzo, C-Ten, Bar.
Subject:	We make holiday; the earth is green, Nature responds, all in praise of our king.
Voice:	Steps, small skips; sequences of short phrases, some longer ones; few rhythmic complications.
Piano:	Chordal, with fairly elaborate decorations.
Comment:	Repeat optional. A nice straight-forward song; a good introduction to the contrapuntal style. Also printed in *EH*, 1600. Watson's refrain was 'O beauteous Queen', changed here since Elizabeth was dead when this song was published. It was headed: 'The Nimphes meeting their May Queene, entertaine her with this Dittie.' St. 1, line 3: clime = region. St. 2, line 3: dight = adorned. St. 3, line 4: weeds = garments.

(21) Come, come, all you.

        D minor. d'-e". [d'-d"]. 4/4. 2'10", [1'45"]. 2 St. V/me, P/me.

For:	Mezzo, C-Ten, Bar.
Subject:	An Elegy on the death of Thomas Leighton, 'who was Music's delight'.
Voice:	Steps, small skips, broken chords; varied rhythms, mostly rather long phrases; good sustaining ability needed.
Piano:	Chordal, but with considerable decoration throughout.
Comment:	Repeat optional. A much more successful lament than **70** (**10**). St. 2, line 2: sith = since; line 3: dreariments = expressions of a dismal condition.

THOMAS ROBINSON
fl. 1589 – 1609

71 NEW CITHAREN LESSONS 1609. Coll 4.

(47) Now Cupid, look about thee.

        G major. d'-g", [g'-d"]. 4/4. 25". 2 St. V/e, P/me.

For:	Sop, Ten.

Subject: Young men consider love out of fashion; the second stanza,
              added by the editor, blames this on tobacco!
Voice: Scales and broken chords; one d′ and rising scale, one g″ and
              descending scale, otherwise within middle 5th.
Piano: Contrapuntal; the bass line being given in small print, for
              singer or viol, is difficult to read at the keyboard.
Comment: Can be sung as a duet with bass.

PHILIP ROSSETER
1568 – 1623

72 A BOOKE OF AYRES Set forth to be sung to the Lute, Orpharion,
and Base Violl. 1601. S & B edition by E.H. Fellowes, 1923. Revised by
Thurston Dart, 1970 (*LS* 15). Tablature provided. The words may be
by Campion, but this is by no means certain; Vivian accepts them, but
Davis does not.

(1) Sweet, come again. Coll 6.
              G major. g′-g″, [g′-e″]. 2/2. 50″, [35″]. 4 St. V/e, P/e.
For: Sop, Ten.
Subject: Please return soon, but if you love me as I love you I am
              content to wait.
Voice: Steps, small skips; simple but varied rhythms and
              phrase-lengths.
Piano: Chordal, with hints of counterpoint.
Comment: Repeat optional. A fine poem with a charming setting.
              Words printed in Davison, 1602, where they are ascribed to
              Campion. St. 1, line 8: vouchsafe = grant. St. 2, line 8:
              annoys = annoyances.

(2) And would you see my mistress' face. Coll 29.
              G minor. g′-f ″. 2/2. 25″, [15″]. 5 St. V/e, P/e.
For: Ten; Bar.
Subject: Description of Mistress in terms of the beauties of nature.
Voice: Steps, sequence of falling 4ths; simple rhythm.
Piano: Chordal with decorations.
Comment: Repeat optional. Some stanzas could be omitted. Printed in
              Davison, 1602, ascribed to Campion. St. 3, line 3: Idaea – a
              nymph of Mount Ida; the ideal.

(3) No grave for woe.
              G minor. d′-d″, [f′-d″]. 2/2. 1′20″, [1′]. 2 St. V/me, P/me.
For: Mezzo, C-Ten, Bar.
Subject: Everything is against me, yet I live.

Voice: Mostly by step; 6th leap; one long phrase, one broken into pairs.
Piano: Chordal, with much contrapuntal elaboration.
Comment: Repeat optional. Musically more ambitious than most of Rosseter's songs. St. 1, line 2: Sighs lack air, and inflamed desires lack pity's showers.

(4) If I urge my kind desires. Coll 21; Coll 20, *A major.*
            G major. f'#-e", [g'-d"]. 2/2. 35", [25"]. 3 St. V/e, P/me.
For: *Ten*; C-Ten, Bar.
Subject: She rejects my desires, says she loves me and does not act; but she may change, since my love is true.
Voice: Mostly by step; regular simple rhythms.
Piano: Chordal with much decoration, not lying under the fingers.
Comment: Repeat optional. St. 1, line 4: affect = love. Colls 20, 21: accompaniment and introduction to each stanza by Keel.

(5) What heart's content.
            G major. f'#-e", [g'-e"]. 2/2. 1'25", [1'05"]. 2 St. V/me, P/e.
For: Mezzo, C-Ten, Bar.
Subject: Guilt will cause misery; love and pity, happiness.
Voice: Steps, broken chords; 6th leap; varied phrase-lengths with interesting breaks and extensions.
Piano: Chordal, a little decoration; some imitation with voice.
Comment: Repeat of last lines optional. St. 2, line 10: enured = accustomed.

(6) Let him that will be free.
            G major. f'#-e", [g'-d"]. 2/2. 50", [35"]. 3 St. V/e, P/e.
For: Mezzo, C-Ten, Bar.
Subject: If you would be free and happy, live alone, for then you can forget your troubles.
Voice: Steps; simple fairly regular rhythms.
Piano: Chordal with some decoration.
Comment: Repeat optional.

(7) Reprove not love.
            G minor. d'-d", [f'-c"]. 2/2. 1'05", [50"]. 2 St. V/me, P/e.
For: Mezzo, C-Ten, Bar.
Subject: Love may reduce ambition, but makes life worth living.
Voice: Steps, sequences; long phrases needing careful choice of breathing points to match the sense of the words; some subtle rhythms.
Piano: Chordal with some decoration; much use of sequence.
Comment: Repeat optional. A fascinating vocal line.

(8) And would you fain the reason know.
G minor. g'-f ", [g'-e"b]. 2/2. 30", [20"]. 7 St. V/e, P/e.

For:	[Sop], Ten; [Mezzo], Bar.
Subject:	Why am I sad and silent? Because I am in love.
Voice:	Steps, sequences; simple regular rhythm and phrasing.
Piano:	Chordal, with hints of counterpoint.
Comment:	Repeat optional. Some stanzas could be omitted, only stanza 2 specifies that it is a woman who is loved. St. 1, line 1: fain = gladly. St. 3, line 2: confute = convict of error. St. 4, line 1: admire = wonder; admire = admire. St. 6, line 3: lie = be untrue.

(9) When Laura smiles. Colls 19, 21, 26; Colls 7, 20, *A major*; Colls 6, 8, *F major*. Published separately by S & B in *F major*, H 186.
G major. d'-e", [g'-d"]. 3/4. 50", [35"]. V/me, P/e.

For:	*[Sop], Ten*; [Mezzo], C-Ten, Bar, *[Cont], Bass*.
Subject:	Happy praise of Laura's many charms.
Voice:	First part skips and short runs, in crotchets and quavers; second part by step, crotchets and minims, varied accentuation.
Piano:	Chordal with some decorations.
Comment:	Repeat optional. A marvellous exercise in phrasing controlled by words rather than music, which can have almost magical results. St. 2, line 1: two syllables, possibly three, are missing here; Colls 6, 7, 8, offer *See where*; *EMV*, *The wanton*; Coll 19, *The dainty sprites that still remain*; Coll 26 gives the original *The sprites that remain*, with a note: 'In singing, the word sprites should come on the second beat of the first bar and be carried on through the second bar'; line 2: underlay must be: *pas-* (four quavers) *-time* (crotchet) *to* (two quavers crotchet). St. 3, line 2: *lists = lifts*, *EMV* and Colls 20, 21, and 26; lists = desires; sport = amusement; lure = entice. Coll 19: bar 4, beat 2, voice: all other editions give f' sharp, not f' natural. Colls 20, 21: accompaniment and introduction to each stanza by Keel. St. 4 omitted. No words added to St. 2. St. 1, line 7: *everlasting = everflowing*, all other editions. St. 3, line 6: loure = lure, as given in all other editions except Coll 19.

(10) Long have my eyes gaz'd with delight.
G minor. f'#-f ", [g'-e"b]. 2/2. 1', [45"]. 3 St. V/me, P/me.

For:	Ten; Bar.
Subject:	I have loved long, but must now despair; I would not mind were she not beautiful; but there is still hope.

Voice: Steps; three-fold descending sequence; much variety of
             rhythm and phrasing.
Piano: Somewhat contrapuntal.
Comment: Repeat optional. Barlines are misleading as to rhythm. St. 2,
             line 4: desert = merit.

(11) Though far from joy. Colls 6, 28.
             G minor. f'-f ", [g'-f"]. 2/2. 1', [45"]. 2 St. V/e, P/e.
For: Mezzo, Bar.
Subject: Praise of holding the golden mean between joy and sorrow.
Voice: Steps, small skips; short runs and sequences; simple
             rhythm.
Piano: Chordal; some imitative counterpoint in second part.
Comment: Repeat optional, written out in Coll 6. St. 1. line 5: *so is = is
             so, EMV*. Bar 3, beat 4 – bar 4, beat 3: Coll 28 phrases both
             stanzas crotchet slurred to quaver, three quavers, crotchet;
             LS 15 and Coll 6 phrase St. 1: crotchet, four quavers,
             crotchet; Coll 6 phrases St. 2: crotchet (*they en-*) four
             quavers crotchet (*-dure*).

(12) Shall I come if I swim. Colls 6, 28.
             D minor. d'-d", [e'-c"]. 3/2. 40", [25"]. 2 St. V/e, P/e.
For: C-Ten, Bar.
Subject: I would brave water and air for you, if you would return my
             love as Hero did Leander's.
Voice: Steps, small skips; a short sequence of descending runs;
             some interesting rhythms.
Piano: Chordal with decorations.
Comment: Repeat optional. St. 2: Leander swam the Bosphorus to meet
             his mistress Hero, a priestess of Aphrodite, who set a candle
             in the window as a guide for him. Music rebarred in Coll 6.

(13) Ay me that love. Coll 26.
             G minor. f'#-f ", [g'-f "]. 3/2. 40", [30"]. 2 St. V/me, P/me.
For: Bar.
Subject: When Laura looks on glass or water she sees her beauty, but
             not her thoughts, which cause me so much grief.
Voice: Steps; sequence of dropping 3rds; rather complex rhythms.
Piano: Chordal.
Comment: Repeat optional, but recommended. Barlines highly mis-
             leading as to rhythms.

(14) Shall then a traitorous kiss. Coll 30.
             G minor. f'#-d", [g'-d"]. 2/2. 40", [30"]. 3 St. V/e, P/me.
For: Mezzo, C-Ten, Bar.

Subject: Will false love always be rewarded and true service be neglected? One mistake is fatal; love and fortune are both blind.

Voice: Steps, small skips; sequence in 3rds; slightly chromatic.

Piano: Chordal with decoration; second part a little complicated to read.

Comment: Repeat optional. Accentuation of second part unexpected – first four accents come on the weak beats. St. 3, line 1: desert = merit. Coll 30: Bar 2, beat 1, LH: f ° for g° of *LS* 15; St. 1, line 3: *Shall the virtue of feign'd love* for *LS* 15 and *EMV*'s *Shall the vow of feigned love*.

(15) If I hope I pine. Colls 6, 30.

    G major. f'#-d". 3/2. 50", [35"]. 2 St. V/e, P/e.

For: Mezzo, C-Ten, Bar.

Subject: If I am afraid to express my love I cannot expect to have it returned.

Voice: Steps, small skips; simple rhythms with a couple of long notes.

Piano: Chordal with some decorations.

Comment: Repeat optional. A remarkably close match of words and music in both stanzas. St. 2, line 2: conceives not = does not comprehend. Coll 30 has quite different rhythms in the last line: bars 15-16, voice: dotted minim, minim two quavers, where *LS* 15 and Coll 6 have (bar 9) semibreve tied to crotchet, two quavers; bars 17-18, RH, treble: minim crotchet tied to quaver two quavers crotchet, alto: minim crotchet quaver dotted crotchet two quavers; LH: dotted crotchet quaver crotchet tied to quaver quaver tied to minim. The other editions have (bar 10) treble: minim minim quaver two semiquavers crotchet; alto: minim dotted crotchet quaver crotchet two quavers; LH: dotted crotchet quaver minim minim. Note that Coll 30 is in 3/4, not 3/2, with twice the number of barlines.

(16) Unless there were consent.

    G minor. f'-e"b, [g'-d"]. 2/2. 1'30", [1'05"]. 3 St. V/me, P/e.

For: [Mezzo], C-Ten, Bar.

Subject: I cannot reconcile your beauty with your cruelty; your eyes promise what you will not give. Tell me whether I am to be saved by your eyes or condemned by your heart.

Voice: Steps, small skips; longish slow phrases, with great variety off accentuation and rhythmic detail.

Piano: Chordal with some decoration and imitation.

Comment: Repeat optional. St. 2, line 1: *her* could be changed to *him*; even = balance. St. 3, line 5: contemned = held in contempt.

(17) If she forsake me. Coll 28; Colls 9, 20, *A major*; Colls 6, 10, *Eb major*; Coll 21, *F major*.

G major. d'-e″, [f'-e″]. 2/2. 35″, [25″]. 3 St. V/e, P/e.

For: *Ten*; C-Ten, Bar; *Bass*.

Subject: My love is vain. I would give it up if I could, but I cannot, although my gifts are all rejected.

Voice: Steps, small skips; simple rhythms with slight extension in last phrase.

Piano: Chordal, some imitation.

Comment: Repeat optional. The music suggests a certain degree of self-mockery. St. 2, line 4: remove = go away; line 6: eschew = avoid. Colls 20, 21: accompaniment and introduction to each stanza by Keel. Bar 7 of each stanza: should be 6/4 bar, note 5 of voice minim followed by crotchet rest.

(18) What is a day. Coll 29.

G minor. f'-f″, [g'-d″]. 2/2. 45″, [35″]. 2 St. V/e, P/e.

For: Mezzo, Bar.

Subject: Worldly success is fleeting; only virtue can bring us to heaven.

Voice: Steps, small skips, three-fold sequence; simple fairly regular rhythms.

Piano: Chordal, some counterpoint.

Comment: Repeat optional.

(19) Kind in unkindness. Colls 6, 30.

G minor. f'-d″, [g'-d″]. 3/2. 50″, [35″]. 5 St. V/e, P/e.

For: C-Ten, Bar.

Subject: A plea to the beloved to return his love.

Voice: Steps, small skips; almost entirely in minims, with varying accentuation controlled by the words of each stanza.

Piano: Chordal with some decorations.

Comment: Repeat optional, written out in Coll 6. Some stanzas could be omitted. Barlines are somewhat misleading. St. 2, line 3, and St. 4, line 2: deserts = merits; line 4: relish = give taste to. St. 5, line 4: his poem will be held in her hand, see St. 1, line 4. Coll 30: bar 18, beat 3, RH: d' and f' should be f' and a'.

(20) What then is love but mourning. Colls 6, 11, 26; Coll 12, *D minor*.

G minor. g'-f″. 2/2. 35″, [25″]. 3 St. V/e, P/e.

For: Sop, Ten; *Mezzo, C-Ten, Bar*; *Cont, Bass*.

Subject: Love is of no use unless returned, and we are getting older; so come away my darling.
Voice: Steps, small skips; a short rising sequence; simple but varied rhythms.
Piano: Chordal, some passing notes.
Comment: Repeat optional but recommended. As Warlock said, an absolutely perfect miniature. It can be taken in many different moods and tempi. Copied in BL Add. MS 24665, with some variants, including St. 2, line 3, *wheel* for *while*.

(21) **Whether men do laugh or weep**. Coll 29.
              G major. d'-e", [d'-d"]. 2.2 30", [20"]. 3 St. V/e, P/e.
For: Mezzo, C-Ten, Bar.
Subject: Nothing on earth really matters, so be happy.
Voice: Steps; one broken chord covering an 8ve; regular simple dance.
Piano: Chordal, a little decoration.
Comment: Repeat needed for balance. Well suited to end a group.

GUILLAUME TESSIER
fl. late sixteenth century

73 In a grove most rich of shade (Sir Philip Sidney, the eighth song in *Astrophel and Stella*, 1591). Coll 1.
              G minor. d'-f ", [g'-d"]. 4/4. 40". 26 St. V/e, P/e.
For: Mezzo, Bar.
Subject: Astrophel and Stella meet and confess their love; Astrophel pleads with her to act upon it, but she rejects this in the name of honour.
Voice: Steps, broken chord, scale; simple but varied rhythms.
Piano: Chordal.
Comment: A pleasant tune, and the poem could easily be heavily cut. In fact, Robert Dowland omitted St. 18-25 of the 26 stanzas himself, though this makes the last verse rather an abrupt conclusion. On the other hand, these stanzas were not in the 1591 version of the poem, being added in *Arcadia*, 1598. Music originally composed for Ronsard's 'Le Petit enfant l'Amour' in 1582.

LEONARD WOODSON
c. 1565 – 1619

74 The marigold of golden hue. Coll 3.

        G major. g'-g". 3/4. 55". 4 St. V/e, P/e.

For:	Ten.
Subject:	My beloved is only happy when I am with her, therefore I love her above all.
Voice:	Steps, some skips; simple repetitive rhythms.
Piano:	Chordal; some imitation of voice in bass.
Comment:	Editorial accidentals in bass justified by imitation. Copied from Christ Church MS 439.

75 A MUSICAL BANQUET. Furnished with variety of delicious Ayres, Collected out of the best Authors in English, French, Spanish, and Italian. Published by Robert Dowland, John Dowland's son, in 1610. Containing ten songs in English, see **2, 14, 28, 53, 48 (1-3), 54, 64, 73,** and ten songs in foreign languages, given below. Translations by Keith Statham unless otherwise stated. S & B edition by Peter Stroud, 1968 (*LS* 16). Coll 1.

PIERRE GUEDRON
c. 1570 – ?1619

(11) Si le parler et le silence. From 'Airs du Court', first printed in Gabriel Bataille's *Airs de différents autheurs*, 1608.

        C minor. c'-f ", [d'-e"b]. 3/4,4/4. 1' [40"]. 4 St. V/me, P/e.

For:	Mezzo, Bar.
Subject:	Let us keep our love secret from rumour-mongers, and laugh at their ignorance.
Voice:	Steps, a few skips, several short melismas; rhythm very variable, with several surprises.
Piano:	Chordal.
Comment:	Repeat optional. Translation by Edward Filmer, 1629.

(12) Ce penser qui sans fin. From 'Airs du Court', 1608.

        C minor. c'-f ", [e'b-e"]. 3/4,4/4. 1'05", [40"]. 5 St. V/me, P/e.

For:	Bar.
Subject:	Loving her has caused me endless misery; however hard I try I can't forget her.
Voice:	Mostly by step; long rising scale; a few melismas; variable unexpected rhythms and metres.
Piano:	Chordal.
Comment:	Repeat optional.

(13) Vous que le bonheur rappelle. From 'Airs du Court', 1608.

C minor. e′*b*-f ″, [e′*b*-e″*b*]. 4/4,3/4. 40″, [25″]. 7 St. V/e, P/e.

For: Mezzo, Bar.
Subject: Rejoice that your once cruel mistress has now conquered you.
Voice: Steps, some skips, a few melismas; varied but simple rhythms.
Piano: Chordal.
Comment: Repeat optional. Translation by Edward Filmer, 1629. Robert Dowland omitted the last three stanzas.

ANON

(14) Passava amor so arco desarmado (Jorge de Montemayor, *Diana*, III, 1574). First printed in Gabriel Bataille's *Airs de différents autheurs*, 1608.

F minor. f′-f ″, [f′-e″*b*]. 3/4,4/4. 1′20″, [50″]. V/e, P/e.

For: Mezzo, Bar.
Subject: Love was passing me by, but Fate made him stay, and now I suffer.
Voice: Almost all by step; one melisma; varied but fairly simple rhythm.
Piano: Chordal.
Comment: Both repeats or only the first.

(15) Sta notte mi sognava.

G major. d′-f ″, [g′-e″]. 4/4. 1′15″. 2 St. V/m, P/e.

For: Bar.
Subject: I dreamt of hell, and women's faithlessness.
Voice: Almost all by step; many highly elaborate cadenzas which require considerable flexibility.
Piano: Chordal.
Comment: Rhythm must be free to accommodate the decoration, which is very attractive, if somewhat instrumental in style.

(16) Vuestros ojos tienen d'amor. First printed in Gabriel Bataille's *Airs de différents autheurs*, 1609.

G minor. d′-b′*b*. 9/8,2/4,3/4. 1′40″, [55″]. V/me, P/me.

For: Mezzo, C-Ten, Bar.
Subject: The love in your eyes torments my heart.
Voice: Steps, many repeated notes; very varied and unexpected rhythms and metres; a patter-song.
Piano: Broken chords in varying rhythms.
Comment: Both repeats or only the first.

DOMENICO MEGLI
fl. early seventeenth century

(17) **Se di farmi morire**. From *Le seconde musiche del Dom. Maria Megli*, 1602.

	G minor. d'-f ", [g'-d"]. 1'50", [55"]. V/me, P/me.
For:	Mezzo, Bar.
Subject:	If you are cruel my love will die.
Voice:	Steps, skips, 6th leap; short sequences and melismas; free rhythms.
Piano:	Chordal, over bass in counterpoint with voice.
Comment:	Both repeats or neither. A rather charming song.

GIULIO CACCINI
c. 1545 – 1618

(18) **Dourò dunque morire** (Giulio Caccini). From *Le Nuove Musiche*, 1602.

	G minor. d'-d". 4/4. 1'55". V/me, P/me.
For:	Mezzo C-Ten, Bar.
Subject:	Must I die before seeing my beloved?
Voice:	Recit. style: steps, skips, sequences; some elaborated cadences, free rhythms.
Piano:	Contrapuntal and fairly chromatic.
Comment:	A very worthwhile song.

(19) **Amarilli mia bella** (Giulio Caccini).

	G minor. d'-e", [f'#-d"]. 4/4. 2'30". V/me, P/me.
For:	C-Ten, Bar.
Subject:	Amarillis, if I die for love of you your name will be found written on my heart.
Voice:	Steps, small skips; decorated cadences and other melismas.
Piano:	Chordal, but a fair amount of added counterpoint.
Comment:	One of the most famous of all early songs, deserving its popularity; it is interesting to have a near contemporary realisation to compare with the usual nineteenth-century versions.

ANON

(20) **O bella più**.

	G major. d'-g", [f'#-e"]. 4/4. 1'30". V/me, P/e.
For:	Ten.

Subject: Sun, moon, and stars must bow to Diana, whom I love in vain.

Voice: Nearly all by step; varied rhythms, some slow phrases, some almost patter; elaborated cadences.

Piano: Mostly chordal.

Comment: A surprisingly cheerful treatment of this conventional sad subject.

Select Bibliography

Composers

Campion

Kastendieck, Miles Merwin, *England's Musical Poet, Thomas Campion*, New York, OUP 1939.

Lowbury, Edward, Timothy Salter and Alison Young, *Thomas Campion: Poet, Composer, Physician*, London, 1970.

Ratcliffe, Stephen, *Campion, On Song*, Routledge and Kegan Paul 1981.

Dowland

Poulton, Diana, *John Dowland*, Faber & Faber 1972, revised and corrected 1981.

General reference

Dictionary of National Biography

Oxford English Dictionary

New Larousse Encylopedia of Mythology, Hamlyn 1968.

Day, C.L. and Murrie, E.B., *English Song-Books 1651-1702*, The Bibliographical Society, at the University Press, Oxford 1940 (for 1937).

Mulgan, John (revised by Dorothy Eagle), *The Concise Oxford Dictionary of English Literature*, OUP 1979.

Northcote, Sidney, *Byrd to Britten: A Survey of English Song*, John Baker 1966.

Pattison, Bruce, *Music and Poetry of the English Renaissance*, Methuen 1948.

Sadie, Stanley, ed., *New Grove Dictionary of Music and Musicians*, Macmillan 1980.

Spink, Ian, *English Song: Dowland to Purcell*, Batsford 1974.

Stapleton, Michael, *The Cambridge Guide to English Literature*, CUP 1983.

Stevens, Denis, ed., *A History of Song*, Hutchinson 1960.

Tilley, Morris P., *A Dictionary of the Proverbs in England in the 16th and 17th Centuries*, University of Michigan Press 1950.

Warlock, Peter, *The English Ayre*, OUP 1926.

Music

Cheerful Ayres or Ballads, printed by W. Hall, for Ric. Davis, 1660.
English Lute Songs, series ed. E.H. Fellowes (revised and continued by T. Dart *et al.*) Stainer & Bell 1920-.
English Madrigalists, series ed. E.H. Fellowes (revised and continued by T. Dart *et al.*) Stainer & Bell 1915-.
Forbes, John (printer), *Cantus, Songs and Fancies,* Aberdeen 19662; 2nd edition 1666; 3rd edition 1682.
Musica Britannica, Stainer and Bell for the Royal Musical Association, 1954-.
Playford, John (publisher), *A Brief Introduction to the Skill of Musick,* 1660, reissued 1662.
————*An Introduction to the Skill of Musick*, 1672.
————*The Musical Companion*, 1667; revised edition 1673.
————*Select Ayres and Dialogues*, 1659; reissued as *The Treasury of Music*, 1669.
————*Select Musical Ayres and Dialogues*, 1652; revised edition 1653.
Songs Compleat, see next entry.
Wit and Mirth, or Pills to Purge Melancholy, vol.1, 1699, 1704, 1707, 1714; vol.5, 1714; vol.6, 1720; new edition, also issued as *Songs Compleat*, vol. 3, 1719.

Anthologies

Ault, Norman, ed., *Elizabethan Lyrics; from the original texts*, Longmans, Green and Co, 1925, revised and corrected 1949; republished Faber & Faber 1986.
Breton, Nicholas, *Britton's Bowre of Delights*, 1591, ed. Hyder E. Rollins, Harvard University Press 1933.
Bullen, A.H., ed., *Lyrics from the Song-Books of the Elizabethan Age*, Sidgwick & Jackson 1896.
Chambers, E.K., ed., *The Oxford Book of Sixteenth Century Verse*, Clarendon Press 1932.
Chambers, E.K. and Sidgwick, F., eds, *Early English Lyrics*, Sidgwick & Jackson 1907 (1947).
Collier, John Payne, ed., *Lyrical Poems, selected from Musical Publications between the Years 1589 and 1600*, London, The Percy Society, 1844.
Cotgrave, J. *Wit's Interpreter*, 1655; 2nd edition 1662.
Davison, Francis, *A Poetical Rhapsody*, 1602, ed. Hyder E. Rollins, 2 vols. Harvard University Press 1931-32.
Doughtie, Edward, ed. *Lyrics from English Ayres, 1596-1622*, Harvard University Press 1970.
Earle, Giles, *His Booke*, 1615, ed. Peter Warlock, Houghton Publishing Co. 1932.
Edwards, Richard, *The Paradyse of Daynty Devises*, 1576, ed. Sir Egerton Bryges, Triphook & Sancho 1810.
England's Helicon (1) ed. Hyder E. Rollins, 2 vols, Harvard University Press 1935; (2) ed, Hugh Macdonald, Routledge and Kegan Paul 1949.
Fellowes, E.H., ed., *English Madrigal Verse*, 3rd ed. revised F.W. Sternfeld and David Greer, Clarendon Press 1967.
Filmer, Sir Edward, *French Court Airs with their Ditties Englished*, 1629.
Gardner, Helen, ed., *The New Oxford Book of English Verse*, OUP 1972.
Johnson, Richard, *Golden Garland of Princely Pleasures*, 3rd ed. 1620.
Phoenix Nest, The, 1593, ed. Hyder E. Rollins, Harvard University Press 1931.

Quiller-Couch, Arthur, ed., *The Oxford Book of English Verse, 1250-1900*, Clarendon Press 1912.

Rollins, *see* Breton, Davison, *England's Helicon* and *Phoenix Nest* above.

Poets

Beaumont and Fletcher, *The Works*, ed. A.R. Walker, CUP 1905-1912.

Breton, *The Works in Verse and Prose*, ed. A.B. Grosart, 1879, reprinted Hildersheim 1969.

Campion, Thomas, *The Works*, ed. Walter R. Davis, Doubleday 1967.

————*Campion's Works*, ed. Percival Vivian, Clarendon Press 1909.

Constable, Henry, *The Poems*, ed. Joan Grundy, Liverpool 1960.

Daniel, Samuel, *The Complete Works*, ed. A.B. Grosart, 5 vols, 1885-96 (privately printed), reprinted New York 1963.

Davies, Sir John, *The Poems*, ed. Robert Krueger, Clarendon Press 1975.

Dekker, Thomas, *The Dramatic Works*, ed. F. Bowers, CUP 1953-61.

Donne, John, *The Poems*, ed. Herbert J.C. Grierson, 2 vols, OUP 1912.

————*The Elegies and the Songs and Sonnets*, ed. Helen Gardner, Clarendon Press 1965.

————*The Complete English Poems*, ed. C.A. Patrides, Dent 1985.

Drayton, Michael, *Poems*, ed. John Buxton, 2 vols, Routledge & Kegan Paul 1953.

Gascoigne, George, *Complete Works*, ed. J.W. Cunliffe, 2 vols, CUP 1907-10, reprinted Scholarly Press 1969.

Gorges, Sir Arthur, *The Poems*, ed. Helen Estebrook Sandison, Clarendon Press 1953.

Greville, Fulke, *Poems and Dramas*, ed. Geoffrey Bullogh, Oliver and Boyd 1939.

Herrick, Robert, *The Poetical Works*, ed. L.C. Martin, Clarendon Press 1963.

Hewood, Thomas, in *The Best Plays of the Old Dramatists*, ed. A. Wilson Verity, Fisher Unwin 1923.

Jonson, Ben, *Works*, ed. C.H. Herford, Percy and Evelyn Simpson, 11 vols, Clarendon Press 1925-51.

————*The Complete Poems*, ed. George Parfitt, Penguin Books 1975.

Lodge, Thomas, *Rosalynde*, ed. W.W. Grey, OUP 1931.

Lyly, John, *The Complete Works*, ed. R. Warwick Bond, 3 vols, Clarendon Press 1902.

Nashe, Thomas, *The Works*, ed. Ronald B. McKerrow, 5 vols, 1904-10, revised F.P. Wilson, Basil Blackwell 1966.

Ralegh, Sir Walter, *The Poems*, ed. Agnes Latham, Constable 1929.

Shakespeare, William, *The Complete Pelican Shakespeare,* ed. Alfred Harbarge, 3 vols, Penguin Books 1969.

Sidney, Sir Philip, *The Poems*, ed. William A. Ringler, Jr., Clarendon Press 1962.

————*The Countess of Pembroke's Arcadia* [*The Old Arcadia*], 1580, ed. Katherine Duncan-Jones, OUP 1985.

————*The Countess of Pembroke's Arcadia* [*The New Arcadia*], 1590, ed. Maurice Evans, Penguin English Library 1977.*

Southwell, Robert, *The Poems*, ed. James H. McDonald and Nancy Pollard, Clarendon Press 1967.

---

* In 1593 *The New Arcadia* was published with books 3-5 of *The Old Arcadia*. In 1598 this composite *Arcadia* was published with *Astrophel and Stella* and *Certain Sonnets*.

Index of first lines

Foreign texts

Index of authors

Bold type indicates a book of songs; *italic* indicates doubtful attributions.